AUTHORS AT SEA

MODERN AMERICAN WRITERS REMEMBER THEIR NAVAL SERVICE

Authors at Sea

EDITED BY
ROBERT SHENK

Naval Institute Press
Annapolis, Maryland

LIBRARY OF CONGRESS CATALOGING-IN-PUBLICATION DATA

Authors at sea: modern American writers remember their naval service
/ edited by Robert Shenk
p.   cm.
ISBN 1-55750-799-6 (alk. paper)
1. Sea stories, American. 2. United States—History, Naval—20th century—
Literary collections. 3. Naval art and science—Literary collections.
4. Authors, American—20th century—Biography. 5. American literature—
20th century. 6. United States. Navy—Biography. 7. War stories, American.
I. Shenk, Robert, 1943–
PS648. S4A95   1997
810.8'0162—dc20   96-30519

Printed in the United States of America on acid-free paper ∞

04 03 02 01 00 99 98 97   9 8 7 6 5 4 3 2

First printing

Page 319 is a continuation of the copyright page.

To Peter, Henry, Stephanie, Mary, and Paula

I was out there in the Pacific, on the bridge of
an old destroyer-minesweeper. I had just
become a new Officer of the Deck, qualified to
stand a watch at sea, and I had the conn. But
my mind was on this book I was writing,
Aurora Dawn, my first novel. I was leaning on
the pelorus, thinking of a turn in the plot,
when I suddenly noticed a rapidly
approaching transport broad on the bow.
Groping to remember the rules, I exclaimed,
"My God, we're on a collision course!
Holmsman, Right Full Rudder."
And the helmsman, without batting an eye,
and vigorously spinning the wheel counter-
clockwise, said, "You mean, 'Left Full
Rudder,' sir. Left Full Rudder, aye, aye, sir."
And that's why I stand here tonight and I'm
not at the bottom of the sea.

HERMAN WOUK
Address to the U.S. Naval Institute,
July 27, 1995, answering a question from the floor

CONTENTS

NAVAL HISTORY AND RESEARCH

PACIFIC WAR—II

GOING HOME

AUTHORS AT SEA

INTRODUCTION

A SURPRISINGLY WIDE variety of modern American writers saw naval duty during World War II. Some of their stories are minor legends. Shortly after the bombing of Pearl Harbor, for example, the Harvard historian Samuel Eliot Morison proposed to go on active duty to become the Navy's official historian of the war. Initially, Morison was rebuffed by the secretary of the Navy, but when he addressed President Franklin D. Roosevelt, Roosevelt agreed, and the eventual result was Morison's seminal fifteen-volume *History of United States Naval Operations in World War II.*[1] James Michener, in his own way a man almost as experienced as Morison though not nearly so distinguished, wrote short stories in the evenings while serving as a naval staff officer in the Pacific.[2] The stories became *Tales of the South Pacific,* a book that won the Pulitzer Prize for fiction and launched Michener on his fifty-year career as a popular novelist.

On the other hand, many recognized authors have written so little specifically about the Navy that until they drew attention to it, few readers knew they had any naval experience at all. Nevertheless, noted authors or journalists such as Louis Auchincloss, Lewis Thomas, and Russell Baker appreciated their naval service enough to pay it tribute in chapters of their autobiographies, and the eminent literary critic Alvin Kernan penned a book-length memoir about his enlisted service.

Each selection in this book comes from the writings of a modern American author who, like those mentioned above, saw active duty in the U.S. Navy (or Coast Guard) during World War II and who later reflected upon that experience, usually in a memoir or a short retrospective essay. All the selections are directly autobiographical. Even though many of the authors represented here are novelists, none of the selections is fictional. In addition, all the selections are written by individuals with earned reputations as authors. It is true that celebrities such as baseball star Yogi Berra and actors Richard Boone and Jason Robards (and many others) served in the Navy during the war, and that no fewer than six modern presidents have seen naval service. Some of these men have written about their naval duty. Their writing is not exceptional, however, and because these figures are primarily known for achievements other than authorship, they are not represented here.

The authors who are included come from many modern professions. Not only do novelists, journalists, and historians speak in these pages, but so do literary critics, a philosopher, two science writers, and a few career naval professionals who successfully turned to authorship during or after their seagoing careers. As a result, this book manifests something of the breadth of American society that has been influenced by naval service. It also hints at the great differences in character, personality, and general outlook that can be found within the naval uniform.

Why collect the autobiography of authors? Of course I have several reasons. First, about eminent writers there is a natural curiosity. We are drawn to know what lived experience an author actually had—and how it relates to that author's work. How, for instance, did James Michener manage to visit all those forty-nine South Pacific islands while serving in the midst of a war? What was his billet, anyhow? Did Herman Wouk pattern Captain Queeg on any real-life naval officer? How did Samuel Eliot Morison's idea of "participatory history" work, and how was he received by the service?

To put it a different way, in the case of a novelist, we read autobiography in part to hear about experience as it actually was—not as dressed up or dramatized (as fiction is popularly conceived to be). True, novelists try to represent common humanity, and by adroit depiction of situation and incident attempt to portray the characteristic within the individual. Nevertheless, we suspect that their personal experiences somehow led these writers to choose the kind of stories they tell, and we would like to hear the real-life stories too. In the case of authors other than novelists, we naturally wonder to what extent their personal experiences shaped their mature intellectual perspectives.

There is another reason for focusing on authors' personal narratives. One of the main reasons for reading autobiography—outside of seeking the hidden reasons for historical events or the scoop on celebrities' secrets—is to hear of decisions made when someone confronted difficult circumstances, choices a person has had time to live with and reflect upon. Such revelations can be instructive; they can lead us to recognize ourselves. And we reasonably believe that when authors write about their past, they can be as insightful and articulate as they so often are in other types of writing.

One might go further, asking why the focus on military autobiography. In answer, I would point to the recent anthologies of good writing about World War II and the widely expressed opinion which their positive reception underscores, namely, that the experience of war is more important than to be left just to the generals, the admirals, and the politicians. Thoughtful people from all walks of life, including excellent writers, might have something meaningful to say about such a conflict.

For example, Mordecai Richler's 1991 book, *Writers on World War II: An Anthology,* is an excellent collection of fiction, poetry, letters, diaries, and journalism by fine writers of many nationalities. It comprises a kind of "mosaic" and succeeds in its stated aim of providing a "big picture" of the war.

And the recent two-volume collection of writing by war correspondents, *Reporting World War II,* is a welcome and interesting project. Note, however, in particular reference to this last collection, that there is naturally a great difference between those who cover war as journalists and those who have been enlisted or commissioned. Both of the latter not only undergo basic and advanced military training, but they also agree to obey all orders given them, to be sent where their commanders decree, and to face combatant or other dangerous service whether they like it or not. (Alternatively, they may have to deploy on heartbreakingly dull, apparently meaningless assignments without any real recourse.) Those in uniform are also often responsible for the safety and morale of those serving with or under them, and sometimes answer not just for their own military work but for the jobs to which their units are assigned—that is, they must answer to some degree for the actual conduct of the war.

Let me put it another way. The typical authors in this volume certainly differ, say, from the famous journalist Ernie Pyle, who during the war lived with and told the stories of the ordinary people in uniform he met, people who had to confront the multifarious troubles of war and military service. But a comparison to Pyle is not invidious. Although the writers here all saw naval service, and most were officers (Pyle usually traveled with the Army and wrote mainly about enlisted men), still, in their recollections, these authors *are* just ordinary people in uniform, and they tell *their own stories* of the troubles of war and military service. The writers presented here have two other advantages Pyle did not have: mature personal reflection and a sense of the importance of their wartime naval duty in their long careers and in their lives.

Why focus on naval authors in particular? I am partly drawn to this subject, of course, through my own longstanding naval interests, and partly because American naval experience is often given short shrift in collections of wartime military writing. But the primary reason is my conviction that the naval profession has a special character of its own. It involves unique challenges that make for exceptionally interesting and informative recollections.

When one enters the Navy, one receives a set of uniforms, a set of traditions (many more so than in most other professions), and a set of strange tasks to perform. But that is not all. Several deeper realities stand beneath and order those on the surface, and these must be confronted as well. Very few naval enlistees or officer candidates have been to sea prior to entering the service, for one thing; virtually none of them has gone into battle, for another. And few have faced the leadership challenges of the forecastle or of the boiler room or of general military life. All these challenges—to say nothing of the concomitant problems such as leaving home, being ordered around, and enduring long periods of celibacy, unaccustomed labor, continually interrupted slumber, seasickness, and universal discomfort—make for early, forced maturation. And they tend to pose dilemmas to be thoughtfully, ruefully, or humorously remembered later in life.

Those who join the service primarily because of a war, particularly those from academic rather than technical backgrounds, often experience a relative lack of competence compared with veterans, which often results in an initial loss of confidence and some stumbling. When this is compounded by insistent authority, one must learn to rely upon moral resources within. On the other hand, occasionally (after long effort) one suddenly realizes, "I can do this job too"—and maybe even better than the person presently doing it. Many of the authors represented here encountered through their naval duty their initial real-world success. A consequent self-confidence and growth in character was a quite common result.[3]

To be sure, naval experience has many dimensions. The selections in this text comprehend all major branches of the U.S. Navy of the forties (surface, naval aviation, submarine, and various naval specialties), and include both officer and enlisted reflections. I have included two pieces from veterans of a kindred seagoing naval service, the wartime Coast Guard, but have omitted reminiscences from United States Marines, who, although often operating with the Navy, ever retain the most inimitable military character whether at sea or ashore. Nor are there any selections from wartime Merchant Mariners except one (Kenneth Dodson)—and he joined the Navy not long into the war.

Yet, while all the authors in these pages had naval experience, they are not all combat veterans, nor are all their reminiscences about sea duty. In the wartime era the Navy came to be a broad, complex institution. Military experience of all kinds—frontline, backwater, technical, shore duty, administrative—can be challenging or instructive to those who undergo it. Besides line officers and enlisted sailors, a few officers who had administrative or technical assignments relate their experiences in these pages. *Human nature,* as illuminated by the unique challenges of naval service, is the central subject of this text. Although modern academics sometimes deny there is such a thing as human nature, I believe that had they spent three or four years struggling with recalcitrant wills on gun mounts or on mess decks, or fighting with petty tyrants in the bureaucracy ashore, or struggling to control themselves while attempting to land on a pitching flight deck in towering seas (low on fuel, or in the dark, or with damaged equipment), they might have a different opinion.

One other question naturally arises: why focus on writers just from the World War II era? On the one hand, why not reach farther back? After all, the U.S. Navy has a long pedigree in American literature. Of classic American writers, the most renowned former bluejacket is Herman Melville, "that persuasive advance man for the sea," as the poet X. J. Kennedy calls him (Kennedy himself having listened to Melville's call and become for a time an enlisted naval journalist).[4] Melville not only wrote about the sea, but he also wrote semiautobiographically in *White-Jacket; or, The World in a Man-of-War* about his fourteen months of naval service aboard the frigate USS *United States.*

And James Fenimore Cooper served three years as a midshipman in the U.S. Navy in the early nineteenth century and went on to pen no fewer than eleven sea novels which rivaled his other works of fiction in popular appeal, including, among them, a book about the naval exploits of John Paul Jones (*The Pilot*). Cooper also wrote an important early history of the Navy, a history which Capt. Edward L. Beach (one of the authors in this collection) literally read "to pieces" in his childhood and then (after a long and highly successful naval career) imitated by writing his own U.S. naval history.[5]

I could go on to cite other American authors who served in the Navy in the nineteenth or early-twentieth centuries and somewhere in their works described that experience. For instance, Richard Byrd, who served in naval uniform during all his Arctic and Antarctic explorations, wrote at least one minor classic (*Alone*) about his adventures, along with several other popular books, books that include interesting accounts of his early experience as a naval aviator.[6]

Or I could have gone forward and included pieces from naval-veterans-turned-authors from the Korean, Vietnam, or Cold War eras. To cite just one phenomenon, in the last few years several Naval Academy graduates have become best-selling popular novelists, experts at technological naval thrillers. The ex-naval aviator Stephen Coonts has written several books (including *The Flight of the Intruder, Final Flight,* and *The Minotaur*) which inimitably capture the experience of jet flying in the Vietnam era, just as the surface naval expert David Poyer has written several excellent novels of modern frigate and destroyer duty (*The Med, The Gulf,* and *The Circle,* to mention a few). P. T. Deutermann spent a whole career as a surface line officer (he retired as a captain in 1989 after twenty-six years of active service) before turning his hand to writing. He was immediately successful with novels like *Scorpion in the Sea* and *The Edge of Honor.* And Dick Couch, a Navy SEAL who served in Vietnam and who also worked for the CIA, has put his varied background to use in best-sellers like *SEAL Team One* and *Pressure Point.*

The successes of these authors (to name a few) in what was a completely new field for them is striking, and one or two of them have also written short autobiographical sketches which might have been included here.[7] But it is the generation of World War II authors whose naval experience is perhaps most instructive. Among other things, there were far more of them than in other periods, and they came from wider backgrounds. World War II put many more Americans of all kinds in uniform than before or since, many of them would-be or soon-to-be authors. Indeed, as we will see, some of them were authors even before they entered the service. Others wrote poems or stories or the better parts of novels or histories while in naval uniform, or even while serving aboard ship.[8]

The majority, of course, only turned to writing well after the war. Yet whatever literary or academic or journalistic career they later

pursued, many of them regarded their wartime experience as particularly significant.

On the whole, these men—and, perforce, all selections in this
volume are by men[9]—have attained an equipoise that is unusual,
especially so in our post-Vietnam War times, when academic and
intellectual culture can be so leery of all things military. These
authors provide a balance; they show an understanding, and a way.
In spite of all the absurdities they went through—the chaotic nature
of war, the stiffness of military ritual, the hard-bitten pettiness of
some naval authority, inevitable military misjudgments—they
speak with a positive voice. By and large, although they were subject to a variety of intense emotions and exasperations while in the
service, they are not cynical. They have retained their humor, their
optimism, their perspective.

To be sure, these authors can excoriate the Navy thoroughly. In
a section of his autobiography not included here, J. P. Donleavy
found that political favoritism was rife and cheating was cavalier
at the Naval Academy Preparatory School in the last year of the
war.[10] Louis Auchincloss was so revolted at the naval establishment
he encountered while on intelligence duty in the Panama Canal
Zone that he did everything he could to get to sea duty, and then
he wrote a novel (*The Indifferent Children*) which depicted some
naval authorities as self-serving bureaucrats. And many of these
authors—here or elsewhere—deplore the color line that existed in
the Navy, a policy which meant that, for the most part, even those
few black Americans who were able to get aboard ship could serve
only as stewards or "mess boys."[11]

But almost all of these authors also found some basic worth in
the institution in which they had once served. Not that they are
mindlessly saluting or marching in step: authors of quite different
political and cultural positions are represented in this volume. But
whatever their postwar outlooks or life-styles, these writers typically pay tribute to the Navy. In fact, most of these veterans who
later became novelists or journalists or academics (but who also in
the forties had been pilots or sailors or officers of the deck or even
ships' captains) speak of their naval service with some pride. The

closest thing to the anti-institutionalism of *Catch 22* in naval literature is probably that found in Gordon Forbes's *Goodbye to Some,* a novel that describes the progressively terrifying and demoralizing experience of bombing strategically unimportant targets in the far Pacific just at the war's end. Although relatively little known, *Goodbye to Some* is an excellent book; its description of bombing attacks, air combat, and long-distance flying—and associated emotions—rings with authenticity. But few of the authors represented in this text would acknowledge that the extremes of terror, despair, and revulsion into which that novel's characters devolve were typical of their own emotional experiences, let alone of their mature reflections about those experiences.

Several subthemes run through the varied selections in this text. Besides the ubiquitous conflicts between veteran and raw recruit there is an occasional tension between regular and reservist. The many attempts at leadership chronicled in these pages provide a kaleidoscope of impressions. Trials of long periods without women (for some) or the sexual expectations fostered by immersion in a sailor's culture (for others) produce their own kinds of drama or at least fantasy. And in this collection of writings by fine American authors there is the repeated phenomenon of serious humanistic writing being attempted in the war, either officially—in billets employing fine historians—or unofficially. Whether shipboard in the Pacific or in odd locations like the Philadelphia Navy Yard, which employed several American science fiction pioneers in uniform and out,[12] many aspiring authors kept whiling away vacant hours attempting to get published or to establish a literary reputation—this at the same time they were in naval employ.

But mainly these selections comprise a set of personal expressions of the confrontation of intelligent and empathetic human beings with the difficulties of wartime naval service. They do so, often with humor, sometimes with weariness or regret, and occasionally with wonder or awe—but they also do it with style. Literary experts often argue that there was very little good writing that came out of World War II. And to be sure, these recollections reflect somewhat less of the intense crucible of combat than is customary in

Science fiction pioneers *(left to right)* Robert Heinlein, L. Sprague
de Camp, and Isaac Asimov at the Navy Yard in Philadelphia in
1944. Sprague de Camp served as a naval officer, Asimov and
Heinlein as civilians.

much military fiction. But it is not poor writing for that. Sometimes
criticism would seem to insist that writing about warfare must
express outrage at the utter senselessness of such inhuman activity
and revulsion at all things military. Yet the experience of the writers represented in this volume is that literary sensitivity and military discipline can coexist.

Despite military uniformity and required obedience and dulling
routine and killing and battle—all of which we normally regard as
quite foreign, even antithetical, to literary or intellectual voca-
tions—these authors in retrospection give full measure to both sides
of the wartime naval equation. In their writings they manifest something of the enormous destruction and personal tragedy of warfare,
but they also credit professionals who can fight well. They can be

highly critical of naval institutions and officials, but they can be genuinely self-critical too. In the end, whether they be amateur or polished, whether early works or late, what these writings suggest is that you can have intelligence and sensitivity and wit and still be a sailor. And they also manifest at least this much: Some excellent writing can come from American authors who have taken the time to reflect on the personal roles they played in the naval side of a war.

NOTES

1. For an account of Morison's attempts to have his project approved, and a fairly detailed scholarly discussion of his whole naval history project, see Gregory M. Pfitzer, *Samuel Eliot Morison's Historical World: In Quest of a New Parkman* (Boston: Northeastern University Press, 1991), pp. 170–192. For Morison's own perspective and that of his "principal assistant," see the selections from Morison and Henry Salomon Jr. in this volume.

2. Michener's selection in this volume tells of the welcome positive support he received from one enlisted critic. But Michener also had a decidedly negative critic (an officer) and several other readers for his stories. Cf. John P. Hayes, *James A. Michener: A Biography* (Indianapolis: Bobbs-Merrill, 1984), p. 66, who quotes from several Michener letters.

3. Science fiction writer James Gunn avers that while the struggles he went through as a naval officer trainee might seem to have produced no benefit: "[O]ne thing they accomplished . . . is that I learned what I was capable of doing. Nothing afterwards seemed difficult. College became easy; that was one reason, along with an impatience to get on with their lives and careers, the returning veterans changed the nature of the college classroom forever. It was not simply that, with their G.I. Bill benefits, they doubled enrollments overnight. [The returning veterans] were different." From "James Gunn," *Contemporary Authors Autobiography Series,* vol. 2, p. 245.

4. "X. J. Kennedy," *Contemporary Authors Autobiography Series,* vol. 9, pp. 81–82.

5. *The United States Navy: 200 Years* (New York: Henry Holt and Company, 1986).

6. For example, in *Skyward* (New York: G. P. Putnam's Sons, 1928), pp. 43–58, Byrd chronicles his flight training at Pensacola and his service on the "crash board" by which he and others would visit accident sites to try to determine why their fellow fliers had just died.

7. Couch describes his unit's liberation of a Vietcong POW camp in "My First Firefight," Naval Academy Alumni magazine *Shipmate,* November 1987, pp. 23–26.

8. For example, Louis Auchincloss began a draft of *The Indifferent Children* while commanding an LST in the Pacific; Herman Wouk worked on *Aurora*

Dawn while on a destroyer-minesweeper; and the naval aviator William Meredith wrote and published a book of poetry about his experiences flying from a carrier escort—*Love Letter from an Impossible Land,* foreword by Archibald MacLeish (New Haven: Yale University Press, 1944).

9. Few of the 90,000-plus women who served in naval uniform during World War II (as Waves or nurses) seem to have become authors of reputation, and almost none of those (to my knowledge, at least, and to the knowledge of several women-in-the-Navy experts I've consulted) has reflected upon her naval duty in print. One woman's experience is perhaps illuminating. Grace Person Hayes (BA, Wellesley; MA, Columbia) worked as an officer in the Waves at a Navy blimp base during the war, decrypting classified information. When the war ended, she received orders for duty in Washington as a historian. She accepted, and eventually was assigned to write a two-volume classified history of the Joint Chiefs of Staff and their prosecution of the war against Japan.

When she finally completed the second volume in 1953, having married in the meantime, she decided to leave the service because she was pregnant. When she went back to show off the baby in early 1954, she was shown the second volume, which had just been printed. But she was not allowed to open it because it was classified—and she no longer had a security clearance.

Hayes finally got a declassified copy in 1971; the work was published (as one volume of 964 pages) in 1982 by the Naval Institute Press. It has become a basic source document of the Pacific war. Hayes went on to author and co-author other books. See Thomas Allen, "Grace Hayes and Her Joint Chiefs," *Naval History* magazine, Nov.–Dec. 1995, pp. 31–33.

10. *The History of the Ginger Man* (Boston: Houghton Mifflin, 1994), pp. 168–75.

11. Blacks were also recruited into a few other enlisted rates—Seabees and pharmacist's mates, for instance. But these personnel usually performed shoreside jobs or served with the Marines.

Late in the war a few more selected ratings were opened up. The Navy also commissioned a few black naval officers, some of whom got to sea; see Paul Stillwell, ed., *The Golden Thirteen: Recollections of the First Black Naval Officers* (Annapolis: Naval Institute Press, 1993), and the selection by journalist Carl Rowan in this volume.

12. Robert Heinlein, a 1929 Naval Academy graduate who had to leave the service in 1934 because of tuberculosis, was recruited by a former academy classmate (Albert Scoles) to work in the R&D labs at Mustin Field, Philadelphia, during World War II. Heinlein then recruited Isaac Asimov for the program. Both Heinlein and Asimov worked as civilians; L. Sprague de Camp was to join the staff as a naval lieutenant. The first two books of Asimov's "Foundation" series were written while the writer was a chemist in the labs at Mustin Field. See the "Afterword" to "Searchlight" in Heinlein's *Expanded Universe: The New Worlds of Robert A. Heinlein* (New York: Grosset & Dunlap, 1980), pp. 452–57.

REPORTING
ABOARD

SLOAN WILSON

SLOAN WILSON realized he might have some talent as a writer when, late in World War II, a poem he had composed while serving aboard a Coast Guard vessel was accepted by the *New Yorker*. He left the service in 1945 and tried his hand as an editor at Houghton Mifflin (rather unsuccessfully: he recommended *against* publishing *Mr. Roberts*). He also worked as a writer and editor in various other capacities. His 1955 novel, *The Man in the Gray Flannel Suit*, was his most successful book; it became part of the popular culture of the era. Wilson also has written many other books (mostly novels).

Wilson is unique among the authors represented in this book in that he had extensive command experience during the war. Having taken an exam to become a Coast Guard officer just after the attack on Pearl Harbor, he was immediately sent to sea on the U.S. Coast Guard cutter *Tampa* (WPB-48). After escorting convoys on the Greenland Patrol for several months, he put in for command of a trawler, and soon he was given the small American trawler *Nogak* (WYP-171). He based his 1979 novel, *Ice Brothers*, upon this tour of duty. Wilson then spent a few months ashore at antisubmarine warfare school before taking command of a newly commissioned Army supply ship, the *FS-158*, a small vessel which he skippered from Long Beach to New Guinea and to other ports in the South

Pacific. (His first novel, *Voyage to Somewhere,* published in 1947, is based upon this experience.)

Having contracted pneumonia, Wilson had to relinquish this command, but when he recovered, he was given charge of a gasoline tanker, the *Y-14.* In 1982 he wrote his most directly autobiographical (and probably his best) Coast Guard novel in imitation of this experience; he called the book *Pacific Interlude.* The novel recounts the madhouse of a ship whose crew daily had to face the terrifying possibility of being blown literally to pieces by a stray spark, flame, or bullet.

Wilson wrote one other work that took into account his service background. Some of the best reading of his charming memoir can be found in the eighty-some pages that describe his early days in the Coast Guard—especially his initiation aboard small ships in the ice, cold, and storms of the North Atlantic. That experience began the day that he reported aboard the *Tampa,* as described below.

from

WHAT SHALL WE WEAR TO THIS PARTY? THE MAN IN THE GRAY FLANNEL SUIT TWENTY YEARS BEFORE AND AFTER

In those days, when there was such a need for young officers, it was possible to get a commission in the coast guard by taking a twelve-hour examination in navigation and seamanship at M.I.T. I had learned the navigation before I dropped out of the Naval Reserve unit at Harvard to look after my own vessel, and I had picked up a little seamanship during our summer cruises. I passed the examination with such high marks that I began laboring under the dangerous illusion that I was an experienced old salt.

With the notice that I had met the requirements for a commission, the coast guard sent me a list of clothes and equipment I should buy. My mother gave me the money for this, and I bought the full regalia, including an impressive sword.

"Why in the world do they make you buy a sword?" [my wife] Elise asked. "Are you going to try to fight submarines with that?"

"I think they sometimes use swords in parades," I replied. "Anyway, it will make a nice souvenir for our children."

In those days we had fallen into the habit of talking about "our children" as though they already existed. The concept of them lying in wait to be born somehow comforted us.

In our apartment I tried on the handsome dress uniform, the blue uniforms with their single gold stripe and the gold shield, which was the coast guard emblem, on the cuffs. One thing I couldn't figure out was the way to attach the shoulder boards to the great coat and the khaki uniforms. It somehow seemed right to have the tapered ends out and the broad ends in. That's the way I fixed them, and when my orders came a few weeks later, that's the way I wore them when I went aboard the United States Coast Guard Cutter *Tampa,* which was moored at a shipyard in Boston. Somewhere I had learned that one is supposed to salute the quarterdeck when one boards a cutter. I had very little practice at saluting, and instead of making it an informal gesture as most officers did, I stopped in the middle of the gangway, assumed as statuesque a position as possible and snapped my hand from the visor of my cap to my side. To the men who were watching me from the deck of the cutter, I seemed typical of all the reserve officers who were pouring into the service. I had my shoulder boards on backward and exaggerated the salute to the quarterdeck so much that I was burlesquing it.

Surprised by the laughter which greeted me, I asked the quartermaster who stood at the gangway where I could find the officer of the deck. This—*The Naval Officer's Guide* had taught me—was the correct procedure.

"He's in his stateroom," the quartermaster replied. "The exec will want to see you if you're coming aboard for duty. He's up on the flying bridge."

The quartermaster told a seaman to show me the way to the flying bridge. After climbing several steel ladders, I found myself standing on a broad deck where a stocky man about fifty years old was pacing in circles. On the cuffs of his uniform he wore two gold stripes which were so worn that they had turned almost to silver. His close-cropped hair was also silvery, and his wrinkled face resembled that of an English bulldog.

Without a word the messenger left me there and disappeared. For perhaps a minute—which seemed very long—the executive officer paced without seeming to notice me.

"Sir," I said finally.

"Now what the hell do you want?" he demanded.

"My name is Wilson, sir. Ensign Wilson is reporting aboard for duty."

"Oh no!" the exec said, and clapped his hand to his forehead.

"Sir?"

"I asked for an officer, god damn it, and they send me a boy with a gold stripe. Did you get that along with the gold stars the teacher used to give you in school?"

"No, sir."

"Have you ever had any experience with this big pond out here which we call the North Atlantic ocean?"

"I have had considerable experience, sir, with small vessels."

"What the hell kind of small vessels?"

"Yachts, sir."

"Oh, sweet Jesus Christ!" the exec thundered. "They've sent me a yachtsman! Dear sweet Jesus Christ, what have I done to deserve this?"

The man's rage was so great that he was making faces at me. His lips drew back in a snarl and his shaggy eyebrows almost covered his piercing blue eyes.

"A yachtsman," he repeated. "Yachtsmen are what the coast guard has to go out saving every day. If they have to commission yachtsmen, why in hell don't they give them to the other side? All of Hitler's admirals put together couldn't run a navy if they had yachtsmen for officers."

"Yes, sir," I heard myself saying.

"Now how did you get that gold stripe on your arm? It took me twenty years as a chief boatswain's mate to get a gold stripe. How did you get yours?"

"I took a twelve-hour examination at M.I.T., sir."

"Jesus, *sweet* Jesus, sweet Jesus Christ," the exec thundered, and he actually clawed his hair as though he were trying to pull it out.

"It took me twenty years to get a gold stripe, and it took you twelve hours. Now where did you get the book learning for that examination?"

"Harvard College, sir."

"Harvard! *Harvard!* I ask for a coast guard officer and they send me a Harvard boy. Are you a fag, boy? They say they got a lot of fags over there at Harvard. We'll have no fags aboard this ship. How could we sleep at night knowing there was only a Harvard fag standing watch on the bridge?"

"Sir! I'm not a fag. You have no reason to worry about that."

"Not a fag, eh? Well, I bet you're a rich little bastard. A snotty rich little prick. That's what they *specialize* in at Harvard, isn't it? That and fags. Of the two I think I'd prefer the fag."

He resumed his pacing and started circling around me like a wolf ready to close in for the kill. His face was still contorted with rage. At first I had thought that this was only some kind of hazing that met all newcomers, but I realized now that the executive officer's anger was real.

"I've only got two officers on this goddamn ship now that are good enough to stand a watch at sea," he continued. "How long do they think it will take me to make a coast guard officer out of a Harvard boy? This is only the second world war, boy! Even if I worked day and night, I doubt whether I could get you ready in time for the third one!"

I couldn't think of anything to say to this. I made a timid attempt to smile.

"What are you laughing for, boy? Jesus Christ, look at you. You've got your shoulder boards on backward. By god, you're an *original,* I'll say that for you. How dare you walk aboard a coast guard cutter all ass backwards like that?"

To my horror the blood rushed to my face.

"I don't know anything about uniforms, sir, sir," I stammered. "The examination was only in navigation and seamanship."

"Book navigation and book seamanship, you mean. You think you know seamanship, eh? Can you launch and pick up a whaleboat in thirty-foot seas?"

"No, sir."

"Well, what the hell can you do? Please enlighten me. The government is giving you more pay than I got after my first twenty years in the service. Now, god damn it, you must know something. It stands to reason. The people up there in Washington are crazy, but they can't be *this* crazy. What can you do to justify that gold stripe?"

"I think I can learn fairly fast, sir."

"*Learn!* You go to school to learn! On a coast guard cutter we save lives! We sink submarines! We stay out in hurricanes to send weather reports. This is no schoolhouse, boy! Maybe you got confused because we got a ship's bell. That's not a school bell, boy! We just ring that when we're anchored in a fog."

"Yes, sir."

"What can you do besides learn?"

"I can navigate fairly well, sir, but I need more experience in identifying stars."

"So, you've come here to learn and to get experience. Can you piss in the head, boy, without missing it when the ship is rolling forty degrees?"

"I hope so, sir."

"Can you keep your vomit off my decks when we get out of this harbor? I'll have no Harvards vomiting on my decks. Makes them too slippery. We had a Yale aboard here once, and all he did was vomit on the decks. Had seamen sliding all over the place. I hear the Harvards are even worse than the Yales, more faggoty. Can you keep from vomiting on the decks, boy?"

"I'll try, sir."

"Oh Jesus, sweet Jesus Christ! Get out of my sight, boy! I have worries enough without you. I have this whole ship to put in shape, and they've given me only a week. I got women welders aboard. Have you ever heard of a woman welder? They sent two aboard to weld them twenty millimeters on the deck. I got women welders and I got Harvards and Yales, and who knows what's going to happen next? You know, it wouldn't surprise me one goddamn bit if they sent me a *monkey* in an ensign's uniform tomorrow. I got to get out of this port or we'll have the whole fucking zoo aboard here, all decked out in brand new uniforms!"

His ferocity was such that there was no temptation to laugh.

"Get out of here!" he finally said. "Go below! Hide! At least I don't have to *look* at you, do I?"

"No, sir," I said, and quickly skinned down the ladders to the deck. A thin, craggy-looking lieutenant junior grade came up to me.

"I see you're still alive," he said. "I'm sorry I didn't get a chance to warn you about the terrible tempered Pop Hart."

"Pop Hart?"

"That's what everybody calls him. He's great with the enlisted men, but he's hell on junior officers, especially us reserves."

"You mean he puts on that sort of display for every ensign who comes aboard here?"

"I don't know just what he did for you. He had one ensign locked up in the brig five minutes after he came aboard."

"What was the charge?"

"Impersonating an officer. He acted real surprised when the guy turned out to be legit."

I laughed.

"Come and I'll show you your stateroom," the lieutenant junior grade said. "My name is Carter. I'm glad to see you come aboard. Frankly, I hope you turn out to be completely incompetent. That might keep some of the heat off me."

*   *   *

I am writing these words thirty-three years after I walked aboard the United States Coast Guard Cutter *Tampa*. Although I was aboard the vessel only about six months, I have many more memories of her than I have of the four years I spent at Harvard College, and I think she taught me more.

The *Tampa* had been old even before the start of World War II. Two hundred and forty feet long, she had a plum stem and a stern like the tail of a seagull, a graceful configuration which showed its recent descent from sailing vessels. The ship had not yet acquired the Arctic camouflage of pale blue and white. She was painted battleship gray, which was really the only warlike thing about her. Partly because of the heavy construction which made her an efficient rescue ship, the *Tampa* was painfully slow for an escort vessel. When the engines were running well, she could reach a speed of only thirteen knots—a limitation which meant that she could barely get out of the way of her own depth charges. To make matters worse, there was no modern method for aiming the two 3-inch and two 5-inch guns that had recently been welded to our decks. When we tried to sink a derelict barge, we couldn't hit it even when we sailed right alongside it. When we used a small iceberg for target practice, it survived intact. These displays did little to improve the morale of the crew.

The duty of the *Tampa,* during that spring of 1942, was to escort merchant vessels from Sydney, Nova Scotia, to our air bases in Greenland. As soon as the *Tampa* got to Greenland, she was ordered back to Sydney to meet a new convoy. Rarely did her crew get ashore.

Conditions at sea were so difficult that few men of the *Tampa* had time to worry about the German submarines which were reported in our area. During the summer months, those Arctic seas were foggy most of the time, and in winter the endless night and almost endless gales reduced visibility as much as the fog did. In those early days of the war, the *Tampa* had no radar and only the most primitive sonar. Completely blind, the ship had to zigzag around a convoy which was itself zigzagging. In retrospect, the fact that the ship did this without collisions appears to be a miracle.

It was a miracle which few of the *Tampa*'s men expected. On the starboard side of a deckhouse, some profound student of military morale had placed a bronze plaque in memory of the first *Tampa,* a coast guard cutter which had gone down with all hands during World War I. The men made grim jokes about the fact that one plaque could be used to commemorate both *Tampa*'s if we sank.

When I first went aboard the *Tampa* and was lambasted by Pop Hart on the flying bridge, I assumed that this was some sort of hazing which was dished out to all newcomers, or that the grizzled executive officer was insane. I was wrong on both counts. Pop Hart's difficulty was simply that he understood the situation. He knew what it was like to convoy ships through Arctic seas, and he also knew that the *Tampa* had no more than four competent deck officers in addition to an ever growing swarm of reserve officers who had been hastily commissioned before the coast guard even had a chance to start effective training programs.

"Do you know what this is like?" Pop Hart said to me the day after I had come aboard. "This is like going to some goddamn football stadium and dressing everybody in the audience up like players. You can put old ladies and fat men in helmets and jerseys, but, god damn it, that's not going to make them play ball!"

I never saw the commanding officer of the ship until a few minutes before we were to get under way and leave Boston harbor for Nova Scotia and Greenland. Our skipper appeared to be the direct opposite of Pop Hart. Small, delicately made and dapper, he used as few words as possible. I watched the two of them in action, for I was stationed as a junior watch officer on the wing of the bridge.

The captain seated himself on a stool near the wheel. He gripped his knees, and the three gold stripes of a commander looked too big for his short arms.

"Mr. Hart," he said in a voice that was barely audible. "You may get under way when ready and proceed to the fuel barge."

"Aye, aye, sir!" Hart bellowed. At the top of his voice he began to give orders as he paced back and forth on the bridge.

"Quartermaster! Tell the engine room to stand by. Messenger! Ask the chief if the decks are secure and ready for sea. Pipe mooring stations! Mr. Wilson! Please get your ass off the bridge. The one thing I had hoped is that you at least would know enough to stay the hell out of the way!"

"I was told . . ."

"Never mind, god damn it. Get out of my sight. I got work to do."

I retreated to a ladder leading to the deck, where I could hide but still see a good deal of what was going on.

"Right full rudder," Hart bellowed to the helmsman as though he were standing a thousand yards away. Coming to the wing of the bridge over my head, he called, "All right, Boats, take in one, three and four."

"One, three and four, sir," the chief boatswain's mate repeated.

The heavy lines splashed. Mr. Hart started bawling orders to the quartermaster who stood by the engine room telegraph. The ship trembled to the rhythm of her heavy engines as we backed away from the wharf and headed out of the slip.

That first short journey from the wharf to the fuel barge in Boston harbor taught me a lot. The channels were crowded with tugs, barges, tankers and every other kind of wartime shipping. Mr. Hart stood on the port wing of the bridge and barked brief orders to the helmsman and quartermaster as we threaded our way through the traffic. He stood straighter than I had ever seen him and his voice had lost its fury. He was, I realized as he threaded his way past a tug's string of barges and an aircraft carrier which occupied most of the channel, a superb ship handler. He smiled as we passed the carrier with only a few feet to spare at the very edge of the channel.

"Boy!" he said to me, despite the fact that I had thought myself safely hidden halfway down the ladder.

"Sir?"

"I doubt if it will ever happen, but if you ever learn enough to conn this vessel in crowded waters, you just remember that that uniform of yours is the uniform of the United States Coast Guard, and this is the United States Coast Guard Cutter *Tampa.* Other ships can walk or run, boy, but a United States Coast Guard cutter has to *dance!*"

And dance the old *Tampa* did as we zigzagged through the crowded harbor and finally arrived at the fuel barge, from which a destroyer was just pulling clear. A tanker was made fast to the other side of the barge, her ensign flat in a brisk breeze which was coming from the mouth of the harbor. As we passed a buoy I saw that it was leaning to a swift current. With such a wind and tide it would not be easy to take a single-screw vessel alongside a barge, and the task would be harder because the barge itself was anchored to long lines, on which it was slowly swinging in a broad arc.

"Ahead slow," Mr. Hart said, and almost immediately added, "Ahead half."

The cutter approached the barge briskly.

"Mr. Hart," the captain said in his oddly dead voice. "Don't try a smart mooring now. I just want a safe one. Reduce your speed."

"Aye, aye, sir," Mr. Hart said, and he made a face, a fierce grimace with bared fangs. Fortunately he had his back to the captain. "Ahead slow," he said to the quartermaster, and made his face again.

The curious thing about Mr. Hart was that when he made a face he managed to be truly terrifying, not just funny. There was nothing fake about Pop Hart. He hated all reserve officers because they didn't know enough, and he hated our captain because he was timid and did not act according to Hart's romantic ideal of a coast guard officer. Whether his romantic ideal of a coast guard officer went around making faces at people, I had no idea, but Pop Hart's all-consuming rage was so powerful that it had to erupt somewhere.

I have for some reason some intense need to make the war appear funny. There was, of course, nothing humorous about the half year I spent as a junior watch officer aboard the *Tampa*. In the first place, I was seasick almost all the time. Summer cruises on yachts had not fitted me for Arctic gales. To obey Pop Hart's command that I keep his decks clean, I carried a bucket on my arm when I went on watch and quietly retched into it every few minutes. No food would stay down. Soon my uniform hung on me as loosely as though my shoulders were a wire hanger.

Worse than the seasickness was the fear of death. A large troop-ship, the *Chatham*, was sunk in Davis Strait just before we got there. Submarines appeared to me to be lying in wait for us everywhere. Thousands of icebergs seemed to me to constitute an even greater menace. It seemed clear to me that the odds were much in favor of my getting killed, and though I knew I should be brave, I was obsessed with thoughts of what it must be like to be on the deck of a ship when she was hit by a torpedo. Everyone said that a man couldn't live more than thirty seconds in the freezing seas of Davis Strait. What did he think about for those thirty seconds?

Lying in my bunk, retching in my bucket and trying to imagine death, I felt unabashedly sorry for myself. Damn it, I was much too *nice* to die, and actually, I was too nice to be seasick month after month. Somehow God had got his plans all mixed up. Here I was going to be eaten by sharks and crabs and even minnows, while evil old men prospered ashore. My wife would soon remarry someone smart or sick enough not to go to war. I would be erased without a memory. Even the sharks and crabs and minnows would soon be hungry for more.

Worse even than the seasickness and the fear was the realization of my own incompetence, my own worthlessness as an officer and as a man. Every day brought me new problems which I could not solve. Handicapped by my seasickness and by the murky skies, I hardly ever could make my star sights work. I couldn't read Morse code or signal flags. I knew nothing about the maintenance or use of the ship's guns. On and on the list of my inadequacies ran. When on watch I hid as much as possible behind a door on the bridge, and the rest of the time I retreated to my bunk.

When we were in Sydney, Nova Scotia, that autumn, the *Tampa* took aboard a load of six-hundred-pound depth charges—twice the normal weight. They were said to be effective against submarines, but almost every man in our crew suspected that because of her slow speed, the *Tampa* could not drop such large amounts of TNT without blowing off her own stern. Almost every man jack was just as scared as I was, I realized with some relief. In fear at least I was not alone.

At general quarters, I was stationed four decks down in the stern of the ship, where I was supposed to supervise five black steward's mates who were passing ammunition up to the 5-inch gun overhead. Pop Hart told me to be sure to wear the .45 automatic which every officer was supposed to wear during general quarters.

"It doesn't take much to make those niggers panic," Mr. Hart said darkly. He was, among other things, a cornucopia of racial prejudice. When he told me that he wanted me to shoot the steward's mates if they panicked, I was not a bit surprised.

Among the many things I didn't know was how to shoot a .45 pistol, and I had been unwilling to pull the gun from its holster for fear it might go off and hit me in the leg. Beyond this, I rather liked the steward's mates, who brought food to my stateroom when I felt well enough to eat, and who were the only people on the ship who did not keep sneering at my incompetence. Every time we went to general quarters, the steward's mates sat in the magazines waiting for the call for ammunition, and I sat a few steps up the companionway presumably waiting to shoot them. There was only one small blue bulb down there in the magazine, and the eerie light it cast contributed to the lack of reality I felt. Once when all our machine guns opened up overhead, the steward's mates leapt to their feet and looked as though they might panic, but then I found myself backing up the companionway toward the deck—a reaction which was quite involuntary, and which was interrupted when one of the steward's mates said, "Suh, I think you better stay down here."

The machine guns, we soon learned, had been sinking a floating mine which probably had drifted over from Europe. None of us had expected to encounter a floating mine in the middle of Davis Strait, and the discovery of such a menace, in addition to all the others, did little to increase our sense of well-being.

Only a few days later, another coast guard cutter which was helping us to escort the convoy signaled a submarine alert and began dropping depth charges. We went to general quarters, and I again found myself sitting in that blue light with the five steward's mates, who appeared to be taking all the excitement so philosophically that they prepared to light cigarettes, until I reminded them that we were surrounded by ammunition. That was my most officer-like deed of the entire voyage, and I felt quite proud of it. Down there in the bowels of the ship, we felt the thump of the other cutter's depth charges in addition to hearing them. Then our own engines suddenly speeded up.

"Here we go," the tallest of the steward's mates said. "Now we going to find out if we can drop them six-hundred-pounders."

"Oh, we can drop *one*," a small, lighter-colored man said. Dark laughter.

There was a lot of clatter on deck, followed by silence broken only by an increase of the engines to what I guessed was flank speed. The motion of the ship changed as she shifted course. I vomited into my trusty bucket—my way of meeting all maritime emergencies. While I was still suffering from the dizziness of nausea, there was the loudest explosion I had ever heard, and the stern of the vessel was thrown so high in the air that the decks became almost perpendicular. The blue light went out. In the complete darkness I was kicked several times as the steward's mates climbed over my body to bolt for the deck. I knew that this was when I was supposed to shoot them, but I was hanging precariously from a ladder, and it was too dark to shoot anybody, even if I had had any real stomach for that kind of military activity. The steward's mates did not seem very important, because the ship obviously had received an enormous blow, either from her own depth charges or a torpedo, and I was sure that I was about to die. The stern of the ship suddenly came down as violently as it had gone up, and all my strength was necessary to hang tightly to the ladder. I was surprised to find that my head was clearer than it had been in weeks, and I felt oddly calm. My calmness in the face of death delighted me. It would of course be a short-lived triumph, but at least I could die with the first glimmering of self-respect. As the ship steadied into a normal position, which is to say, a heavy roll, I listened to see if I could hear a rush of water through a hole left by the explosion, but there was none. All I could hear was the rolling of heavy objects on the deck below. It dawned on me that the steward's mates had dropped the explosive shells they were supposed to be passing to the gun overhead. Rolling about, they of course constituted a danger almost as bad as a torpedo. Feeling highly heroic, I captured the shells and stowed them. As I ran my fingers over the pigeon holes in which bags of powder and the shells were kept, it occurred to me that only a crazy man would start shooting a pistol in a magazine. That is what I would tell Pop Hart if he asked me why I had not shot the steward's mates.

Only a few minutes later I heard the signal to secure from general quarters. In the wardroom, where the unrepentant steward's mates were serving sandwiches and coffee, I heard the cause of the enormous explosion: when the signal had been given to drop a six-hundred-pound charge, a frightened seaman had held the big "ashcan" back by putting his hand on it. Whereupon the signal had been given again, and in the end, two of the lethal charges had been dropped together. Pop Hart was furious about the mix-up, but his anger was lightened by pride in the fact that the old *Tampa* had survived without serious injury.

"You tell me what ship except a coast guard cutter can survive twelve hundred pounds of TNT under her ass when she's only making thirteen knots!" he said.

I was apprehensive for days, but he never found out about the panicking steward's mates, or my dereliction from duty in allowing them to escape. In the lightheadedness induced by my continued seasickness, I sometimes imagined being ordered by Pop Hart to stalk through the ship, shooting steward's mates wherever they could be found. I even imagined a citation I might be given by President Roosevelt himself.

> For shooting all six steward's mates aboard the United States Coast Guard Cutter *Tampa* while engaged in combat with German submarines off the coast of Greenland, the Distinguished Service Cross is hereby awarded to Ensign Sloan Wilson, USCGR, who bagged his men despite extreme seasickness.

Despite the lack of such a citation, I found that the memory of my performance in the after magazine of the *Tampa* gave me pleasure to help combat the depression of seasickness. There had, after all, been about three minutes there when I actually had been brave, the only three minutes in which I could feel pride during the months I had been aboard the *Tampa*. The nonsense about shooting the steward's mates was the first example I had of the fact that war is ridiculous far more than it is heroic. When one came right down to it, I saw, the steward's mates had been sensible enough to panic when the *Tampa* had come close to sinking herself with two giant depth charges while pursuing a whale, for that is what the man on the sonar machine finally decided that his target was. The only good thing about this whole burlesque was that despite the explosion of twelve hundred pounds of TNT, both the steward's mates and the whale had got away.

TRAINING

RUSSELL BAKER

RUSSELL BAKER, journalist and humorist, became a reporter upon finishing college in 1947. He developed an eye for the humor of events first while working on the Baltimore *Sun* (in Baltimore and in London) and later while serving in the Washington Bureau of the New York *Times*. In the latter position, he often sensed something of the absurdity of political events, and in 1962 began writing "The Observer," a column that was syndicated and came to appear in hundreds of papers. Baker won the Pulitzer Prize for distinguished commentary in 1979.

In the 1980s Baker turned a gentle satire upon his own life in two memoirs. The following passage is drawn from the first, the acclaimed biography *Growing Up,* which won several awards, including another Pulitzer Prize. Baker was in the midst of college at Johns Hopkins when he entered the Navy Air Corps in 1943, and about that time the Navy began to string out the pilot pipeline because too many pilots had been recruited. As a result, he never got to the war, and he was quickly discharged at the war's conclusion.

His short service, however, was nevertheless eventful. Baker's chief subjects in this passage, which begins just after he leaves home, are his initial naval training, flight training, and his continuous "struggle to get rid of my accursed virginity." The latter subject,

incidentally, fills page after page of modern naval memoirs—though
few such descriptions are quite like Baker's.

from

GROWING UP

For the next eighteen months, while old friends and schoolmates
were discovering the face of death on battlefields from Bastogne to
Okinawa, the Navy sent me on an extended tour of Dixie. After four
months at Pensacola came three months at the University of South
Carolina. I was in Miami living the good life at Coral Gables when
Eisenhower sent the armies ashore on D-Day, and at pre-flight
school at the University of Georgia when Patton was racing for the
Rhine. I was at Memphis waiting to take off on a flight to Arkansas
when a mechanic climbed onto the wing and shouted: "President
Roosevelt is dead!" Germany surrendered three weeks later and I
was sent back to Pensacola. Because the Navy had overestimated
the number of flyers it needed to fight Japan, flight training slowed
to a crawl. The Navy had kept one of its promises—it had put thirty-
five pounds on me—but its promise of glory remained unfulfilled.

By the summer of 1945 we were flying out of Whiting Field. It
was a broiling expanse of cleared land in the north Florida boon-
docks, one of those ugly, barren, temporary training bases that had
been nailed together overnight. The South was strewn with them
during World War II. A couple of runways and acres of stark wooden
barracks surrounded by a perimeter of back-shadowed piney
woods. A water tank on four steel legs. A flag hanging limp in sul-
try air. Pensacola was an hour away by slow bus. I made the trip to
town and back several nights a week on account of Karen, an Indi-
ana girl at the local nursing school. I was in love.

It was a chaste romance. We held hands in the movies and walking the streets. Under a subtropical moon we sat in the grass and
Karen confided her dreams, which had to do with owning a horse
farm and having a large family, and I talked of mine, which had to
do with shooting down Japanese warplanes. We kissed without feel-

ing any fire and went to Walgreen's drugstore for milkshakes, and she went back to the nurses' quarters while I rode the bus back to Whiting Field. I considered our love too fine to be fouled by lust and was offended when my roommate Ozzie, awakening as I returned, leaned down from his upper bunk to ask as he always did, "Did you get deflowered tonight, Bake?"

A big part of my Navy career by then had been spent in the struggle to get rid of my accursed virginity. This had been harder than learning to swim or learning to fly. The swimming had been surprisingly easy, thanks to the Navy's policy of dealing with fear by ignoring it. My fear of deep water left the Navy simply uninterested. On the first day in the pool an instructor with a voice like a bullhorn ordered fifty of us to climb a high board and jump in feet first. The board looked about two hundred feet high, though it may have been only twenty or twenty-five. A line was formed to mount the ladder and jump. I drifted to the end of the line, then stepped out when the splashing started and introduced myself to the instructor.

"I'm a nonswimmer," I said. "You want me to go to the shallow end of the pool?" At City College I'd spent four years in the shallow end of the pool.

"This pool doesn't have a shallow end," the instructor said.

"Well, what am I going to do?"

"Get up on that platform and jump," he said.

The pool depth was marked as fifteen feet at that point.

"I'm not kidding. I can't swim a stroke."

"Up! Up!" he shouted.

"But I'll drown."

"This pool's got the best lifesaving equipment in the Navy," he said. "Don't worry about it."

"Come on."

"I'm giving you an order, mister. Up!"

Quaking in every fiber, I climbed the ladder, edged out onto the board, took one look down, and unable to faint, stepped back.

"Jump!" the instructor roared.

I stepped to the edge, closed my eyes, and walked into space. The impact of the water was like being smacked on the bottom by

Russell Baker as a naval air cadet.
COURTESY OF RUSSELL BAKER

a two-by-four, then I was sinking, then—my God!—I was rising irre-sistibly to the surface. My head broke water. The water was actu-ally supporting me, just as everybody had always said it would. The instructor glared.

"You didn't keep your legs straight," he shouted. "Get back up there and do it again."

Astonishingly, I was able to make a little progress dog-paddling through the water, and, hauling myself out of the pool, I went back up the ladder and did it again. Again I popped to the surface like a cork. Again I was able to move a little through the water. Fifteen feet of water too. I was swimming. Swimming! A lifetime of fear ended in those few moments. By the end of a year I was able to swim, fully clothed, for hours at a stretch in deep water.

Flying was trickier. My early instructors tried to put me at ease by saying it was a lot like driving a car. I was afraid to tell them I didn't know how to drive a car. Didn't every young man know how to drive by the time he was sixteen? Not knowing how to drive by eighteen seemed shameful. I feared the Navy would wash me out of flight training and send me to scrub decks if they learned about it.

On my first flight the instructor took me to three thousand feet in a Piper Cub before letting me handle the stick.

"Goddamn it, don't swing it like an axe handle!" he shouted when I yanked the plane violently up and down. "You wouldn't handle a steering wheel like that, would you?"

This was when we were flying out of a field south of Miami where the instructors were all civilian pilots under Navy contract. Mine was a nervous, middle-aged pilot named Jim, a natty little man with bulging eyeballs usually bloodshot from hangover, a handsome cavalry mustache over his lip, and fear of student flying in his soul. After our seventh flight together, he landed the plane, stepped out, smiled at me, and said, "You take her around."

I was appalled. He was telling me I was ready to "solo." I knew I wasn't. He'd demonstrated the basics during our seven flights and then had me practice while he sat in the front seat. Theoretically I knew how to take off, maintain altitude, bank, recover from a stall and a full spin, and land. Actually I'd never done any of these things. Jim was so nervous about having a beginner at the controls that he'd never yielded either stick or rudder to my command. When I had been supposed to be doing the flying, I'd felt the stick and the rudder pedals doing things that were not my doing. The plane had dual controls, which operated simultaneously in front and rear seats. Jim had been "riding the controls" up front; that is, instead of leaving me free in the back to handle the plane, he'd been actually doing all the flying for me. Several times I had tested him by taking my feet off the rudder pedals, and I'd noticed they kept making the right moves, in and out, as if operated by ghostly feet. Occasionally Jim had even congratulated me on the skill with which he had executed a landing. I'd certainly never made a landing while he'd been in the front seat. Nevertheless when Jim said, "Take her around," I closed the door, pushed the throttle forward, and started to take her around.

The takeoff wasn't too bad, though I nearly skidded off the runway before getting airborne. All I had to do was climb to eight hundred feet, turn 180 degrees, turn again, put the nose down, and land. It was exhilarating not having Jim riding the controls, but I was surprised too. The plane seemed to have acquired a mind of its own. It insisted on going all the way to twelve hundred feet when I wanted it to level off at eight hundred, then when I tried to get back down it dived all the way to six hundred feet before leveling off. It finally consented to circle the field, and I got the nose pointed toward the runway and headed for earth at a civilized speed. When the wheels touched down it looked as if I might survive, and, feeling solid runway underneath, I slammed on the brakes. The plane spun violently through a 180-degree ground loop and wound up fifty yards off the runway in the grass. Since my ground loop hadn't flipped the plane and destroyed a wing, the jury that weighed my case decided to give me a second chance instead of washing me out of the program.

For the longest time, though, I flew and flew without ever being in control of any airplane. It was a constant struggle for power between the plane and me, and the plane usually won. I approached every flight like a tenderfoot sent to tame a wild horse. By the time I arrived at the Naval Air Station at Memphis, where Navy pilots took over the instruction, it was obvious my flying career would be soon ended. We flew open-cockpit biplanes—"Yellow Perils," the Navy called them—which forgave almost any mistake. Instructors sat in the front cockpit, students behind. But here the instructors did not ride the controls. These were courageous men. Many were back from the Pacific, and they put their destinies in my hands high over the Mississippi River and came back shaking their heads in sorrow.

"It's just like driving a car, Baker," a young ensign told me the day I nearly killed him trying to sideslip into a farm field where he wanted to land and take a smoke. "You know how it is when you let in the clutch? Real smooth and easy."

I knew nothing about letting in the clutch, but didn't dare say so. "Right," I said. "Smooth and easy."

I got as far as the acrobatic stage. Rolls, loops, Immelman turns. Clouds spinning zanily beneath me, earth and river whirling above.

An earnest young Marine pilot took me aside after a typical day of disaster in the sky. "Baker," he said, "it's just like handling a girl's breast. You've got to be gentle."

I didn't dare tell him I'd never handled a girl's breast, either.

The inevitable catastrophe came on my check flight at the end of the acrobatic stage. It was supposed to last an hour, but after twenty minutes in the sky the check pilot said, "All right, let's go in," and gave me a "down," which meant "unfit to fly." I was doomed. I knew it, my buddies knew it. The Navy would forgive a "down" only if you could fly two successful check flights back-to-back with different check pilots. If you couldn't you were out.

I hadn't a prayer of surviving. On a Saturday, looking at Monday's flight schedule, I saw that I was posted to fly the fatal reexamination with a grizzled pilot named T. L. Smith. It was like reading my own obituary. T. L. Smith was a celebrated perfectionist famous for washing out cadets for the slightest error in the air. His initials, T. L., were said to stand for "Total Loss," which was all anyone who had to fly for him could expect. Friends stopped by my bunk at the barracks to commiserate and tell me it wasn't so bad being kicked out of flying. I'd probably get soft desk duty in some nice Navy town where you could shack up a lot and sleep all day. Two of my best friends, wanting to cheer me up, took me to go into Memphis for a farewell weekend together. Well, it beat sitting on the base all weekend thinking about my Monday rendezvous with Total Loss. Why not a last binge for the condemned?

We took a room at the Peabody Hotel and bought three bottles of bourbon. I'd tasted whiskey only two or three times before and didn't much like it; but now in my gloom it brought a comfort I'd never known. I wanted more of that comfort. My dream was dying. I would plumb the depths of vice in these final hours. The weekend quickly turned into an incoherent jumble of dreamlike episodes. Afterwards I vaguely remembered threatening to punch a fat man in a restaurant, but couldn't remember why. At some point I was among a gang of sailors in a hotel corridor, and I was telling them to stop spraying the hallway with a fire hose. At another I was sitting fully dressed on what seemed to be a piano bench in a hotel room—not at the Peabody—and a strange woman was smiling at me and taking off her brassiere.

This was startling, because no woman had ever taken her brassiere off in front of me before. But where had she come from? What were we doing in this alien room? "I'll bet I know what you want," she said.

"What?"

"This," she said, and stepped out of her panties and stretched out flat on her back on the bed. She beckoned. I stood up, then thought better of it and settled to the floor like a collapsing column of sand. I awoke hours later on the floor. She'd gone.

With the hangover I took back to the base Sunday night, I would have welcomed instant execution at the hands of Total Loss Smith, but when I awoke Monday morning the physical agony was over. In its place had come an unnatural, disembodied sensation of great calm. The world was moving much more slowly than its normal pace. In this eerie state of relaxation nothing seemed to matter much, not the terrible Total Loss Smith, not even the end of my flying days.

When we met at the flight line, Total Loss looked just as grim as everybody said he would. It was bitterly cold. We both wore heavy leather flight suits lined with wool, and his face looked tougher than the leather. He seemed old enough to be my father. Wrinkles creased around eyes that had never smiled. Lips as thin as a movie killer's. I introduced myself. His greeting was what I'd expected. "Let's get this over with," he said.

We walked down the flight line, parachutes bouncing against our rumps, not a word said. In the plane—Total Loss in the front seat, me in the back—I connected the speaking tube which enabled him to talk to me but didn't allow me to speak back. Still not a word while I taxied out to the mat, ran through the cockpit checks, and finished by testing the magnetos. If he was trying to petrify me before we got started he was wasting his efforts. In this new state of peace I didn't give a damn whether he talked to me or not.

"Take me up to five thousand feet and show me some slow rolls," he growled as I started the takeoff.

The wheels were hardly off the mat before I experienced another eerie sensation. It was a feeling of power. For the first time since first stepping into an airplane I felt in complete mastery of the thing. I'd noticed it on takeoff. It had been an excellent takeoff. Without thinking about it, I'd automatically corrected a slight swerve just before becoming airborne. Now as we climbed I was flooded with a sense of confidence. The hangover's residue of relaxation had freed me of the tensions that had always defeated me before. Before, the plane had had a will of its own; now the plane seemed to be part of me, an extension of my hands and feet, obedient to my slightest whim. I leveled it at exactly five thousand feet and started a slow roll. First, a shallow dive to gain velocity, then push the stick slowly, firmly, all the way over against the thigh, simultaneously putting in hard rudder, and there we are, hanging upside down over the earth, and now—keep it rolling, don't let the nose drop—reverse the controls and feel it roll all the way through until—coming back to a straight-and-level now—catch it, wings level with the horizon, and touch the throttle to maintain altitude precisely at five thousand feet.

"Perfect," said Total Loss. "Do me another one."

It hadn't been a fluke. Somewhere between the weekend's bourbon and my arrival at the flight line that morning, I had become a flyer. The second slow roll was as good as the first.

"Show me your snap rolls," Total Loss said.

I showed him snap rolls as fine as any instructor had ever shown me.

"All right, give me a loop and then a split-S and recover your altitude and show me an Immelman."

I looped him through a big graceful arc, leveled out and rolled into the split-S, came out of it climbing, hit the altitude dead on at five thousand feet, and showed him an Immelman that Eddie Rickenbacker would have envied.

"What the hell did you do wrong on your check last week?" he asked. Since I couldn't answer, I shrugged so he could see me in his rearview mirror.

"Let me see you try a falling leaf," he said.

Even some instructors had trouble doing a falling leaf. The plane had to be brought precisely to its stalling point, then dropped in a series of sickening sideways skids, first to one side, then to the other, like a leaf falling in a breeze, by delicate simultaneous manipulations of stick, rudder pedals, and throttle. I seemed to have done falling leaves all my life.

"All right, this is a waste of my time," Total Loss growled. "Let's go in."

Back at the flight line, when I'd cut the ignition, he climbed out and tramped back toward the ready room while I waited to sign the plane in. When I got there he was standing at a distance talking to my regular instructor. His talk was being illustrated with hand movements, as pilots' conversations always were, hands executing little loops and rolls in the air. After he did the falling-leaf motion with his hands, he pointed a finger at my instructor's chest, said something I couldn't hear, and trudged off. My instructor, who had flown only with the pre-hangover Baker, was slack-jawed when he approached me.

"Smith just said you gave him the best check flight he's ever had in his life," he said. "What the hell did you do to him up there?"

"I guess I just suddenly learned to fly," I said. I didn't mention the hangover. I didn't want him to know that bourbon was a better teacher than he was. After that I saw T. L. Smith coming and going frequently through the ready room and thought him the finest, most manly looking fellow in the entire corps of instructors, as well as the wisest.

Though I'd succeeded in sky and water by the time I was flying out of Whiting, I still had not triumphed with women. In a world where every man boasted of sexual conquest after every trip to town, my innocence was like a private shame. All of my efforts to escape it, though, seemed doomed to failure. This wasn't because I lacked a powerful lust. Once the Navy freed me from the sexually stifling atmosphere in which I'd been growing up, the madness of that mania clamped me in a terrible grip. This was inflamed to white heat by the tales told by the Casanovas who infested the barracks.

Listening to this talk, I was paralyzed with envy and desire. There was scarcely a woman alive, it seemed, who could resist the urge to haul men down onto beds, car seats, kitchen floors, dining-room tables, park grass, parlor sofas, or packing crates, entwine warm thighs around them, and pant in ecstasy. There were many older men among us, Marines who had survived Guadalcanal, Navy petty officers from ships sunk in the Pacific, men who went to town with chests blazing with combat ribbons. I envied those ribbons. They had the power to turn women into groveling slaves subservient to their wearers' vilest desires, or so I judged from the stories that came back on Sunday nights.

Burns, a handsome Marine sergeant of astonishing strength, boasted of having a local debutante so enchanted she would make love dangling from a parlor chandelier. Costello, a chief petty officer, never passed a weekend without having several officers' wives beg him to slake his appetite for flesh in delightfully squalid hotels. Powers, a machinist's mate who'd survived the sinking of the carrier *Wasp,* preferred to have three women bedded simultaneously to perform a variety of sexual services and, he said, seldom had trouble filling the quota.

I discounted a good deal of this talk but believed enough of it to give me pain. If the world was a sexual carnival, I wanted to be admitted, yet all my efforts failed. At first I spent liberty nights standing on street corners in towns packed with sailors, waiting for overheated women to claim my body. All I saw were thousands of other uniformed bodies standing on street corners waiting to be claimed. After midnight, when we all rode buses back to celibate barracks, I lay in my bunk angry and puzzled. If there were so many women out there with smoking armpits and steaming thighs, why did they not search me out? Wasn't I handsome enough, suave enough, desirable enough? Where were all those hot-blooded women anyhow? All I ever saw were five thousand sailors standing on street corners waiting for something exciting to happen, and nothing ever did. That was Pensacola in 1943.

In Miami there was promise. Lovely Miami, sexy Miami, the hot moon hanging over beautiful Biscayne Bay, the girls so juicy under their light summer dresses, the hot little beads of sweat bedewing their upper lips in that tropical heat. A lush girl picked me up on the street in a Cadillac convertible. A car dealer's daughter, she was game for lippy nuzzling on the front seat but timid about hands fumbling along her thighs, full of "Behave yourself now" and "Be a good boy." I was sick of being a good boy. "It's too public here" was always her final complaint. "Somebody will see us."

I located a very private place south of Coral Gables. We passed it each day en route to the airfield. On a Saturday night I told her to drive that way. She seemed willing enough. We pulled off the highway into marshy ground overhung by great spreading limbs and vines. She switched off the headlights and we embraced in the blackness, hungry for sin. The mosquitoes arrived immediately. Not in squadrons or battalions, not in divisions—the mosquitoes came in flying armies. She was screaming that they were eating her legs. I could feel them tattooing the back of my neck.

She pushed me away, threw on the headlight beams, and crying, "They'll eat us alive!" backed out and roared top-speed back to Miami cursing mosquitoes.

Anticlimax waited to mock me at the end of every encounter. In Atlanta a spare young woman with thick eyeglasses agreed to come to my hotel room after midnight, plopped on the side of the bed, and said, "If you touch me I'll scream for help." I'd heard in the barracks about such women. They wanted to be treated forcefully. I touched her. She screamed. I'd heard of men wrongfully hanged because nervous women cried, "Rape!" I wanted to get her out of the room as quietly as possible, but it wasn't easy. She was determined to stay until I knew her life story. It was long and uneventful.

In Athens, Georgia, a girl spoke to me in a drugstore on Sunday afternoon. "Like to walk?" We walked idly hand in hand. She was young, maybe sixteen or seventeen, and communicated a sense of moist heat. We walked to a ramshackle part of town. "Here's where I live," she said.

It was a small tumbledown frame house, not much more than a shack.

"Like to come in?"

We went into a small parlor. It was separated from an adjoining room only by a sheet hung on a rod. I sat on a sofa with ruined springs. She sat on my lap, closed her eyes, offered her lips, and placed my hand under her skirt. Here was paradise at last. In a moment she was making incoherent noises which I took to be the music of feminine ecstasy. She seemed to be entering a deep swoon. With her body shuddering on my lap, I was near swooning myself when her cries became urgent. "Can't you get out of those pants?" she asked.

I was struggling to loosen my belt buckle when I heard pots and pans clattering on the other side of the sheet.

"There's somebody out there!"

"It's just Mama getting ready to cook dinner," she murmured and gave in to another onset of passion sounds. These had delighted me a moment earlier, but realizing that Mama was not eight feet away, handling pots on the other side of the sheet, took all the music out of them. Now they just sounded like very loud grunts and groans.

"Quiet! Your mother will hear you," I whispered.

"She won't bother us. She never does."

Since I still had Mama's daughter on my lap in a rosy condition, I could only imagine what would happen if Mama didn't run true to form this time but decided to stroll through the sheet. At this point a terribly masculine voice on the other side of the sheet boomed out: "Where'd you put them shoes I left out on the back porch?"

"That's just Pa," the girl said. "He won't bother us."

I hurled her off my lap, stood up, and grabbed my cap. She replied by arranging herself flat on the sofa, opening her mouth wide, and running the tip of her tongue over her lips. She'd seen Lana Turner inflame men that way in the movies, but it didn't work with me. The fire in my blood had turned to ice. Pa had one of those backwoods voices that usually came supported with a shotgun.

"Come on back here," she said, raising her legs to let the skirt fall back to her hips. That did it. I was two blocks away moving at a pace just short of a gallop before I looked back and saw that Pa wasn't on my heels.

Fate seemed to have sentenced me to virginity. There had been the chance to overcome it that weekend in Memphis when the curtain parted briefly on my alcoholic haze and I'd seen the strange woman in a strange hotel room undressing and lying on the bed to initiate me. Where I had met her or where she'd acquired me I couldn't even remember, but bourbon had obviously made me do something right—as it had in aviation—before it turned the tables and left me snoring helplessly on the floor. My sex life was a running joke.

Returning to Pensacola early in 1945 to fly the heavy planes and learn the mechanics of killing, I was resigned to chastity. From my 1943 tour there I knew the odds were hopeless: a thousand Navy men for every female on the streets. Waiting for the bus back to the base with my friends Nick and Carson one night, I was startled when a car pulled to the curb and a handsome woman asked if we wanted a ride. There were two other women in the car. None of the three looked like a casual pickup. Of course we wanted a ride.

The woman driving had a house in the fancier section of town. We ended up there. "For a drink," everybody agreed. But it was soon clear there would be more than a drink. The three women shared the house. They were older women. Women of twenty-five, twenty-six, maybe even twenty-seven, and all married to Navy officers now in the Pacific. They didn't talk much about their husbands. They'd been in the Pacific a long time. We made civilized talk, quiet ladies-and-gentlemen talk. By two A.M. the last bus to the base had left. "Why don't we sleep here tonight?" suggested Nick. Matter-of-factly, the women thought that was the only sensible thing to do. Two of them led Nick and Carson toward the bedrooms and nobody returned. I sat with the woman who'd been driving and had another drink and she finally said, "I'll make up a bed for you on the cot on the sun porch."

When she did I told her good night and she left. I undressed and lay wide awake in the dark for a long time, wondering if she was awake in her own bed expecting me to come to her room. Not likely, I told myself. These were women, real women, good women who missed their husbands and were being kind to three lonely boys who probably reminded them of the men they loved. She came through the sun-porch door and closed it quietly behind her while I was still musing on the nobility of good women.

"Are you still awake?"

She sat on the cot peering down at me in the darkness. I smelled perfume in her nightgown. I was scared. I believed in the distinction between good women and bad women. Good women were to be respected and loved purely. That's what they expected of a man. It was all right to wallow in lust with bad women but not with a good woman, not with a woman who was married to a man, possibly a Navy hero facing death for his country, for his wife, for me, in the faraway Pacific. I didn't want my belief in the good woman shattered. Now, as she sat in her gown on the edge of the cot, saying she couldn't sleep and did I mind if she stayed long enough to smoke a cigarette, I was scared of what she might do. I wanted her only to go away and continue being a good woman.

"Tell me about your husband," I said.

She touched my forehead lightly with her fingertips. "Not right now," she said.

"You must miss him."

Her fingertips brushed my cheek and neck. "It gets lonely sometimes."

"How long were you married before he went overseas?"

"Are you nervous about something?" she replied.

"Why?"

"Do I make you nervous?"

"Not a chance."

"I'm not much older than you are," she said. Her fingertips were now like feathers under my Navy-issue T-shirt.

"How old's your husband?"

"Doesn't matter," she murmured, fingertips still busy.

"Your husband must be quite a guy," I said.

She removed her hand and straightened her back. There was a silence. Finally, "You're really just a kid, aren't you?" she said.

It was very gentle, almost reflective, as though she were talking to herself.

"I guess so," I confessed.

"Don't worry about it," she said, standing up. "You'll grow up soon enough."

"I guess so."

She leaned over and pressed her lips lightly on my forehead. "You're sweet," she said. "I'm glad I brought you home. Sleep well." And she was gone, taking with her my golden opportunity. For weeks afterwards I was torn between feelings of nobility and suspicion that I had acted like a childish idiot.

J. P. DONLEAVY

ALTHOUGH HE HAS written many books, J. P. Donleavy's reputation rests largely upon his first novel, *The History of the Ginger Man,* which he completed in 1951. Book editors who first read this sexually explicit work found it highly entertaining but unpublishable, because obscene. Donleavy was unable to get the book published until 1955, when he placed it with the Olympia Press in Paris, in a series with a reputation for pornography. Only later did the mainstream literary world acknowledge the novel as a kind of comic masterpiece and come to regard the novelist as a stylistic innovator. By then, disillusioned with America, Donleavy had determined to move to Ireland and change his nationality.

His roots were decidedly American, however. The author not only had been born in America (to Irish immigrant parents) and grown up in Brooklyn, but he had also once enlisted in the U.S. Navy. Eventually he even talked his way into the Naval Academy (he apparently didn't actually attend there, but he did take classes at the Naval Academy Preparatory School). That Donleavy would have been able to get into such a select program is curious, for he had been rather outrageous as a sailor. In fact, some former servicemen have found the author's self-portrait in the following selection—lazy, always trying to get out of things, lying, consistently breaking the regs—extremely offensive. In their view, even Donleavy's characteristically run-on and fragmental syntax is a piece with his youthful behavior as a sailor: it is slovenly rather than innovative.

But if the sailor as described in the selection is indeed a sort of malingerer, he is clearly a classic of the kind. Donleavy's description of his brief but energetic naval service is taken from his 1994 memoir.

from

THE HISTORY OF THE GINGER MAN

It was true, as [my classmate] Izzy said, that out of the amphibious corps our lives were saved. One had been assigned as a radar man to one of the amphibious landing ships medium, which had been converted to a rocket ship. Such vessels were stationed off a beach, having for three hours the firepower of a battleship, and were, with their hundred tons of rockets, chosen as a priority target to be blown out of the water by kamikaze suicide pilots during the amphibious landings. And the English teacher to whom Izzy alluded was one of the few exceptions to all the Naval Academy Prep's insubordination on the part of some of its students. . . .

John Hall Wheelock['s] . . . English class provided its wonderful hour of pleasure with this marvelously entertaining gentleman, a chief petty officer, opening up the day's proceedings by telling his latest received risqué jokes, which, despite their banal simplicity, always reflected a verity of life. His suggestions of subjects to write upon were always original, and one responded to them. And from these assignments, he chose a selection to have read aloud by his visiting friends at gatherings at his house. Aware that I was ghost-writing several other students' themes, he never brought me to book or complained. Instead he seemed to be amused and encouraging, several times suggesting I let him show copies of my class essays to publishers with whom he had been associated in civilian life. And I had the temerity to think, as Izzy did, that he was in fact referring to me when he said that there was someone writing in the class that they would hear of one day.

However, in already presuming I was a writer, I was shy to put myself forth as one. Branded and called Shakespeare in navy boot training camp, I had been the acknowledged company poet, which mostly involved writing requested love letters to fellow seamen's girlfriends, to whom, with cynicism reeking between the lines, I would unleash salvos of marvelously sentimental endearments, which brought forth equally fervent replies. However, my similar attempts at flowery embellishment on behalf of my fellow Naval Academy prepsters often embarrassingly resulted in highly disgruntled customers, who would, chagrined, present me with a loved one's unnice response, telling them, in more flowery words than mine, to fuck off and to go shove their crap up some other gullible girl's ass. Even I myself, getting such a reply from a sophisticated young lady, Joy Calverton Corbett, with whom I had attended the Ford Theater in Baltimore and who later wrote from Antioch College that if I wanted to continue my ridiculous letter writing to her, I would be getting back the same ridiculous replies.

But while there was a growing dissension to my letter writing, when instructor Chief Petty Officer Wheelock alluded to overtones of James Joyce in my ghostwritten efforts, I was alacrity itself in repairing to the Tome School library. This always singularly empty place was where I often foraged alone and on this occasion went to find out about this man Joyce, who might be imitating me. When after a long search, I finally found mention of him, it was with a certain sense of mystical awe that I read that his obscene work was banned and that he had been a dissolute undergraduate, who, frequenting houses of ill repute, consorted with medical students and led a drunken existence, carousing through the street of the ancient capital city of Dublin. With it being three thousand miles away across the Atlantic and the country of origin of both my mother and father, news of this alleged dissolute writer aroused my first interest in Ireland. Plus the awareness that someone somewhere was producing literature banned as obscene.

But all was but a miracle in my getting an appointment to Annapolis and arriving at the Naval Academy Prep in the first place. My naval career being full of recalcitrant behavior of an almost insane

and suicidal kind, ruled by my nearly hysterical refusal to do anything I considered menial, and an assault upon one's dignity. In
such resolve I was helped by being a mile runner and my ability to
cover any training obstacle course in pronto time. At boot camp, I
had won extra leave by winning races over these prescribed hur-
dles and hazards. Not that difficult, as no one else was looking to
overly strain himself. However, there were bases offering twenty-
five-dollar war bonds as prizes, and on these I would try to break
the obstacle course record. In any event, when arriving at an amphibious base located on a barren sand flat at the mouth of the Chesapeake Bay at Little Creek, Virginia, my escapes from receiving unit
working details recruited for the day became legendary. Effected as
they were following morning muster in front of thousands of men.
Rather than have some sadist cook relish overseeing me wash pots
and pans and then exercise a further authority to inspect them to
see if they were clean, I would, still, even after another daredevil
one or two had abandoned the idea, bolt out of the massed group
of sailors while a presiding officer from a raised podium screamed
over an address system in a voice I can hear even now ringing in
my ears,

"Get that man. Get that man. Get him."

Of course, not ever having washed a pot or pan before, I had no
idea what such cleanliness that cooks insisted upon meant. So even
when extra shore patrol were put waiting for this man to burst forth
from the assembled sea of navy blue, and were stationed on the long
road fronting the dozens of Quonset huts which ran parallel to the
base obstacle course, I still made a run for it. And the rousing cheer,
which went up from three thousand or so naval personnel, did nothing to calm the anger of the lieutenant in charge. It was nearly
becoming a matter now not to disappoint all those anticipating as
the seconds would tick away and the suspense would mount. But
as the days went by and I went uncaught, I was not to know that
further shore patrol had now finally been put lurking with their
truncheons at the ready and patrolling the sandy alleyways between
those moundlike, corrugated, circular-roofed iron barracks. And
upon the day I discovered that this further additional naval enforce-

ment had been posted everywhere, it was too late. As a crescendo of voices rung out, "Go, go, go," I really went, for now actual hands were reaching out and one could feel the breeze of wielded truncheons as I dodged, ducking and weaving, in every direction. Literally now, running for my life. But luckily, just as the trap was closing, and, in the fraction of a second it took to do so, I finally got unseen into a Quonset hut. With doors at either end, I ran through taking off my tunic and skivvy shirt to emerge out the opposite door and to plunge both under the tap of a washing facility between the huts. And to be seen scrubbing away just as a dozen shore patrol came running from every direction. I even found a piece of old soap to add authenticity to this desperate moment. One of the posse even stopping to ask me did I see a guy running by.

"Nope, can't say I did."

It was my last attempt at outrageous escape. Leading to my final adoption of more subtle means involving less stress and considerably less energy. As a result of my appointment to the Naval Academy and the belief that this indicated above-average intelligence, I was summoned on the base to meet one or two of the powers that be. In the amphibious corps, where lieutenants were captains of substantial-sized landing ships, even the lowest-ranked of petty officers and naval ratings wielded considerable authority. And in one signal case, there existed a first-class yeoman who simply seemed to wield influence over and above everybody, and run the entire base. This gentleman was the marvelously erudite Roger Parr. Who, with the looks of a matinee idol and possessed of many civilian academic degrees and an authority on Shakespeare, was also a humorous humane man. With a generous sympathy, he helped many through tragedy and difficulty. And in my case, as a deserving intellectual, I was, instead of being chased by the base's entire shore patrol, able now to devise a phone call each day to the receiving unit to be called out to attend this or that facility, which enabled me to instead retire for the day to the library. Parr was also responsible for my achieving a major practical advantage in pursuing a writing career. One day seeing me peck away one-fingered over the typewriter, he insisted that I become a proper touch-typist and assured me I would never regret the time spent drilling in the initial tedium of five-finger exercises.

Parr and his cohorts were a welcome blessing from the anonymous mass of sailors who frequented the nearby city of Norfolk, surrounded as it was by military installations and one of the world's largest naval bases. On a night out on liberty, even the toughest of old salts would be seen next morning lying in their bunks wreathed in bandages. One debonair gent for whom the ladies easily fell in his bell-bottomed tailor-mades had even boasted of a date he'd made with a girl he'd met in the city's library but then found that evening when he called on the lady at her address with a bouquet of flowers, he was number seven waiting in the queue on a hall staircase. Amused by his own presumption and happily undismayed, he said that when his turn came he presented the roses, which earned him an extra kiss on the cheek for which the lady made no extra charge. And indeed agreed to let him take her out to dinner when she had finished with the last of her customers.

But from this and other stories, one was mighty glad to be able to repair to the clublike atmosphere of this base welfare office and talk away the evenings, run as it was like a Paris café, coffee brewing and cake at the ready. In turn I did one of the powers that be a favor and sat the high school exams for a man who never graduated and wanted to qualify to go to mortician's school when he left the navy. Embarrassingly, this gentleman, a first-class boatswain mate and a most impressive disciplinarian in his manner of commanding men, was also the petty officer who directly oversaw the very section of the receiving unit from which one had been so conspicuously bolting each day. He also had a glaring clue to my identity with my name on a nearby sign in gold letters for having broken the record and won a war bond on the obstacle course. If he recognized me, and I had a suspicion that he did, he never gave any indication. On the contrary, he spent hours describing his dream mortuary to me. Ah, but when I duly, fraudulently sat his high school exams for him, this inspired gentleman who had such wonderful plans for dealing with the dead, just barely passed.

Although I had now resorted to more subtle means to avoid menial tasks in the navy, I had previously in my reckless disregard for authority actually once been caught. Which resulted in my being briefly criminalized and imprisoned for having gone absent without leave. And had it not been for an anonymous man behind a desk who had, without my knowing it at the time, done me an immense favor, my return to academia and my brush with literary matters at the Naval Academy Prep would never have happened. Having completed radar training school in a beachside hotel in Fort Lauderdale, Florida, and endured a hurricane, which involved me in what could have been a lethal fight with a giant bully over a bunk to sleep in, I had now more peacefully been sent with a crew to the city of Miami to a receiving unit in a hotel converted to naval use to await being shipped out. As the first few days passed, I was able to leave and play golf on one of the marvelous local golf courses. Then, as an announcement was made that the transfer of the crew was imminent, we were confined to barracks, and guards posted at the hotel front door no longer allowed personnel to exit. I had long got used to this hurry-up-and-wait treatment in the navy as a quite frequent convenience adapted as an option while the navy carried out other more urgent plans, needlessly confining personnel to barracks until it suited them. This always struck me as being highly inconsiderate behavior on the part of the navy. And gauging that there were at least three days left before we would be shipped out, and too precious not to indulge in good golfing excursions, I decided to make a break for it.

The day, as they usually were in Florida, was balmy, sunny and warm. To avoid detection by the guard at the front entrance, as there was no longer free exit out the hotel front door, I repaired to the back of the hotel and a high balcony from which, holding by my fingertips, I was able to at least eliminate six feet from the fifteen or so feet to the ground. I dropped and escaped the barracks out through a back alley to a parallel street. From there in a taxi, I was off to play golf on a course where it was given free of charge to servicemen. Shooting my eighteen holes, I took a further leisured few hours dining and wining in the members' clubhouse. Returning that night to the hotel sunkissed and alcohol-refreshed from one of Miami Beach's most beautiful golf courses, I discovered I had been wrong. This single one time, the navy for once absolutely meant what it said. The naval shore patrol were there already waiting to arrest me.

However, although more than a little worried I was assured by my captors that I wouldn't be shot immediately, and as we raced through the nighttime Miami streets in an open jeep, I found my nighttime tour full of fascination. In the brig, pleasantly located on an inland waterway near the sea, I was locked in a communal cell with what seemed to be an unrepentant group of murderers, rapists and thieves. On my prison dungarees was printed back and front of my shirt and on both thighs a big P for prisoner. My fellow criminals seemed to be charming conversationalists, philosophizing about life's untrustful vagaries and of the main things to pursue in avoiding them. One murderer, pacing back and forth reading the Bible and occasionally providing a quote. Because the prison dining room also catered to officers, served on the other side of a partition, I sampled the best food I'd ever had in the navy. Then put alone in a single cell, I was after four days suddenly given a ticket and my records and released. Instructed to take a train on which I was booked north to Washington, D.C., and from there on to an amphibious base called Solomons, I was told that I had better get there.

Although full of foreboding with the realization that my whole future in the navy was now doomed by my felony, boarding the train that evening out of Miami I entered a carpeted sanctum of mahogany elegance. I was to later learn that my crew four days previously had been shipped north, slumped in broken seats, sitting the night away in a rattling old sooty cattle car. Here in my private berth the Pullman porter had pillows puffed up and my blanket folded back on the clean sheets stretched smooth. With a decanter of chill water within hand's reach, his smiling black face inquired as to one's comfort. I said I was fine. But as I was removing toothbrush and toothpaste from my ditty bag, a naval officer with scrambled egg on his cap visor of a full commander arrived. He couldn't help but notice from the two tiny lines around my tunic cuffs that I was next to the lowest ranking sailor in the navy. When he found himself having to climb into the upper bunk above mine, his only observation of my inconvenient presence was a comment said to me with a certain amused resentment.

"Who do you know."

I was tempted to slip the commander the truth that I was a prisoner in transit. But I promptly thought better of it. Instead, by the time we reached Washington, I was by all the demeanor at my command, pretending to be, if not a nephew of President Roosevelt, at least a cousin of the secretary of the navy and on urgent top-secret naval business. Such imagined privilege must have gone to my head because I even chose on my arrival to commandeer a taxi and avail of a whole morning's leisure viewing the generously wide and beautiful boulevards of Washington, D.C. And as I was on my way to be sentenced at summary court-martial, to no doubt serve further time in the brig, I thought at least I might enjoy a last few moments of freedom out in civilian life. For, back in Miami, as we paraded as prisoners out of doors under armed guard and within sight of civilians, I had already learned what it felt like to be a marked criminal. And it sure wasn't nice.

On my arrival back at this vast train station to catch a naval bus to Solomons and with the doom of my situation now descending, it would have been of immense reassurance, had I any way of knowing then that one day many years hence I would have a limousine pulled up next to the train in this same station and would be chauffeured out with the voice of John Lehman Jr., the then actual secretary of the navy, inquiring over the car's sound system if I were comfortable and had a good trip. But now this day I traveled by uncomfortable bus to this naval base located about fifty miles southeast on an isolated toe of land sticking out into the Chesapeake Bay. With some trepidation, on arrival I handed my orders across the counter at the base's reception office to a naval yeoman. Who, in turning through the pages of my record book, looked at me quizzically. And then looked back at my papers as I assumed to look back with as much bravery as seemed appropriate while waiting for him to summon the shore patrol to put me under arrest. Finally he said,

"Hey, this is really none of my business, but you traveled all this way up here with these further orders for trial and disciplinary action just like this in your hand."

"Yes."

As I persisted to look back uncomprehendingly at him, he realized that I simply did not know what he was talking about or what I could have done if I had known. I had traveled the night along the coast of Florida, a thousand miles north, traversing these sea-level lands over the Okefenokee Swamp, through Jacksonville, Savannah and Richmond. A bell clanging as the train slowed to cross the street crossings through these sleeping villages and towns, and one peeked out to read the name of the lonely, empty passing stations. Carrying all this way with me a small slip of paper upon which was typed a naval directive toward the sentencing and doom of yours truly, seaman second-class, serially numbered 909 59 08. For a few further foolish seconds as I waited, the yeoman behind the counter suddenly tore a page out of my orders and simply said: "You don't want this little sheet of paper in here. You just go and join your unit."

I now realized that what any old salt would have done in carrying his own records had now been done. I thanked this man I had never met before and have never seen since. And I now thank him again. For without a clean discipline record, I could never have succeeded in getting a fleet appointment to the Naval Academy. Which in itself had nearly been a lost battle. For when I heard it announced at the amphibious naval base at Little Creek, Virginia, that one could sit exams to get such an appointment, I submitted my academic school record in order to do so. But on this fairly abysmal report being reviewed, I was turned down by the officer in charge as not having a ghost of a chance. And as I stood before his desk in a gloomy Quonset hut on a sunny Virginia day, it may have been the first time in my life that I ever persisted in an effort to be let do something and especially in this case anything as unappealing as being allowed to sit an exam.

The officer, wanting to go out to play golf, finally standing and reaching for his cap, said with the utmost weariness, "OK, sailor, if you want to take the exam that badly, I'm not going to stop you."

The mental and physical exams were spread over four days, finally ending with an interview in front of a board of officers. At this latter, one was advised to present oneself as one of the under-privileged who, through the democratic process afforded by the navy, was now given a chance to pursue the hope one always held dear of being a career naval officer. I may have even alluded to grow-ing up in an old shack on the edge of a polluted canal where I first dreamt of a seafaring life. And also possibly described being the son of Irish immigrant parents, who although honest and hardworking didn't have a clue as to wielding influence in opening doors to the higher attainments available in American life. I could not discern any moisture in any officer's eyes, but there was no doubt that at the time I was desperate enough to absolutely believe what I was saying. And, if nothing else, I was at least free for four days of my ordeal in escaping working parties. But out of this base called Little Creek and from the ten thousand men there, only one man ended up getting an appointment. And that was me. And appropriate enough, as my old prep school pal Tom Grill was already at the Naval Academy, and considering the many times we'd both fought admi-rals around the ring at the New York Athletic Club, it was time now to become one of them.

But then again, it was the existence of this curious American characteristic of dispensing fairness to an underdog that one seemed to look for and expect to find on my return from Europe. And also the trait of humanity in giving somebody a break whose despera-tion in requesting it or needing it should have instead alerted cau-tion in the giver to whom it might even cause serious risk. It was a pleasant practical quality one continued to recall when an officious European would go to all lengths to make life difficult and which made me have to regard Americans as being the fairest of all nation-alities. Knowing that among them there were those principled with genuine compassion. Which, if it weren't the case, one would not now be writing these words.

But this day I had retired to my unit at the amphibious naval base at Solomons, which, despite my good samaritan friend who saved me from the brig, had a reputation for a certain lawless toughness.

Between the constant stream of profanity, as it was generally in the navy, it was rare to hear a word of English spoken which conveyed any meaning and one was warned that these sea duty-hardened amphibious personnel were skilled at all the ruses the navy offered. I found myself the next day at morning muster standing beside a man who, as we turned right to salute, was now in front of me, as the band played the national anthem and the flag was raised. As he held his arm up, his sleeve slipped down, revealing watches worn from his wrist to elbow. Assuming that he must be either a collector, watch repairer or eager to have the correct time, I asked him what he was doing with so many watches. He said that some of his friends in the navy were careless and just not looking, so he stole them. When I showed shocked surprise at this open admission he smilingly turned to say,

"When you find a friend who is good and true, fuck him before he fucks you."

EDWARD P. STAFFORD

E DWARD P. (for Peary) STAFFORD was commissioned
an ensign in the Naval Reserve three months before the 7
December 1941 attack on Pearl Harbor and was assigned instructor
duty. After about a year, he underwent Subchaser Training, and
before his training was finished he was unexpectedly given command of *SC 692,* a small vessel that he skippered for a year in the
Atlantic and Mediterranean. In 1944 Stafford transferred to the
destroyer escort USS *Abercrombie* (DE-343), in which he served as
first lieutenant and executive officer. He was still serving in the
Abercrombie at the end of the war.

He was soon mustered out, finished a BA at Dartmouth, and then
returned to the Navy. Stafford served as executive officer of an
Atlantic Fleet radar picket destroyer before entering pilot training.
As an aviator, he went through a variety of operational and shore
tours, becoming at one point a "hurricane hunter" in a land-based
airborne early-warning squadron. He happened at one point to see
a television program called "The $64,000 Question." Having earned
an MA at George Washington University in American literature
while in a shore assignment, he thought his background might be
interesting to the producers. It was, and his weeks of success on
this program led in a roundabout way to his being asked to write

the history of the USS *Enterprise*—a book which in 1962 became the best-seller *The Big E.*

Stafford retired as a commander in 1963. Since then he has seen various writing jobs—for example, he was recalled to active duty in 1966 to be Pacific Fleet historian during the Vietnam War, and when that war wound down he returned to civilian life first as a speech writer for the secretary of the Navy, and later as a speech writer for Bicentennial and NASA administrators.

In the 1980s Stafford reflected on his wartime tours of duty on the subchaser and the destroyer escort. By using deck logs and after action reports, and by interviewing surviving crew members, he composed lively, accurate, and highly interesting histories of these two vessels, both of which saw much action in their respective theaters of war.

In the selection below, Stafford recounts the moment he was given his first (and only) command.

from

SUBCHASER

If any further motivation for learning was required beyond the news of losses at sea reported daily in the press and on the radio and the natural desire of red-blooded young men to defend their nation against threats of tyranny from a powerful enemy, it was provided by the commanding officer (CO) of SCTC [the Submarine Chaser Training Center] in the form of a prominently displayed lifeboat, riddled by machine-gun fire and stained with blood. To each new class of student officers and men, the CO personally delivered a fiery lecture at the site, relating in detail the slaughter of survivors in the boat and dwelling heavily on the callousness and brutality of the enemy his listeners were soon to face. Subtle it was not, but memorable and effective it surely was.

With such [an intense training] program and the necessary three to four hours of study required each evening, the sixty days went by with astonishing rapidity. And, as it turned out in my case, not everyone completed the full two months.

I had reported to SCTC on 20 November. At 1500 on 8 January I was called out of a navigation class and ordered to report to the operations officer. I found him at one of several desks in a large room on the second floor of the training center building. The masts of some SCs and the larger, steel PCs were close outside the windows. The operations officer was a lieutenant commander. I was a lieutenant (junior grade), a "jaygee." Although only two grades separated us, it was a chasm. I stood before his desk. He remained seated behind it.

There were no preliminaries. "Mr. Stafford," he said, "I need a commanding officer for an SC. Can you take command and get under way for Key West by 1800?"

The abruptness of the question, the offer, the order, momentarily severed the link between my brain and my tongue. Command? Of course I wanted command. I was twenty-four years old, the sea was in my blood, and there was a war on. But was I really ready, really qualified? For a year I had been instructing in seamanship, navigation, and gunnery, but that was "book learnin'"; the only time I had been at sea in the Navy was one summer as a midshipman on a battleship. I had to be honest.

"Sir," I answered when I finally got my tongue and brain hooked up, "I think I know all I need to know from the books, but I've never applied that knowledge at sea."

I had wasted my breath. The operations officer's voice was cold and impatient, his eyes level and searching. I was being tested.

"Never mind all that bullshit, Stafford," he said. "Yes or no?"

"Yessir" (no hesitation this time), and with those two syllables a door opened and closed; behind it in that instant, the land, home, family, young wife, peace; ahead, the sea, the war, the responsibility of command, the unknown.

"Good!" The operations officer's voice became normal, with perhaps even a hint of friendliness. "We've been watching your work here. You've done well. Don't worry, you can handle it. Now here's the situation. There's a new SC just in from the builder's yard, a good ship with good men aboard. Skipper is a good seaman, a yachtsman, but he and his XO haven't been able to pull their men together into a crew, a team. Drills and exercises here have been unsat. We

Lt. (j.g.) Edward P. Stafford, captain of *SC 692*, and members
of his crew during a swim call in the Bay of Tunis, shortly after the
subchaser's Atlantic crossing from Bermuda to Gibraltar.
COURTESY OF EDWARD P. STAFFORD

are relieving all three officers. The new XO and gunnery officer have
been aboard only a couple of days. I wish I could give you a few
days of shakedown here but they need escorts in Key West pronto.
You'll have to whip the crew into shape at sea, between assignments, whenever you can. We'll try to get you back up here and give
you a hand in a few weeks. Right now you just about have time to
inventory and sign for the registered publications and Title B gear
and get your personal effects aboard. Good luck."

That was a lot to swallow, but I was beginning to adjust to this
incredible afternoon, and there was something important the ops
officer had better know. "Thank you, sir," I said, "but there's one
thing you should know. I've never had the conn of an SC, only the
YPs during docking drills."

That news didn't upset him in the least. "That right?" he said. "Hey
Joe, take Stafford here out in the turning basin on our SC and let him
turn her around a couple of times and bring her back alongside."

With Joe, a lieutenant in the SCTC's operations department, I went aboard an SC kept at the school for training; the crew manned their special sea details stations, and Joe backed her away from the dock and into the narrow western end of the harbor. There I took over and, with coaching, went ahead on the starboard engine and astern on the port with full left rudder, adjusting RPM on both engines so that she turned completely around to port without moving either ahead or astern more than a few feet. Then we reversed the procedure, turning this time to starboard. It wasn't hard. In fact it was fun. The SC responded instantly to her rudders and engines and was a pleasure to handle. After perhaps twenty minutes I took her back to the dock, coming in slowly, port side to, at a shallow angle and backing the starboard engine to stop her and swing the stern in so she paralleled the pier.

Then Joe walked me down the long dock to berth H, where my new command was moored. Even in the mild state of shock engendered by the events of that busy afternoon, I knew that my first glimpse of her would be one of the memorable moments of my life. Under the weight of the afternoon sun, the pier smelled of diesel fuel and fresh paint. We passed several other subchasers; then Joe said, "There she is." We approached her from the stern. The gray paint was new on her fantail and on the heavy pipe screw guards on each quarter. Half a dozen depth charges were lined up in each of her stern racks and they too were shiny with fresh black paint. Abaft the pilothouse a dark-haired young sailor was working on the starboard 20-millimeter machine gun, its heavy coiled recoil spring shiny with lubricant. On the fo'c'sle forward of the short-barreled, 3-inch gun, a heavily tattooed sailor and a younger, huskier, darker man with curly black hair were splicing eyes to manila mooring lines. On the port side of the sharp, high bow, all the way forward, was her number—her name—five characters I would never forget, "SC 692."

The feeling I got from my first sight of the *SC 692* was of her newness and innocence, nubility—an unexpected feeling toward a warship of whatever size. She was complete, with all the equipment she would need to fulfill her destiny, and beautiful in the way an

armed yacht would be beautiful, but so new, so obviously inexpe-
rienced and untried! Even the sailors on her decks, with the exception of the tattooed man, had the smooth, fresh faces of youth. A
French phrase I had read once in a Hemingway novel sprang to
mind: *"Fraîche et rose comme au jour de bataille."*

PACIFIC WAR–I

ALVIN KERNAN

ALVIN KERNAN is a distinguished academic whose teaching and books—on such subjects as Samuel Johnson, Shakespeare, and literary theory—have engaged scholars and students for decades. Kernan studied at Williams College and at Oxford, taught at Princeton and Yale, held important administrative posts at both the latter institutions, and then moved to the Mellon Foundation. But prior to beginning this long academic career, Kernan had served four years in the U.S. Navy, working up through the enlisted ranks until he left the service in 1945 as an aviation chief ordnanceman— a chief petty officer—at the age of twenty-two.

Kernan's service was all in the Pacific, where he saw many great events from a special angle and endured a great deal as well. He was on the USS *Enterprise* (CV-6) loading bombs during the Battle of Midway (see the account reprinted below); he was on the *Hornet* (CV-8) carrying wounded as it was being sunk by bombers near Guadalcanal; and he was an aerial gunner in torpedo planes during the first night-fighter action off carriers in 1943. He narrates these episodes, along with much else about enlisted life, the Navy, carriers and torpedo planes, sex and gambling, and family tragedy, in his excellent memoir, *Crossing the Line: A Bluejacket's World War II Odyssey,* published by the Naval Institute Press in 1994.

As we pick up the narrative, Kernan has just finished an account of his having been stunned by watching a Dauntless dive-bomber accidentally hit the ship and fall in the water, immediately killing both the pilot and radioman. From long-suppressed fear, no one really wanted to talk about the incident. But then they all hear of a far greater loss.

from

CROSSING THE LINE:
A BLUEJACKET'S WORLD WAR II ODYSSEY

The tightly controlled fear of death was stirred up with the news a few days later that the *Lexington,* commissioned in the early 1920s, had been sunk by aircraft and the *Yorktown* damaged in the Battle of the Coral Sea, the first of the great carrier battles of the Pacific war. The *Lexington* was a much loved ship in the Navy—as her sister ship the *Saratoga* was not, for unknown reasons—a "good ship" it was said, and the news of her sinking was felt as a personal blow, particularly to the many aboard the *Enterprise* (a relatively new ship, commissioned in 1938) who had served on the "Lady Lex." Felt too because she was the first American carrier to go down, making clear our own vulnerability, increasing the odds to at least six Japanese carriers against only three American.

Again, however, our desire for simple revenge was thwarted when the *Enterprise* and *Hornet* turned and began making a high-speed run back to Pearl Harbor. It seemed to us once more like craven cowardice, and there was a good deal of muttering. But as we approached Pearl, where there was, we were told, to be no liberty this time, the rumor mill began to whisper a fantastic story. The Japanese fleet, it was said, was about to attack Midway Island, with a diversionary move on the Aleutians, and we, having broken their code, were going to lie off Midway and surprise them.

The accuracy of this report is not the product of hindsight, for I remember exactly the occasion on which I was told, with full details about ships and dates. Modern historians of the war still assume that secrecy on this critical matter was carefully maintained, that our success at Midway resulted from it, but I can testify that the deepest Navy secret—that we had broken the Japanese code and were reading their messages—was widely known among the enlisted men, and the proposed strategy and tactics for the coming battle learnedly and gravely discussed by the admirals of the lower deck, who were, on the whole, as always, of the opinion that the officers' plan would not work!

A few days out of Pearl a destroyer came alongside with the mail that was our lifeline back to familiarity. My best letters came from my mother, who was a good correspondent, typing long and interesting letters about the dogs, cats, cattle, and horses on the ranch, the neighbors, and plans for the spring and the ranch's new buildings. A few hours later the letters worked their way down to the divisional compartments and were passed out by the mail orderly— "Smith, she's run off with a Marine"—and now, these fifty years later, the feelings are still so hot under the ashes that I can write only with the greatest difficulty of the first letter I opened, from my stepfather (he did not often write), dated April 28, 1942. The words hit me like a hammer:

> I am writing this in Saratoga on Sunday morning following the funeral of our Dear. . . . Then I went over to get in the wood and do the chores. The door was locked. My first thought was it was a joke. I called to her and no answer. Then I tapped the door with my overshoe and asked to be let in. Then I got alarmed and kicked the door in. Mother was laying in the dining room Dead. I ran to her and felt her pulse. She was cold as marble. I felt her head and it was likewise. She had shot herself in the temple with the 22 pistol you gave her. I did not touch the gun. The whole sight was one awful shock and I will not describe the scene further in this letter. I hunted for a note for a few minutes and then lit out for town. I ran until I was ready to keel and then got control of myself to go into a walk.

The old letter still has the burns where I crumpled it and put it in a bulkhead ashtray before I was finished reading it, only to return to dig it, smoldering, out and go through each of the awful details. A letter I opened later from my mother, written a few days before her suicide on April 22, gave no indications of anything particularly wrong, and apparently she had bottled whatever it was up in herself, in the way that in all the old photos of groups she is hard to spot, lurking, I realized long afterwards, in the background, away in the corner. It was, of course, despair, despair with all the many things that had gone wrong in life and could never be put right, but I didn't know that at the time and hunted for particular reasons, including blaming myself for having left her. The telegram telling me of her death arrived in the mail months later.

Feelings of heavy emotional pressure were intensified by being on a ship in the middle of an ocean, on the way to a great battle, trying to deal with a mysterious event, the body already buried a month earlier. Having to do something, I blundered down into the pale green officers' quarters, where enlisted men were prohibited without a pass, and found my way to the Catholic chaplain's rooms. I was not devoutly religious, but I had been raised a Catholic in order to please my stepfather, and now seemed the time, if ever, to call on religion for help not to be found elsewhere. The chaplain was napping. Startled to see a crying distraught young sailor, he asked first if I had a pass, which I did not. Being young, I expected help, and insisted that he provide it in some tangible form like getting me leave to go home, which he could not, of course, provide.

The old chief of the ordnance gang, Murphy, sipping moosemilk, was more sympathetic and more practical. He took me off mess cooking—sending some other poor devil down to the galleys—and gave me a day off, which I spent sitting on a sponson and staring at the ocean rolling by. I slept well, which made me feel guilty that I lacked feeling.

A second day off was not thought good for me by the assembled wisdom of the ordnance gang sitting in solemn conclave wearing the red-cloth helmets that were the symbol of our trade. So I was put to work again along with everyone else, getting .50-caliber ammunition up from the magazines, taking it out of its wooden boxes, opening the greased tin inner containers and paper cartons, and

Alvin Kernan *(second from right)* relaxes with friends *(left to right)*
Richard Boone, Gaffney, and Dutscher in a San Diego bar in 1943.
For a time after the war, Boone and Kernan shared an apartment in
Greenwich Village while Kernan attended Columbia and Boone
performed with the Neighborhood Playhouse.

COURTESY OF ALVIN KERNAN

then using hand and automatic belters to shove the bullets into the
connecting metal links for the machine guns of the fighter planes
in the coming battle. Black tips were armor piercing; blue, incendiary; red, tracer; and plain, ball. We made up different combina-
tions for different purposes, using more tracer where it was important to be able to see from the burning tip of the bullet where the
fire stream was going, more armor piercing and incendiary for the
hits, and ball to keep the barrels of the guns from burning out too
quickly with all this hard, hot stuff.

Working away, eating, sleeping, and in a short time talking and
joking with the rest of the ordnance gang, my mother's death drifted
away from me. We are much simpler mechanisms than we think,
preserving life and seeking what meaning we can find in it. The dead

Professor Kernan in 1993 after years of teaching
at Yale and Princeton Universities.

must bury the dead because no one else pauses long enough to do so. Guilt is inevitable, but the real danger, I quickly found, was in feeling that you cannot move on away from what you cannot endure, letting deep emotions get too tangled and blocked.

On May 26 we were back in Pearl. Halsey, who had been standing for weeks on the bridge in his skivvy shorts trying to cool the allergic rash that was covering his body—he must have been more nervous than he appeared to be—went ashore to the hospital. He had become a hero to the crew by then, for no apparently good reason except that he was familiar, and so his departure seemed ominous. Nimitz came aboard, and we all stood to quarters to watch medals being presented to various worthies. Later, Spruance appeared as the new admiral commanding Task Force 16, built around the *Enterprise* and *Hornet,* for the Battle of Midway.

Someone saw fit to give me a two-hour compassionate liberty after we reached Pearl, time enough for me to race into Honolulu in a taxi to the Mackay office (naval communications were never used for personal matters of enlisted men) to cable some borrowed money home to help with funeral expenses and let my stepfather know that his messages had been received, that grief had spread as far as it was likely to for this death. The brass would never have let me off the ship if they thought I or anyone else had the slightest knowledge about the Japanese plans and the coming battle. How astounded they would have been to learn that everyone in the crew knew about the code and the plans! Even so, all precautions were taken to seal off the ship lest something somehow leak out, and though it was little enough, I was always grateful to whomever it was who made the tremendous argument that must have been necessary to get me ashore in those tense circumstances.

The time in port was short and filled with all-hands details provisioning the ship, refilling the magazines, getting stores and fuel aboard. The bright floodlights burned all night as one lighter after another came alongside, while the workmen from the yard installed new guns and equipment. But no one complained, for once, and excitement shone in the men's eyes. By the late morning of May 28, lighters still alongside, we were under way, steaming out of that deep and narrow channel that leads south out of the great harbor at Pearl to the open Pacific Ocean. Though we were unaware of it, at the same time (May 29 Japanese time), Isoroku Yamamoto on his flagship, *Yamato,* the largest ship in the world—seventy thousand tons, nine 18.1-inch guns—was leading the Japanese fleet out of Yashiro-jima through the Bungo Channel on the way to Midway, twenty-five hundred miles to the east. The *Yorktown* was being patched up in the dry dock at Pearl and would follow in a few days, with yard workmen still aboard making repairs, to complete the American fleet.

Once under way, we continued belting machine-gun ammunition obsessively, like some rite of war, piling up huge mounds of ammunition ready for use in the planes. We also piled up an enormous amount of trash that had to be burned, long tow targets filled with pasteboard cartridge cartons pulled like Chinese festival dragons laboriously down the passageways and ladders to the ship's incinerator to be burned at night when the smoke would not give away the position of the ship to submarines or scout planes. Big jobs always produce new shit details, and the eyes of authority—perhaps because they had overlooked the rules and felt pity for me a few days earlier—found me out instantly and dispatched me to work shoveling tons of paper into the incinerator all night long.

The trash contained bullets here and there, missed in the sorting, and after these lay in the hot fire for a time, they exploded. Since they had no firm backing when they exploded, the bullets lacked the force to go through the insulated steel sides of the furnace, but if by chance one came through the door of the incinerator when it was open, it would maim anyone it hit. The job required two sailors, dressed only in skivvies in the boiling heat that was filled with the stale smell of trash, flames lighting the small space weirdly. One man opened the door of the furnace and then slammed it closed, instantly, once a shovelful of trash had gone in. The other sailor, me, threw a shovel load in the furnace and then quickly dropped to the deck to avoid any rounds that might have cooked off since the last shovelful was thrown in. The pops were loud and frequent, and eight hours of shovel-drop-pop from sunset to sunrise jangled the nerves. But the danger was less, much less, than the frustration of being occupied with trash disposal while going into what we all knew would be one of the great naval battles of all time.

After burning paper all night, I got a few hours of sleep on the morning of June 4 before going up to the ordnance shack to help arm the planes. This was the big day when the tactics of U.S. naval air that had been developed over twenty years were at last put into practice, and failed. Knowing that the Japanese fleet intended to attack and take Midway (whatever for was hard to imagine then and now; strategy and sense often have little to do with one another), the three American carriers—*Enterprise, Hornet,* and the battered *Yorktown,* all sister ships and the only three American carriers left in the central Pacific—had steamed more than a thousand miles and taken up station to the north and east of Midway at the aptly named Point Luck.

Though we were apprehensive, the hubristic Japanese were completely unaware of our presence because, having beaten us so easily for so long, they were careless, and because of poor scouting. Their position was established just after dawn by land-based planes flying out of Midway. The carriers turned into the wind and, once the CAP was in the air, the *Enterprise* and *Hornet* began just about 0700 to launch a model carrier-based air strike.

The torpedo planes from my squadron (VT-6), being slowest, went first: fourteen TBDs loaded with torpedoes to sink ships. Each carried two men, the pilot and the radioman-gunner. The mid-seat observer-bombardiers were left behind that day, presumably to save weight but in truth to save lives, for everyone half knew what was coming. The Douglas "Devastators"—how ironic the name—were obsolete, slow, only about a hundred knots, and not highly maneuverable, in contrast to the Japanese fighter planes, the remarkable Zeros, that would be among them before they came into range of the antiaircraft guns of the Japanese fleet.

Everyone knew that a new, much improved torpedo plane, the Grumman TBF, the "Avenger," was ready for the fleet. One section of the *Hornet* torpedo squadron (VT-8) had already gotten the new planes and had flown out to Midway from where they too attacked the Japanese fleet on June 3, though with no better success than the carrier squadrons.

All the ground crew, aware that this was the big day, were out to see the pilots and crews off, and as he walked by, Winchell, one of the squadron's several enlisted pilots recently made warrant officers, borrowed my cigarette lighter for luck. The commander of the squadron, Lt. Comdr. E. E. Lindsey, was taped from his waist to his neck after a crash a few days earlier. Bad eyesight had caused him to try to land at an odd angle to the flight deck, but he would not give up the attack he had trained for, for so many years.

After the torpedo planes cleared the deck, the dive-bombers of Bombing and Scouting Six, thirty-three in all, went off, the scouts with two one-hundred-pound bright yellow bombs under the wings and a five-hundred-pounder under the fuselage, the bombers with a single yellow one-thousand-pounder. Then the obsolescent little fighters, ten F-4Fs, no match for the Zeros, clattered off. The tactics worked out over the years called for a concerted attack. The torpedo planes were to circle and then attack the Japanese fleet from all directions at sea level, not more than a hundred feet off the water. The dive-bombers were to come out of the sun at twenty thousand feet when attention was focused on the attacking torpedo planes, while the fighters were to fly air cover, engaging the Japanese fighters and preventing them from getting into the dive-bombers and the torpedo planes, lumbering and slow, flying straight and level during the time they were releasing their fish.

Timing and concentration were everything, and despite years of practice, both were bad from the start. The different squadrons got separated at once. As we watched, the torpedo planes, being the slowest, formed up and took off alone to find the Japanese fleet, which they did by an error of navigation. Being low on gas by the time they got to the Japanese carriers some time just after 0900, they started their attack at once without knowing where the dive-bombers or the fighters were. The Japanese Combat Air Patrol of Zeros came down on them as they began their runs. None of our planes made a hit, or if they did, the torpedoes did not explode.

We waited for them on the deck of the *Enterprise,* with an eye toward the *Hornet* nearby and the *Yorktown* several miles away to the west, which launched her air group later to provide a second strike. Our fighters came back first, intact, which seemed odd, and then one, two, three, and finally four torpedo planes straggled in separately, and that was it. The last of the planes was so badly shot up that it was deep-sixed immediately after it landed. One pilot, Winchell, was later picked up out of the water, sixty pounds lighter following seventeen days adrift in a raft after he was shot down. So, the total losses were nine out of fourteen crews.

The size of the loss was unimaginable, and even when the crews in a condition of shock told us what kind of a slaughter it had been, it was unbelievable. It became real when one of the surviving torpedo pilots, a bushy-mustached warrant officer, came out of his cockpit with his .45 automatic out and charged up the ladder to the bridge shouting that he was going to kill the lieutenant who had commanded the fighter escort. He was prevented by force from doing it, but the whole mess was out in an instant; that the torpedo planes had attacked alone; that the fighters had remained at a high altitude where there were no Japanese fighters—they had all gone down to shoot up the TBDs at sea level; and that while VT-6 was dying, the fighters decided there was no opposition that day and turned around and flew back to the *Enterprise.* The whole matter has remained, I understand, an issue in naval aviation to this day, but on the *Enterprise* on the morning of June 4, 1942, there was no doubt that the fighters had failed badly, and the torpedo planes had paid the price.

Around noon came the clanging alarm, the bugle call, "All hands man your battle stations," and then a few minutes later, "Bandits at twenty miles and closing, stand by to repel enemy air attack." But we were not the target that day. The *Yorktown,* about ten miles to port, was between us and the Japanese fleet, and she took the full weight of the attack. How glad we secretly were that it was not us. We stood on the deck and watched as in a movie the flashes and smoke from the antiaircraft guns in the distance. The *Yorktown* heeled over in sharp turns, taking evasive action, while near misses exploded around her, and attacking planes blew up in bright flares. Not all the bombs missed, and when it was over in less than half an hour, the *Yorktown* was down on the port side, dead in the water, and there were holes in her flight deck large enough to make it impossible for her to land her own planes. She was patched up at once and by 1400 was moving under her own power again, only to be hit by two torpedoes launched by the second and last Japanese strike. Even then she didn't go down until a submarine finished her off on the morning of the seventh.

Within a few minutes after the first attack on the *Yorktown,* her dive-bombers and ours began arriving in small clusters and singly. Shot up, some landing in the water, out of gas, some crashing on deck with failing landing gear or no tail hooks and being pushed over the side instantly to make room for the others coming in. But now the mood was triumphant. They were shouting and laughing as they jumped out of the cockpit, and the ship that had been so somber a moment before when the torpedo planes returned became now hysterically excited.

The dive-bombers had found the Japanese carriers, and they had sunk three of them, getting to them in classic style, out of the sun while they were trying to launch their own planes and when they were occupied with the torpedo planes and other attacking land-based planes coming out of Midway. It was over in an instant. Each of the three Japanese carriers—caught with bombs and torpedoes on the deck instead of being stored away in the magazines, with gasoline in the lines that ought to have been drained and flooded with CO_2—went up like tinder. And in the afternoon the bombers went back and finished off the fourth and last carrier. Four of the six carriers that had carried out the attack on Pearl Harbor—the *Kaga* and *Akagi, Hiryu,* and *Soryu*—were all burning and would sink before the next morning.

We were exultant, not just at the revenge for Pearl Harbor, sweet as that was, but at our renewed sense of power and superiority over the Japanese fleet. No one doubted by now that it would be a long war, but to everyone on the ships at Midway it was clear that we would win.

But a lot of old ideas were swept away on June 4. For one, our torpedo planes, the old TBDs, were death traps, slow, underarmed, and lacking in maneuverability. The Zeros had shot them down at will, not only the *Enterprise* squadron but also the squadrons from the *Yorktown* and *Hornet* as well. VT-8, the *Hornet* squadron, became famous for losing all of its fifteen planes and men except Ensign Gay, who flew over the carrier he was attacking and crashed on the other side but managed to get out and hide under a cushion in his life jacket all day long, watching the Japanese ships go down. VT-3, off the *Yorktown,* also lost all of its thirteen planes and most of its crews.

In addition to the forty-two torpedo planes from the three carriers, the six-plane section of VT-8 flying the new TBFs out of Midway lost five of its planes and all but two of its men, while four Army bombers, B-26s, modified to carry torpedoes, lost no planes but got no hits. Of the fifty-two torpedo planes that attacked the Japanese carriers on June 4, only nine returned to base, a loss rate of 83 percent, and none did any damage to their targets. The few that got a hit had no effect, for the torpedoes were themselves deficient and either broke up or failed to explode.

The failure of our torpedoes on planes and submarines during the first three years of the war—which everyone in the fleet knew and talked about—and the refusal of the Navy to acknowledge the problem and fix it, remain one of the scandals of the U.S. Navy. All that reckless heroism, with no chance of success even if things had gone well, instead of going about as badly as they could. The Japanese torpedo, the "long lance," worked, and the Japanese pilots put them home, but from that day at Midway on, our Navy used airborne torpedoes rarely.

The fighters were little better. The little Grumman F-4Fs were no match for the Zeros at Midway. It was the dive-bombers that emerged there as the primary weapon of naval aviation, and until the end of the war, dive-bombing with one type of plane or another remained the most effective weapon. Thirty some dive-bombers in the *Enterprise* group and the same number of the *Yorktown* group—the *Hornet* bombers never found the target—were enough to do what was needed.

Even their success, however, turned not on planning so much as on luck and on a piece of rare good judgment by Lt. Comdr. Wade McClusky, the commander of Air Group 6. On the morning of June 4, having not located the Japanese fleet at his utmost range, he had to decide in which direction to turn back. Seeing the wake of a Japanese destroyer eighteen thousand feet below going northeast, he chose to follow it, and over the horizon saw that mighty Japanese fleet below him, taking on aircraft, unable to launch, its fighter protection all down at sea level tormenting the torpedo planes. Bombing and Scouting Five from the *Yorktown* arrived just a little later, and between them the bombers of Air Groups 5 and 6 did the work. I have always thought that if there were one single crucial act in the Pacific war it was Wade McClusky's turn northeast, and though I never heard of him again, I have often wished him a long and prosperous life.

Battles are always well planned, but their outcomes always turn on chance. Many years after the war, the Japanese reports on what happened at Midway appeared and made it clear that we had been a lot luckier there than we had known at the time. Hubris, that fatal overconfidence engendered by easy victories in the early months of the war, made the Japanese eager to draw out and destroy the remnants of the American fleet, which, they believed, would have only one carrier. So they did not worry when one of their scouts from a cruiser was accidentally late in being launched on the fatal morning of June 4. But it just happened to be the scout assigned to the sector that would have discovered our fleet.

After launching their first strike against Midway, still unaware of our presence and thinking that they had all the time in the world, they made a fatal decision to rearm with bombs the second strike that remained aboard for another attack on Midway, rather than arming them with torpedoes and holding them in readiness to strike any American carriers that might appear. To add to their blunders, they brought the first strike, low on gas, back aboard before launching the second. At that point they finally learned that we were out there and began frantically arming and fueling for a strike against our carriers. But it was too late. Our torpedo planes were already attacking them, and though they made no hits, they drew all the Zeros down to sea level from where they were flying CAP at high altitude. When our bombers arrived, there were no fighters to oppose them, and the carrier decks were crowded with planes, gas, bombs, torpedoes, and ammunition just waiting to explode.

The Japanese were brave men, but it is hard not to exult across fifty years at reading about the shouts of their lookouts, "Hell Divers!" and their panic as the crews looked up into the sun and saw the dive-bombers there, with the yellow bombs already in the air beneath the planes and on their way into the big red rising suns painted on their yellow flight decks. Hard too not to admire the way their great pilot and air planner, Comdr. Minoru Genda, met the disaster with the brief word *Shimatta*, "We goofed."

At the end of the first day of battle the *Enterprise* pilots and those from the *Yorktown* who had landed on the *Enterprise* after sinking the Japanese carriers stood in a long line, waiting to be debriefed, just outside the incinerator where I was back to lighting up for the night's inferno and preparing to duck the dull bullets that hadn't made it to the battle. These were heroes dressed in their khaki flight suits, carrying pistols and knives over their yellow Mae Wests, and describing with quick hands and excited voices how they had gone into their dives, released their bombs, and seen the Japanese flight decks open up in flames just below them. The slaves who carried the equipment of the Greek warriors at Salamis, or the rowers chained to their benches at Lepanto—those other epic naval battles where the West turned Asia back—could not have felt more envious or less heroic than I.

The Battle of Midway was fought and won in a few hours on the morning of June 4, and it was finished by sunset when the last of the Japanese carriers, the *Hiryu,* was gutted. But what is clear in hindsight was not certain to either fleet at the time. Before withdrawing, the Japanese tried to force a surface action, and we grappled for their remaining ships like a blind wrestler. An information officer on the *Enterprise* drew a map with chalk on the side of the island so that all on deck could follow the battle, and we were fascinated; but every fifteen minutes the yeoman on the scaffold suspended from the top of the stack changed the location and size of the fleets.

As the information constantly changed and the range to the enemy increased or decreased, so did the armaments. Bomb size went from one-thousand-pounders to five-hundreds and back again on the dive-bombers within the space of an hour. This meant endless work for ordnancemen, which got me at last out of the incinerator. I happily ran back and forth trundling bombs and carrying belted ammunition for the machine guns, a part of the ordnance gang again, hopefully, since I had just been made a petty officer, third class (sixty dollars a month), never to return to the drudgery of general ship's duties again. Nothing in the next two days of the battle could match the first, though the excitement remained high and the level of activity feverish. The Japanese fleet proved elusive. We caught only a couple of cruisers and destroyers and hammered them viciously.

The *Enterprise* returned to Pearl Harbor on the morning of June 13, my nineteenth birthday, but I already knew how quickly memories, even of the greatest things, fade and lose their reality. Aware during the battle that this was probably the greatest event I would ever be present at, I looked for some image to fix Midway in my mind, forever. As I did so, I was waiting for a bomb to come up the forward bomb elevator shaft, about three feet by four. I looked down the narrow shaft going several hundred feet from the bright sunlight of the day on deck to the depths of the ship, where, close to the keel, the bomb magazines were located. At the very bottom, a bright yellow bomb had just been put on the elevator, so that I seemed to be looking down an immensely long tunnel at a bright yellow spot, both beautiful and deadly at once, at the end. To this very moment I can see it as clearly as if I were still there, and for me that image is the famous Battle of Midway.

WALTER SULLIVAN

IN HIS LONG CAREER as a journalist, Walter Sullivan worked on only one newspaper—but it was the New York *Times*. He served that paper in many capacities, joining the staff as a copyboy in 1940 (before he went to war) and later writing as a foreign correspondent in both the Far East and Germany. He was also a United Nations correspondent for a time. But Sullivan was to find his real niche in science writing, and he was the *Times*'s science editor for many years.

As a science writer, Sullivan reported research news for his own paper (for example, he coauthored the New York *Times* report "Project Apollo"), and he contributed articles to various magazines. But he also wrote many books on science, including two McGraw titles, *Quest for a Continent* (1957) and *We Are Not Alone* (1964), and *Black Holes: The Edge of Space, The End of Time,* published by Doubleday in 1979. He won the International Nonfiction Book Prize for *We Are Not Alone.* He has also won many other awards from an impressive variety of scientific and journalistic organizations for his science writing.

Sullivan participated in and wrote about polar expeditions too. But he had embarked on an active life a long time before he took up science. He joined the Navy in 1940 and left in 1946 as a lieutenant commander. He saw combat in the fall of 1942 in the Pacific

as communications officer on board the USS *Fletcher* (DD-445)—
the first ship of that famous class of destroyers. He was aboard the
Fletcher on one dark night when two opposing battle groups sailed
right through one another and engaged in a battle celebrated both
for its confusion and for its fury. The following account of that battle is based on journals, interviews, and Navy records, as well as
Sullivan's own recollections.

"THE SHIP AHEAD JUST DISAPPEARED"

Some believe it was the most critical engagement between surface
ships in World War II. At the time, we called it the Third Battle of
Savo Island, but it came to be known as the Naval Battle of Guadalcanal. One of its participants, our destroyer the *Fletcher,* was the
first of its kind, equipped with a new radar that displayed target
positions on a screen. As the ship's communications officer, I was
technically in charge of the radar but knew almost nothing about
it. That night it was our lifesaver.

The Japanese had established themselves on Guadalcanal, an
island in the Solomon chain with a backbone of huge volcanic
mountains. The U.S. Marines had challenged them, gaining a beachhead and airfield, but both were in peril. Already, we believed, the
Japanese on Guadalcanal outnumbered our Marines by a wide
margin. High-speed Japanese transports laden with reinforcements,
supported by four battleships, eleven heavy cruisers, two light
cruisers and more than three dozen destroyers had assembled at
Truk to the north. At night, warships came down to shell our beachhead at leisure.

On two successive days, in the fall of 1942, our warships escorted
transports into the broad sound off Guadalcanal (later called
Ironbottom Bay) and the troops were unloaded despite repeated
(and generally ineffective) air attacks. Air reconnaissance, however,
had reported that a large Japanese fleet was headed south.

At sundown, the American transports withdrew through Sealark Channel between Guadalcanal and Florida Island, and so did our five cruisers and eight destroyers. We hoped to give the impression that the combat ships were leaving, like mimicking a departure by ostentatiously slamming the door, but we lingered nearby to return after dark through Sealark. The *O'Bannon,* our sister ship with the same new radar, led our line of thirteen ships while we brought up the rear.

Our second in command, J. C. (Bill) Wylie, had placed himself in the chart room on the bridge, contrary to Navy doctrine that demanded that his battle station be aft at a secondary control station in case the bridge was destroyed and the captain incapacitated. Wylie reasoned that it was more important to take advantage of the new radar, a decision that proved to be momentous.

Someone pointed out that at midnight it would be Friday the thirteenth. We were the thirteenth ship in the line. Our ship number was 445 and our task force number was sixty-seven, both adding up to thirteen. Was this a bad omen? It also seemed strange to be facing Admiral Tojo's fleet only a few weeks after waving goodbye to the workmen who had fitted out our ship in the safe and friendly environs of Brooklyn.

On the bridge, it was very dark, since the sky was heavily overcast, and I would have found the night extraordinarily beautiful had it not been for fear. The air was still; the water smooth as glass. The slick sea, rolled over by our bow wave, sparkled with luminous creatures like sequins on black velvet. I could tell land was near from the hothouse fragrance of night-blooming flowers. Thousands of Americans, Navy men and troops about to face combat, came to know that gardenia fragrance and never again would smell it without remembering this prelude to a close encounter with death.

I left the bridge to decipher a couple of new messages, then brought them to Bill Cole, our soft-spoken captain. He ran his dim red flashlight back and forth across each page as he read. They listed two Japanese battleships, four or more cruisers and ten to twelve destroyers on the way down.

"Seems funny to be fighting battleships with destroyers and a few cruisers," he said softly. The crew was not told that we might run into battleships. After midnight, I felt the channel widening as we entered the bay.

The inter-ship radio had remained silent as we steamed in, lest it tip off the Japanese that we were there. Then one of our ships broke radio silence: "Contact bearing . . . looks like a number of ships."

More reports followed, as we pressed onward. Our 5-inch guns trained on the nearest target and we waited for word from Rear Adm. Daniel Callaghan on when to open fire.

In the blackness, I peered toward the enemy ships that I knew were there, but could see nothing. Then suddenly the Japanese ship on which we had our guns aimed turned a powerful searchlight on a ship forward of us. Its side glow illuminated the upper works of what seemed a cruiser and I could see other ships, ahead and astern of it.

For me, the sudden end of darkness, the material appearance of the enemy and the illumination of the water between the two lines of ships was an instantaneous relief, as though a great decision had finally been made.

We didn't wait for orders from the admiral.

"Commence firing!" the captain yelled. It was as though, with the fierceness of his cry, he could make his guns shoot harder and faster. The whole American battle line reacted in the same way; the procession of ships began spouting fire. The searchlight went out. Had the ship been sunk, or even hit? There was no way to tell. We shifted our fire to another target. Several of the Japanese vessels seemed to be on fire and there was an explosion; perhaps a destroyer blowing up.

I wasn't looking when it happened, but suddenly our whole pilothouse was filled with reddish light. I turned and saw a cloud of fire and smoke billowing up from the sea a few hundred yards ahead of us. It obscured all our ships and much of the sky. A moment later, we felt the concussion. The captain elbowed his way among those in life vests to the intercom linking him with Wylie in the radar shack.

"Hey, Bill!" the captain yelled. "The ship ahead of us has just blown up!"

The horror of it curdled my stomach. The captain ran to the engine-order telegraph, swung the handles and ran back to the phone.

"I'm stopping, Bill. I don't want to run through the survivors. I think that was the *Barton*. The *Monssen* and *Aaron Ward* both seem to have been hit and dropped behind." (These were destroyers, the *Monssen* having originally been directly ahead of us.)

The water ahead was brilliantly lighted by flame from the *Barton*'s burning oil. We saw a long, sleek object fly out of the sea, then plunge in again like a great fish with a hook in his mouth.

"Hey, Bill," the captain called, "a torpedo just broached a few yards ahead of us."

"The after gunners report one just passed under us, too, Captain," Wylie answered, "and someone else says he saw a torpedo making a surface run aft. That must be what got our other destroyers."

It was a formidable attack. We may have been spared only because the torpedoes were set to run deep enough to hit below the armor of a cruiser or battleship but too deep for a destroyer. We learned later that the Japanese Long Lance torpedoes were far superior to our own.

We were dead in the water. A few ship lengths ahead was a pool of burning oil and debris. The sky was ablaze: star shells, rocket clusters, parachute flares. We could see that, in the confusion, our line of cruisers had made a sharp turn to the left.

Since we were the last ship in the line, the flagship asked us on the voice radio: "Are you around the corner yet?" The captain jumped for the microphone: "No!"

It was hard moving around; everyone had on bulky life jackets, and it seemed an unusually large number of men had crowded into the shelter of the pilothouse. The captain bounced from man to man.

"Can't we get some of these pregnant women out of here?" he said, and into his squawk box: "Hey, Bill, what do you think we'd better do?"

In the enclosed chart house, Wylie and the radar man, Tom Hollyday, were trying to plot the situation on the radarscope. It may have been the first time that the new surface radar was used in a night battle. Out on the bridge, the captain could see very little. All that Wylie and Hollyday knew of the battle was the noise, most of it from our own guns, and the radio, radar and visual reports coming through earphones connected to the various battle circuits.

The one on Wylie's head had a single earphone, leaving his other ear free. He had squawk box communication with the captain and access to the inter-ship voice radio. In his lap, or otherwise handy, were circuits linking him with the main battery, torpedo crew, fire-control radar and the computer, which was in the bowels of the ship. It was a makeshift arrangement, but described later in a report by the captain, it became fleet doctrine and, ultimately, the Combat Information Center now on all Navy ships. He and Hollyday saw no fireworks, no explosions, no torpedoes. But they counted the "pips" of about twenty Japanese ships.

"There are Jap ships up north of us," Hollyday said (we *never* called them Japanese). "And over to the east, too."

"Yes, chum, and those are Japs to the south and west," Wylie said, in a detached voice.

"Christ, Mr. Wylie," Hollyday said, "what do we do now?"

The exec looked at him with a trace of a smile. "Well, I'm a Presbyterian. I think we'll get through."

"Hey, Wylie, what's the best way out of this?" the captain bellowed again over the squawk box.

"I'll be darned if I know, captain. We're cut off from the rest of our force. There're Japs all around us."

"Right full rudder," the captain yelled. "Port head two; starboard back one." I was happy to feel the ship shudder from the push and pull of the two engines. It hadn't been fun lying dead in the water. The ship started swinging right without advancing into the debris of the *Barton.*

"I got it, captain," Wylie called out. "You gotta come left. Come left and go like hell!"

"Are you sure, Bill?"

"Captain, it's our only chance. Those Japs ahead are going to be coming right over this spot in a few minutes."

"Left full rudder!" the skipper called.

Inside the chart house, Wylie was sweating. It was all his pigeon now. He gave the captain a course to steer.

To hide us, those on the stern were told to activate chemical smoke generators, producing a trail of white smoke as our stern dug in, like a high-speed motorboat at full throttle. Likewise, the engineers were told to adjust the burners so sticky black smoke came pouring out of the stacks. Men on the high platform of the 40-millimeter guns aft of the stacks ducked behind the guns' protective shield, but it did no good. They choked and coughed and the soot clung to their faces. Yet the thicker it was, the happier they were. The Japanese, lobbing star shells into the sky overhead, were trying to illuminate us so their heavy guns could open fire. Men on the stern reported later that shells landed all around us.

We were drawing clear of the fight. The Japanese had forgotten us and were shooting at other ships or at each other. In the confusion, some of our own cruisers may also have fired on one another and a call to our ships on the voice radio ordered: "Cease fire! Cease fire!"

Ahead of us, a vast long shadow loomed. "What the heck is that?" I asked Hamilton, the torpedo officer. My sense of direction was jumbled.

"You nut, that's Guadalcanal," he replied. We were on the wing of the bridge and did not hear the captain's order to the helm, but we saw the wake curve and felt the ship heel over as we sped around in a sharp turn. We slowed; high speed was not needed. We were going back in.

"Stand by for torpedo attack," the captain called to Hamilton.

"Aye, aye, sir," Hamilton replied and alerted his torpedo gang. For months they had been preparing for this moment, sometimes working in tropical downpours, their dungarees soaked, sustained by large quantities of coffee and the glib, Tennessean chatter of their boss, Chief Torpedoman Anglin. The torpedo is a fickle instrument of war, requiring constant attention and overhaul to be sure it runs

"hot, straight and normal" when the time comes for the destroyer
to use its most potent weapon. All during our approach up Sealark
Channel, Anglin had paced up and down the catwalk alongside his
torpedo tubes, muttering.

"Don't fail me tonight, girls; this may be your coming-out party;
remember who brung you up," he said, and he tapped them gently
with the hammer he carried to fire them by hand if the remote control failed.

"Bill, there's a great big fellow coming out of the mess up ahead,"
the skipper called to the exec. "Looks like a pretty good target—
maybe a battleship."

"I've got it, Captain," said Wylie, looking at his radarscope, "but
isn't that one of our own?"

"No. I can see it. It's a Jap all right. See if you can pick it up,
Hamilton." Hamilton's fire-control system calculated the course
and speed of the target and adjusted his ten torpedo tubes accordingly. Wylie still was not convinced.

"God. Are you *sure* it's not ours?" Even after the fight was over,
Wylie was fearful, until we learned that not one of our ships was
torpedoed at that time or in that area.

The captain was getting excited and hopping around. "Have you
got a solution yet, Hamilton?" he asked.

"Yes, sir. We're all set up."

"We're going to let 'em have it, Bill," the captain called into the
squawk box.

"Fire when ready," he told Hamilton.

"Stand by!" Hamilton cried.

"Stand by!" Anglin echoed.

"Fire one!" There was a swish; the gleaming metal cylinder of
the first torpedo emerged from the tube, flew gracefully over the
rail and plopped into the water.

"Fire two!" Swish . . . plop.

"Fire three!" Swish . . . plop. Anglin stood by the tubes, mumbling. At first, the torpedomen thought he was praying. Then they
heard fragments.

"Goodbye, darling."

"Give my love to the duchess."

"Send her to the bottom, you bitch."

Ten torpedoes flew over the rail with majestic precision—ten tons of destruction. We could feel a barely perceptible push against the ship as each impulse charge went off, forcing its torpedo out.

"All torpedoes expended—no casualties," Hamilton announced. It had all sounded like our daily torpedo drills.

The torpedomen were counting the minutes needed for the torpedoes to reach their target. There were several flashes at the horizon, followed by increasingly heavy explosions. Anglin was already on the bridge.

"I think we got her, captain," he said.

The shooting had died down, although crippled ships still fired potshots once in a while.

"We've shot our bolt, Bill, let's get out of here," the skipper called to Wylie. "What's a good course for Sealark?" The exec gave it to him; then he and Hollyday lit cigarettes.

"Well, Tom, I think it's over," the exec said.

"I guess I'm a Presbyterian too, now," said Hollyday.

As we retired across the broad bay into Sealark Channel, we could see the glow of what we took to be our burning target. Suddenly the glow brightened, flew apart and disintegrated into darkness. A large ship appeared ahead of us, going the same way. It proved to be the cruiser *Helena*.

"Well, we aren't the only ship still afloat, thank God," the captain said. We pulled ahead of her so our sonar could watch out for submarines, then soon heard another voice on the air, asking who was around. It was the cruiser *San Francisco*. We slowed so it could catch up. Its steering gear had been shot away and it was navigating clumsily with its port and starboard engines. The *O'Bannon* joined us and the shadow of another destroyer appeared ahead. It did not respond to radio calls—its radio had been knocked out— but it correctly answered recognition signals by flashing light, as did another ship, too distant for identification, that later proved to be the light cruiser *Juneau.* Thus six ships steamed out where thirteen had entered the night before, and ours was the only member of the squadron that had not been hit.

After dawn, a scouting plane found others of our ships still afloat in the bay, as well as a Japanese battleship listing badly, its steering gear crippled so it could only steam in circles. Japanese destroyers were beached on nearby islands. Japanese survivors were swimming in pools of oil and debris where other ships had gone down. Most of our ships in the bay were beyond salvage and had to be scuttled. The Japanese battleship was finished off by bombers. The *San Francisco* was in shambles, with hundreds dead and more wounded than she could care for, so the *Juneau*'s doctor went over.

Excitement had kept us going, but now, after daylight, we dropped into sleep wherever we could. I lay on my life jacket on a superstructure deck. Suddenly I found myself standing and shaking. There had been a violent concussion. Aft, a pillar of smoke seemed to reach from the sea almost to the thunderheads in the sky overhead. There were specks of flying debris against the white clouds and heavy smoke rolled out in all directions from where the *Juneau* had been.

The *San Francisco* swung sharply toward the smoke, using her engines to twist and avoid torpedoes in the water. When the smoke lifted from the sea, there was nothing to be seen where the *Juneau* had been except an oil slick.

We wanted to go back and look for survivors, but the task force commander decided that, with a submarine in the area, hoping for a chance to torpedo others, we should all press onward. The *Fletcher* was particularly needed, since its submarine-detecting sound gear was still fully functional. It was a heartrending decision, debated for years afterward. Among the deserted crew (if they survived the explosion) were five Sullivan brothers (no relations of mine) for whom a destroyer was later named. (It is now on exhibition in Buffalo.) Not all the crew perished. A handful reached a nearby island, and were eventually rescued.

The blowing up of the *Juneau* was almost more shattering than the battle of the night before. We sought to settle our nerves in various ways. In his cabin, the captain took out a pack of cards and played Canfield. He won twice in a row, which Wylie said was so momentous it should be entered in the ship's official log. Eaton, the chief boatswain's mate, walked up and down the deck calling out: "There's something lucky on this ship. Don't throw anything overboard, not even the garbage."

In the wardroom, many records of classical music had been broken by the shock of gunfire, but Hamilton found one of Beethoven's greatest and last string quartets—Opus 130. This was usually not the favorite music in the wardroom, but no one walked out. It was as though this was the lyre of David, not the Budapest String Quartet.

When the report from the scouting plane confirmed the damage to the Japanese, the captain must have read it five times. Another particularly eloquent message came from Adm. William Halsey. But it was the one from Gen. Alexander Vandegrift, commanding the Marines on Guadalcanal, that meant the most to us. We learned later that some Marines brought camp chairs to the beach to watch the battle in comfort.

General Vandegrift eulogized the aircraft carriers and battleships for their fighting in the Coral Sea after our engagement, but the supreme homage, he said, must be reserved for our task force, which, on the thirteenth, fought under Admirals Callaghan and Scott (both of whom perished): "Against what appeared hopeless odds they turned back the first great onslaught. To them the Marines on Guadalcanal raise their battered helmets in deep tribute." Only when these dispatches were posted on our bulletin boards did the crew begin to realize what a turning point our battle had been.

Of the five ships that reached Espíritu Santo on the afternoon of November 14, ours was the last to enter the harbor. The others were already at anchor. The stacks of the *Helena* were peppered with holes. The bridge structure of the *San Francisco* had been demolished. Suddenly the captain rushed to the loudspeaker.

"All hands, attention to starboard!" Everyone on the decks of the *San Francisco,* its holds still carrying its dead, was standing at attention, facing us as we passed. It was a grim tribute from the shelltorn cruiser. Our men caught the idea and themselves froze as we passed across its bow. Beyond was a British cruiser. The tars were drawn up in ranks and, as we steamed past, waved their white hats three times in unison. Then the sound reached us across the water: three faint cries of "Hip! Hip!" each followed by hundreds of voices crying "Hurrah!" The *Fletcher* was being cheered by a British cruiser. This was no empty, halfhearted ceremony. There were no bands, no bunting, no dress uniforms. But the battered ships at attention and the British cheers were enough.

BEN BRADLEE

B EN BRADLEE spent some forty-six years as a professional journalist. In early assignments, he served as a reporter for the Washington *Post* as press attaché for the American embassy in Paris, and as European correspondent and later Washington correspondent for *Newsweek*. Later he became managing editor and executive editor of the Washington *Post*. Overseeing that paper's investigations into the Pentagon Papers, Watergate, and other important stories, Bradlee played a major role over two decades in developing the paper into the highly influential institution it is today.

In 1991 Bradlee retired, and among other things began writing a memoir, which was published as *A Good Life: Newspapering and Other Adventures* in 1995. In this book he recounts his formative naval experience during World War II, which began with his commissioning two hours after his graduation from Harvard on August 8, 1942. (He and several of his friends had joined the Naval ROTC at Harvard, partly attracted because this particular program promised its cadets only the choicest of duty—on cruisers or destroyers.) Bradlee was assigned to duty aboard the USS *Philip* (DD-498), which was still under construction, and served two years on this vessel. (According to Bradlee, those were a vitally important two years for him.) He saw his first action in gun duels with Japanese

planes and destroyers in "The Slot," the famous strait near Bougainville. Spending most of its time at sea and often in combat, the
Philip returned to the States in mid-1944 after participating in the
invasion of Saipan.

In January 1945 Bradlee was assigned as a kind of expert con-
sultant in destroyer Combat Information Center (CIC) operations.
He served in this capacity on nineteen destroyers over the succeed-
ing eight months, often in combat and always under way; hence,
he usually transferred from one ship to another by "breeches buoy."
At the war's end, before being released, Bradlee was assigned to
rewrite the Navy's destroyer CIC manual. In an interview with *Naval
History* magazine upon his memoir's publication, Bradlee said he
agreed with those who likened the job of a CIC officer (as he had
described it in the book) to that of an editor. Among other things,
his method was to surround himself with the very best people, and
then to listen to what they had to say.

The selection below is drawn from the thirty pages of Bradlee's
memoir in which he describes his naval duty.

from

A GOOD LIFE: NEWSPAPERING
AND OTHER ADVENTURES

The first time a man goes into battle—making eye contact with
someone trying to kill him—is strangely like the first time a man
makes love to a woman. The anticipation is overpowering; the ignorance is obstructive; the fear of disgrace is consuming; and survival
is triumphant.

For me, that first time came near some forgotten island in the
Strait of Bougainville, or "The Slot," as it will be forever engraved
in the hearts of those who raced—or were chased—up and down it
during most of 1943. We had escorted some LSTs filled with Marines
to make an assault landing on . . . it could have been Vella Lavella,
where the rats were said to be as big as dogs. LSTs were large, cum-
bersome, and slow transport ships, incapable of evasive action. We

had gotten them ashore, when our radar operators reported "a mess of bogeys at twenty, Angels eleven." Translation: Enemy planes twenty miles away, flying at eleven thousand feet. Someone else was directing the small group of F-4U Corsair fighters, flying cover for our little operation. So my job was to relay the changing range and altitude information (which were then cranked into an amazingly unsophisticated fire-control system) until visual contact was made. Then, my job was over, at least for a moment. When I heard the antiaircraft guns of the other ships in our convoy, I ran out of the darkened CIC onto the bridge. The first plane I saw was whizzing along the water about one hundred yards away. Just as I recognized it as one of ours, and cheered as I saw him splash the plane he was chasing, I looked almost straight up, and there it was.

It was a Zero, with its distinctive fixed wheels, covered with equally distinctive streamlined wheel covers. I could see the pilot. And worse than that, I could see the bomb he had just dropped arching lazily down toward us. How far away was the Zero? Maybe 150 feet. How big was the bomb? Somewhere between the size of the Empire State Building and about two hundred pounds, probably closer to the latter. Was I scared? Who knows? I was so exhilarated it didn't feel like any fear I had ever felt.

By the time I was sorting all that out, and noticing with some satisfaction that I had not wet my pants, the bomb smashed into the water so close that the towering splash soaked everyone on the starboard side of the ship—and never exploded. It was a dud. (I have felt strangely ambivalent about Japanese technology ever since.)

After a few weeks of trying to fool the Japanese into thinking we had a lot of carriers out there, instead of just the *Enterprise,* our squadron took up our semi-permanent assignment with three brand-new cruisers. The destroyers (*Philip, Sauffley, Conway, Renshaw, Waller, Sigourney, Eaton*) comprised Destroyer Squadron 22. The cruisers (*Montpelier, Denver, Columbia,* and *Cleveland*) made up Cruiser Division 6, and together we made up a Task Group, under the overall command of the flashy, charismatic Admiral William Halsey, or the brilliant, self-effacing Admiral Raymond Spruance, the admirals who taught our generation the art of "calculated risk."

The officers of the USS *Philip,* including young Ensign Bradlee *(fourth from the left)* were photographed on the destroyer's commissioning day in November 1942 at the Brooklyn Navy Yard.

COURTESY OF BEN BRADLEE

(We all preferred Spruance.) For the next nine months we alternated with a Task Group of older destroyers and cruisers in night raids up The Slot. We would leave Tulagi, an island about twenty miles north of Guadalcanal, in the brilliant sun of a late afternoon.

"Let's go get us some medals, Mr. Bradlee," said our commanding officer, Tommy Ragan. "Yes, sir," replied Ensign Bradlee, hoping that his twenty-one-year-old sphincter would hold.

We would steam fast enough to be abreast of Bougainville by dark, and steam on more slowly in the dead of night toward Rabaul. Our official orders were to look for trouble. Some nights we found nothing, but not many. Some nights we would spot small coastal boats, transporting Japanese soldiers as they retreated up The Slot. Some nights we would be trailed by Japanese night fighters, who would suddenly bracket us in the phosphorous light of parachute flares—presumably to illuminate us for the Japanese submarines known to be in the area. Some nights we bombarded targets picked out for us by the Australian coast watchers, an extraordinary bunch of men, mostly former plantation superintendents who had fled into the jungle when the Japanese arrived.

And some nights our radars would spot a group of enemy ships coming down The Slot from Rabaul, looking for their own medals, and the two groups would shell each other in a blind slugfest for an hour or so. We worried more about Japanese torpedoes, fired from ships or submarines. Our torpedoes were nowhere near as good. Rabaul is the island that a young congressman, somehow a lieutenant commander in the Naval Reserve, flew over one night as an observer, and flew back to Washington immediately. Got himself a Bronze Star for that single flight, as the world would learn later. His name was Lyndon Baines Johnson (D-Tex.).

Unless we were actually engaging the enemy, we would have to leave the waters off Rabaul by two or three in the morning in order to get safely out of range of the Japanese planes in Rabaul by daylight. We'd get back to Tulagi, refuel, and take on new ammunition, just in time to see the other Task Group start up The Slot to repeat the search and destroy mission. Of course, we would have to stand watch—four hours on, four hours off—until we went to General Quarters and started the whole process over again the next day.

Even without the constant concern for survival, it was an exhausting life that discouraged reflection, introspection, or anything more intellectual than reading. We slept in what we laughingly called our spare time—often in bunks that were only eighteen inches above or below someone else, known as your fart-sackmate. Always with a fan only a few inches from your face, since there was no air-conditioning, of course. We played a little cards, mostly cribbage. We used to gamble—for high stakes because there was no place to spend money—but that had pretty much been outlawed by our skipper, Tommy Ragan. My favorite cribbage pigeon was Bill Weibel, from Detroit, the torpedo officer, hence known as "Tubes." Our games ended in a repeat of my college "21" games. All of a sudden "Tubes" owed me more than four thousand dollars, which approximated a year's pay. When the captain heard about the debt, he ordered me to play double or nothing until I lost, and then quit playing for money. Took me three boards.

And we did read—when we weren't too exhausted or scared to read. Boswell's *Life of Johnson* was permanently in a book rack that had been welded to the bulkhead in the officers' head aboard the *Philip.* I got hooked on the anti-establishment works of Philip Wylie, like *A Generation of Vipers.* I remember particularly a book called *Love in America,* a scathing description of the basic relations between men and women by David L. Cohn. Both Wylie and Cohn questioned the soupy sentimentalism that dominated advertising and film. I read a novel by Gladys Schmitt called *The Gates of Aulis.* Bill Cox, an officer on the *Sigourney,* specialized in comics, especially "Terry and the Pirates." He had friends in the States who would clip comics from their newspapers, staple them together in sequences, and mail them out to him.

Bob Lee became my best pal and my model, probably because he was so many things I was not, at least was not yet. First, he was educated and motivated. He read books because he wanted to read books. Up to now, I had read books because I had to read books— except for *Lady Chatterley's Lover.* A couple of years older than I, he had been on a four-stack destroyer before coming to the *Philip,* and so the insignia on his cap had that tarnished look that separated the veteran sailors from the new kids on the ship. He had gone to Amherst on a scholarship, and really learned things. His father had been a carpenter in East Orange, New Jersey. His sister was married to a wholesale Amoco Oil dealer in East Orange, and I had yet to meet a wholesale oil dealer. He shared his destroyer knowledge gracefully and often. When we were still in the Brooklyn Navy Yard being outfitted with things like motor whaleboats, he had asked me one morning to go pick up the one consigned to the *Philip.* He quickly saw I didn't know what a motor whaleboat was (a motor launch), much less where it was, and we went off to pick it up together.

"General," as he was known, was just like the hero of Tom Heggen's great war novel *Mister Roberts*—relaxed, wry, hardworking, and loved by the people who worked under him. He was impressed by the way I had handled my first real people crisis. So was I, as a matter of fact. Before we sailed off to the Pacific, I was standing a night watch one night in the Brooklyn Navy Yard when a young sailor named Frank had pulled a Colt .45 pistol on me, maybe in search of a Section 8 discharge as a mental case. Since I was armed with my own .45, but would never have shot him under any circumstances, I had no choice but to talk him down quietly.

In thousands of hours of conversation at sea over more than twenty-four months, Lee and I shared each other's lives, peeling back layer after layer, until we didn't have to worry about our friendship: it had taken root and flourished.

Along about Christmas 1943, we got orders for Sydney, Australia, for a week of R&R. In conventional terms we hadn't had a day off for almost a year. We had not heard a female voice for the same length of time except in the movies. We talked a lot about Garbo nibbling on Melvyn Douglas's ear in *Ninotchka*. That's how bad it was. And Sydney was the answer to our prayers. As we steamed into Sydney harbor, General and I were standing on the bridge together when Hoppy, the chief signalman, pointed to some flags waving from a distant hill and said, "You're not going to believe this." The flags were actually semaphore signals, and the closer we got, the more easily we could see that the signals were being sent by young persons of the opposite sex. Age sixteen, tops. In fact, they were asking if anyone might be interested in dates that evening.

Lee and I had volunteered to stand watch that first night, moored to the Woolamaloo Docks, so the rest of the crew except for a skeleton force could go on liberty. I knew why I had volunteered: I wanted to put off for as long as possible the critical question, was I going to get laid after only eighteen months of enforced fidelity?

We were duly hailed for our generosity by the rest of the crew, and were sitting alone in the wardroom discussing the liberty we would take next day, when we suddenly realized that the ship was listing obviously and ominously to starboard—away from the dock. The reason for the list was not hard to find: thirty sailors were drooped over the railing talking to three young women who had rowed alongside looking for a little action. Pogies, at a glance.

("Pogies" is Navy slang for very young females, as in "pogey bait"—candy for use to lure "pogies" into the sack.) General and I couldn't come up with any regulation that was being violated, until one of the girls started scrambling aboard and the rowboat was being tied up. Plainly the pogies had accepted an invitation to entertain what was left of the crew, and the sailors looked to see what Lee and I were going to do about it.

General and I were widely respected for the wisdom of our decisions in disciplinary matters. This respect dated from an incident which had occurred one night a few months earlier, while the *Philip* was anchored in Iron Bottom Sound, Tulagi. We had rigged the movie screen forward and were showing a movie when another destroyer signaled for permission to come alongside. This was normally no big deal. We would stop the movie for maybe five minutes, while the other ship came alongside and moored bow to stern, allowing the new ship to rig its movie screen forward and show its movie alongside our stern. The whole process shouldn't take five minutes.

This time, though, the ship moored their bow to our bow. To make matters worse this was our new skipper's old ship, and Jimmy Rutter, our new skipper, was in no mood to ask his old captain for any favors. On top of that, damned if they didn't rig their movie screen forward and start showing their own movie, in competition with ours. Rutter, knowing when he was licked, threw up his hands, canceled our movie, and retired to his quarters. Not our crew, however. Some of them retired to the spud bin, the place between the smokestacks amidships where potatoes were stored—when there were any to store—and started throwing them at the new arrivals. Pretty soon one of our potatoes hit their commanding officer in the back of the neck, and pretty soon after that Jimmy Rutter was invited aboard his old ship for a tongue-lashing from his old skipper. Something about how important it was to take command quickly, and show his new ship who was boss.

Jimmy Rutter returned steaming and sent for General and me, immediately. He had never been so humiliated in his life, he told us. The worst behavior he'd ever seen, and in front of his old commanding officer. What kind of ship was this anyway? And he demanded that we find out who had done this dastardly deed, and tell them they were going to get their asses court-martialed. Lee and I left meekly, knowing we were on a fool's mission. Potatoes, we heard? "Mr. Bradlee, you know we ain't had no potatoes on this ship for months." We went from bow to stern. No one had seen any potatoes thrown. No one had seen any potatoes, period. Plenty of them told us they wished they had found some spuds, so they could have thrown them at those "bastids."

After delaying our report for an extra hour to enforce our claim of thoroughness, we told the captain we had found no culprits, and felt we had no chance at all of finding any. We wished his former skipper had not been hit by a flying potato, but we felt the *Philip* had been trashed, and some defense was explainable if not completely meritorious. Anyway he cooled off and we got credit from the crew for the lack of discipline.

Now we used the same strategy. We did nothing for about half an hour, then asked a chief petty officer buddy by loudspeaker to report to the wardroom. We were worried about the Sydney police, we said. These girls were plainly minors. We were worried about venereal disease, we said. These girls were also plainly pros. And we were worried about the number of Navy Regulations the captain could claim were being violated if he returned to the ship early. And so, we told him, we were going to stroll through the ship on an inspection tour in twenty minutes, and we sure hoped that we wouldn't find any extra passengers, or any rowboats. Right on schedule, we took our stroll. We found no stowaways, and the rowboat had disappeared into the Woolamaloo night.

The next night was our turn ashore, one of the most memorable nights of my life—and I didn't even get laid. We started off in the (men's) bar of the Australia Hotel, downing glass after glass of the great, bitter Aussie beer. Next, we were flipping Australian pennies up over our heads into the large glass bowls, which hung on chains like lampshades under the hanging lights. We were quickly joined at this by a wonderfully tough-looking group of soldiers, a good deal older than we, and much harder. But just as thirsty. We had been told there were no able-bodied men in Australia; they'd all gone overseas to fight in Europe and North Africa. This, we'd heard, was why the women were so friendly. But these were able-bodied men, by God. These were the ragtag remnants of the Second Australian First. The First Australian First had been composed of the first Australians to leave to fight World War I. And these were the first Australians to leave to fight World War II. In fact, they had landed that very day, back home for the first time in five years, after fighting in Crete, fighting Rommel across North Africa, and after crossing the Owen Stanley Range in New Guinea to fight the Japanese. After these incredible battles, they wore no decorations other than the curved metal AUSTRALIA at the top of their shoulders. Despite our callow youth and comparatively limited battle experiences, we had at least one row of ribbons. After listening to their stories, we solemnly pinned our ribbons on them, and they wore them for the rest of the night, as we wore their hard-earned AUSTRALIAS.

As the night slowed into morning, and we slipped in and out of stages of oblivion, our new friends started slipping off quietly—except for one: the towering figure I can recall only as "Shag." "Shag" had taken a piece of shrapnel in his neck from one of Rommel's tanks at Tobruk, and he spoke through a hole in his throat. He'd been repaired and sent back into battle without home leave. He was pretty drunk by now, as drunk as we were, but it gradually dawned on us that he was scared, on top of everything else. Before long he told us why. He hadn't seen his wife for six years! And hadn't dared call to tell her he was home. She lived across Sydney harbor in Manly Beach, but he was scared to go home to her alone, scared that she would think his new voice box would be a fatal disfigurement in her eyes. As the skies lightened he asked us, begged us, to go home with him. We pleaded that would be an intrusion; he insisted he needed us. Were we real mates, or not? What was friendship about, anyway? And finally, as the sun rose over this fabulous city, the three of us boarded the ferry to Manly Beach, Lieutenant junior grade Robert E. Lee, Ensign Benjamin C. Bradlee, and PFC "Shag," all three gloriously drunk, on the mission that scared him more than a desert battle. We wove our way slowly and noisily down this country road of cottages, each with gardens, fenced with rose bushes. And suddenly, "Shag" tottered to a stop, tears stream-ing from his eyes—and as tears streamed down our cheeks—and we knew he was home. None of us said a word as a door quietly opened, a woman appeared, and they slowly walked into each other's arms.

Our next night was more selfish. We rented a flat for a week in Rosalyn Gardens, in a building that housed scores of pretty, friendly young secretaries, as willing to go to bed with us as we were des-perate to go to bed with them. All it took was satisfactory answers to a few questions about VD, and since we were ashore for the first time in a year, we had satisfactory answers. So much for the fidelity problem. I felt such guilt, so fast, that it didn't happen again dur-ing our short stay. I tried one more time, but I found someone who preferred women to men, much to the amusement of General and his girl, who giggled all night in the next room. I remembered my mother and father talking about one of their friends being a "Lesbian" in the hushed tones reserved for all such matters, but in my innocence I had never thought that I might end up trying to seduce one.

Before I could wrestle my way through the subtleties of that par-ticular moral quandary, we departed beautiful, downtown Sydney, waving sadly at our young nymphets, still in position on the hill, and headed back to more months up and down The Slot. We were involved in landings at Rendova, Vella Lavella, Bougainville, firing shots in anger, or being fired at, almost every time we looked for trouble.

Off Bougainville, under air attack, we clipped an uncharted coral pinnacle trying to dodge bombs, and had to steam down to Espíritu Santo to get a new propeller. The Navy had no way of making new charts, and so we had to make do with charts made by someone else, in some other time. Off Bougainville, we were using German charts. Our own private bit of coral lay uncharted sixteen feet below the surface of Kaiserin Augusta Baie. Off Vella Lavella we got jumped by some twenty Japanese planes, which snuck in on us just over the water from the other side of the island. The first wave was over us so fast they couldn't release their bombs. When they came at us again, the *Philip* and the *Waller* were laying a heavy screen of smoke on either side of a column of fat-ass LSTs, trying to scramble to safety at five knots. Suddenly there was a deafening, shuddering crash, and I was sure we had been torpedoed, though I had seen no evidence of the much slower torpedo planes in the attacking force. Much to my relief, a voice broke radio silence, and the skipper of the *Waller* was saying something like, "I'm sorry. That was my fault. I was trying to bring my guns to bear on the bastards." Neither destroyer could see the other because of all the smoke, and the *Waller* had crashed into us amidships trying to get into a position where she could shoot her 40-millimeter and 20-millimeter guns against the Japanese planes. It was an historic admission. In all my time in the Navy, I never heard another open admission of error.

During some other landing our radar operators reported a "shit-load of bogeys" about a hundred miles away. (In Navy parlance, an initial "shitload" could mean anything from two to a hundred; we would worry about details later.) We were particularly vulnerable, operating with the LSTs again, without any air cover this time and without the prospect of any air cover. I was in the Combat Information Center, sifting information from radars, SONAR, and radios to pass on to the captain when I thought they needed it. On the spur of the moment, I pretended I was a fighter director, vectoring nonexistent squadrons of F-4s or F-4Us to attack this particular shitload of bogeys. Like "Code name for fighter squadron, this is code name for *Philip.* We have a mess of bogeys, bearing whatever, at about one hundred miles, or about ninety from you. Vector [whatever course, to intercept]." We kept this up for about five minutes, moving our "planes" up and down, right and left, when damned if the shitload of bogeys didn't suddenly change course and run off. I have no idea whether they even heard us. Lee and the skipper put me in for a Bronze Star for this particular scheme. Never got it.

Another time one stormy night we were fiddling with the fighter-director radio circuits in CIC, when we suddenly heard a distant voice singing "Bless 'Em All." And then a whole lot of different guys singing "Bless 'Em All," with especially good renditions of the final line, "Cheer up, my lads, fuck 'em all." They turned out to be a New Zealand fighter squadron, lost in the storm, getting their courage up to run out of gas and land in the drink. Our radar operators finally found them on their screen, and we interrupted their rendition of perhaps the finest Pacific War song, and sent them to the nearest friendly base.

My first important solo decision came just before dawn one morning, steaming in the middle of a line of the other destroyers in our division, off somewhere after a night in The Slot by ourselves. I was the Officer of the Deck, which meant acting captain since we weren't at General Quarters, when CIC reported an unidentified plane, closing on us fast, almost dead ahead. The blip on the radar screen lacked the pulse below the line on the screen (known as IFF for "Identification, Friend or Foe") which identified friendly planes, but we couldn't see it at first, and the gun crews on watch were tracking it. I was just about to give the signal for General Quarters and wake the captain, when we saw it, about five hundred yards just off the port bow, lumbering along only a few feet off the water, easily identified as a "Betty," the code name for a twin-engined Japanese bomber. None of the ships ahead of us had fired, but when I saw it myself, I felt sure, and shouted, "Commence firing," just as the captain, the medal-hungry Wild Bill Groverman, popped out of his night cabin. (The flame from the 5-inch shots took both his eyebrows off, and he couldn't hear for a week.) We must have fired a dozen shots from the 5-inch guns, and a clip or two from the 40s and 20s, but we missed him. Later, the war historians identified this as a plane taking a high-ranking Japanese admiral to Rabaul.

This kind of responsibility was typical in destroyer war in the Pacific for its youngest officers. You start as J.O.D., Junior Officer of the Deck, helping the O.D. run the ship under way from the bridge. Eight months after I graduated from Harvard, I made Officer of the Deck. That meant that when we were not at General Quarters, ready for battle, I ran the ship on my watch—twenty-one years old, in command of a 370-foot warship, responsible for the safety of more than three hundred people, four hours on watch, eight hours off, during which time you did your regular job running a department. Twenty-one years old, you are almost as scared of telling sailors what to do as you are of a Japanese bullet.

My regular non-battle job involved communications, the care and feeding of the machines which provided raw information to the ship, and of the men who operated and maintained those machines. This responsibility was more educating than Harvard, more exciting, more meaningful than anything I'd ever done. This is why I had such a wonderful time in the war. I just plain loved it. Loved the excitement, even loved being a little bit scared. Loved the sense of achievement, even if it was only getting from Point A to Point B; loved the camaraderie, even if the odd asshole reared his ugly head every so often. For years I was embarrassed to admit all this, given the horrors and sadness visited upon so many during the years I was thriving. But news of those horrors was so removed in time and distance. No newspapers, no radio even, except Tokyo Rose, and of course there were none of television's stimulating jolts. I found that I liked making decisions. I liked sizing up men and picking the ones who could best do the job. Most of all I liked the responsibility, the knowledge that people were counting on me, that I wouldn't let them down.

Many of the reserve naval officers with no obvious technical qualifications were better at their jobs than the regulars. Naval Academy ensigns were mostly electrical engineers. They knew how steam turbine engines worked, but they weren't so sure when to start them or when to stop them. They were better doers than teachers, and in wartime they had to lead and teach.

The first night Jimmy Rutter was in command of the *Philip,* he had had to bring her alongside a tanker to refuel. Mooring a twenty-one-hundred-ton ship to a stationary object—like a dock, or another ship at anchor—isn't all that difficult, even if you studied the fragments of Sappho more than seamanship. But only experience will teach you the exactly right moment to order the engines "All back, One" while the ship is still moving forward, or "All ahead, One" while she is still inching backward. Poor Jimmy Rutter had no such experience. Again and again, he was a moment late with his orders, and twice he snapped mooring lines. I suspect the boys in the engine room were answering the commands a second or two late, screwing the new skipper over just to let him know who was really the boss. But he finally endeared himself to everyone by shaking his head and saying, "Goddamn it, I can't stop this son of a bitch. You do it."

*   *   *

Finally, at the end of the campaign, the *Philip* was chosen to transport all the brass in the area from Saipan up to Tinian for a flag-raising there. Normally on a destroyer, if you saw a four-striper (captain) once a month it was a big deal. We never saw any kind of admiral, much less a general. Destroyers pride themselves on their informality, and flag officers are prohibitively formal. But now, here was all this brass down below in the wardroom, including the great man himself, Admiral Raymond Spruance. Spruance was both Commander Central Pacific Force and Commander Fifth Fleet at the time. Also the legendary Marine General, Holland M. "Howlin' Mad" Smith, and a whole boatload of stars, bars, and braid. Our captain was in the wardroom with the brass, doing everything but stand on his head to occupy his guests. I was on the bridge, as Officer of the Deck, having been told only to "take her up to Tinian." No course, no speed, no nothing. Just "take her up."

It was one of those glorious tropical days that cost so much to enjoy in peacetime. Not a cloud in the sky. That incredible blue-green seawater. And so I thought we would take the brass on a real destroyer spin—like about thirty knots (thirty-three miles per hour). The water was so smooth you could hear only the big waves thrown off by the bow as the ship sped "up to Tinian."

Suddenly, the quartermaster snapped to attention (I'd never seen him do that before) and shouted, "Attention on the bridge. The Admiral is present." I saluted him (I was never awfully good at that), and asked him if there was anything he would like to see. He shook my hand with just the slightest smile, and thanked me, but he would just like to look around. We all watched him as he started thumbing through the file of ALNAVs (directives issued to all ships of the Navy and all the other Pacific ships). In this case, directives issued by Spruance to the *Philip*. Suddenly, he stopped, as if he'd found the one he wanted. As soon as he moved on, I rushed casually to see which one had been left for us to see, and I saw the one that ordered all ships to proceed no faster than fifteen knots, unless specifically ordered otherwise.

I rang Jimmy Rutter in the wardroom for instructions. We came up with a deceptively simple solution: every few minutes, we would decrease the *Philip*'s speed by one knot, all but imperceptibly, and we steamed into Tinian an hour later making a steady fifteen knots.

WRITING

EDWARD L. BEACH

EDWARD L. BEACH wrote *Run Silent, Run Deep* (1955) in spare moments while he was naval aide to President Dwight Eisenhower. This book has become the classic submarine novel, and it was based in great part on Beach's own duty. In writing each of his three novels, however, Beach not only was remembering his own experience but also was basing some of his characters on officers he knew. There are obvious dangers in this for a serving officer.

For instance, in an interview in the summer of 1995, Beach recounted that Adm. Hyman Rickover once called him up and asked, "Who the hell is this Brighting?"—an admiral in *Cold Is the Sea* (1978). Beach had to confess that, in creating the character, he had had the famous admiral in mind (something obvious to the most casual reader). But the novelist then pointed out that Brighting comes up with the best idea at a key conference and, as Beach remembers saying to Rickover, "By the way, admiral, I married you to the best girl in the whole story!" At this answer Rickover grumbled a bit and then hung up.

Whether Beach's career as a novelist had any deleterious effect on his naval career may never be known, although characters in Beach's other novel, *Dust on the Sea* (1978), were also partly based on servicemen Beach had known. In any case, Beach retired at the

rank of captain. He had a most varied and interesting career, beginning with his graduation from the Naval Academy in 1939 and a
tour aboard a destroyer in the North Atlantic. There followed many
war patrols on three submarines, the last of which, the USS *Piper*,
(SS-409), Beach commanded.

After the war his continued service in submarines alternated with
periods of shore duty. Beach was the captain who took the nuclear
submarine USS *Triton* (SSR[N]-586) on the first underwater circum-
navigation of the world in 1960, an experience he also wrote a book
about, *Around the World Submerged: The Voyage of the* Triton (1962).

Beach retired in 1966 to work full time as a writer. In his both
serving in and writing about the Navy, Beach was simply following his father's example, as he tells us in a selection from the introduction to a history of the U.S. Navy he wrote in 1986.

from

THE UNITED STATES NAVY: 200 YEARS

My earliest memories are of the Navy, even though they are in truth
only of my father telling me about it. The first stories I remember
reading were of the Navy, and they were history, not children's sto-
rybooks. Lying on my stomach on our living room rug, I literally
read Father's copies of James Fenimore Cooper's and Edgar Maclay's
naval histories to pieces, for I was less than understanding in my
treatment of books and bindings in those days. Father's own books,
which I discovered at the age of about seven, complete in special
author's bindings, received the same treatment. So did a number of
fine picture books he had acquired somewhere. Some of these books
stand on my library shelves today, professionally and beautifully
rebound as penance for my heedless younger days, and one of the
picture books, which I thought I had completely destroyed and thus
lost forever, has recently reappeared, in the form of an undamaged
copy from a friend who understood how much I would value it.

My father entered the U.S. Naval Academy in 1884, served until
retirement in 1922, and died in 1943. I went to Annapolis in 1935

and was on continuous active service until the end of 1966. Both my father and I loved the Navy, wrote books and articles about it, served on the board of the U.S. Naval Institute (an independent Navy-oriented organization that publishes the highly regarded monthly *Proceedings*), and read naval history as a special area of personal interest. My first knowledge of our Navy thus came in fact at Father's knee, when I was about six years old and he was already a retired captain. As a youngster I built wooden models of our entire battle fleet, with his help as to numbers of stacks and masts (made with big nails), and great guns (small nails)—and such other obvious distinguishing features as clipper bows. My models would not have been acclaimed among the ship-modeling fraternity (most of them ended up as firewood and it was well they did), but in the summer of my seventh year there were some great evening naval battles fought on our large front porch.

To my mind and heart, Father never left the Navy, nor have I, though his days at sea were over when I knew him, and so, now, are mine. In the sense in which I write, we already compass together just about half the entire period of our Navy's existence. It is not an unworthy point of pride. He bequeathed his understanding of our Navy, and his appreciation for it, to me. I am the inheritor of all his history, all his writings (including a few unpublished manuscripts), and everything he knew or felt about the sea service of our country. I have always felt myself to be a continuation of him, a surrogate extension. It has been an abiding emotion in my personal makeup.

In 1898 my father fought at Manila Bay as a junior officer, and in 1918 he commanded the flagship of the American Battle Squadron of the British Grand Fleet, based in Scapa Flow, Scotland. But the second battle of the great fleets, after the disappointing Jutland in 1916, never took place, and he watched the surrender of the German High Seas Fleet from the bridge of his battlewagon, with his crew at battle stations just in case.

I came along at about this time, and by 1941, with only two years of commissioned service in the Navy, felt within myself a strange ambivalence: on the one hand youth and inexperience, on the other

Comdr. Edward L. Beach, naval aide to President Dwight D. Eisenhower,
was present when the president's wife, Mamie, christened the *Nautilus*
—the world's first nuclear-powered submarine—on January 21, 1954.
At that time, Commander Beach was writing *Run Silent, Run Deep*.
U.S. NAVAL INSTITUTE COLLECTION

the excitement of the challenge brought by the most serious crisis
of our time. Would we—would I—be able to master this greatest of
all tests? How would my father's junior officers, now pretty well running things, react to my puny contributions? Would they even be
aware of them? Could anything I did make any difference to the war?

Somehow I felt strangely left behind, almost an outsider looking on. My logical place, it seemed to me, should have been with
the officers my father had helped train, who would be in the fore-
front of the battle—but I had been born late in Father's life, and
they were all oldsters to me. Except in the sense of being welcomed
as my father's son, I was beneath their notice, not truly worthy in
my own right.

In the crucible of the war years, this lack of confidence, while natural enough perhaps, could not last long. I found my niche, and have the glad feeling that I did contribute to the winning of the war. So, in a reverse sort of way, did my father. The submarine of which I was executive officer was within a day of going on patrol when news came that he had died; I could not go home right then, although I did after we got back. I expressed my grief in the only way I could think of, a childish way, but it made me feel better. I quietly penciled his name on the warheads of our torpedoes. One of our chiefs saw me do it, but he knew what had happened, and he must have guessed from the look on my face that I was best left alone.

Being my father's son has also produced warm rewards. "I knew your dad," senior officers have said to me. "I served in the old *Neversink* with him." Or, amazingly often, "I entered the Navy because of your father's books." My favorite such yarn concerns Admiral Nimitz. It was not long after the war, and he was chief of naval operations. I was a lieutenant commander, the most junior member of the inspection party the admiral was taking with him on a long propeller-driven aircraft flight to California. Some hours after we had taken off, the admiral's aide came forward to us in the steerage with the news that the CNO wanted to play cribbage; as the most junior person present, his aide said, it was my duty to oblige him. Never questioning the process by which I had been selected, and blessing Father's foresight in teaching me the game, I moved aft to the admiral's cabin, apologized for not being very good at cards, and settled in to keep my wits about me and do the best I could. Partly with the help of some extraordinary cribs, I won the first game handily. In fact, I nearly skunked the old man, but somehow he managed to peg just enough holes to escape that ignominy. During the game, I thought he handled the cards rather slowly for the inveterate cribbage player I had assumed he must be, and I could not help noticing that his ring finger was missing from his left hand. His Naval Academy ring was on his right hand. The gap in his left hand where a finger should have been was constantly before my eyes; gradually memory stirred, and at last I got up the courage to say, "Admiral, excuse me for asking a personal question, but I can't help noticing that you have lost a finger. When I was a small boy, a naval officer came to see my dad, and he was missing that same finger. I was fascinated and kept asking him about it. He said it had been torn off in a machinery accident in a submarine, and when I asked if it hurt a lot he said no, not right then, but it sure hurt a lot later. Could this have been you?"

There was a little smile on Admiral Nimitz's face. "I was just wondering if you'd remember," he said. "Your father gave me some good advice that day. You were pretty young, but you said you wanted to go to Annapolis, and I see you made it."

It was his turn to deal. This time, he shuffled the cards much more quickly. I cut, and he dealt them out for the second game. But my winning streak had ended.

ALEX HALEY

A LEX HALEY is widely known as the author of *Roots: The Saga of an American Family,* the 1976 Pulitzer Prize-winning novel that traced his family's roots back to his African ancestors, one of whom had been kidnapped and brought to America as a slave. This novel sold millions of copies, was translated into dozens of languages, and was adapted for a television miniseries that became one of the most widely watched TV programs ever. Before this novel made him famous, Haley was best known for *The Autobiography of Malcolm X,* which had originated with an interview Haley conducted while he was writing for *Playboy.* Prior to that, Haley had been a writer for *Reader's Digest.* This was Haley's second career, however. In 1959 he had retired as a chief petty officer after twenty years of service in the U.S. Coast Guard.

Haley had enlisted in 1939, after a couple of years of college. He went through World War II on Coast Guard cutters and other ships as a steward's mate (the typical rating into which black sailors were placed). But Haley also attempted to write for publication in slack hours. After years of effort, he began to have some success. One day, while stationed in the Third Coast Guard District in New York long after the war, Haley was serving coffee to Adm. "Iceberg" Smith, an officer exceedingly proud of his literary taste. Smith pointed out an article lying open before him as a captivating piece, one that had been written by "some colored fellow." Haley hesitated, then replied, "Yes, sir, I wrote it." At a conference of admirals in Washington a few months later, the Coast Guard established a rating of journalist, and Haley became a journalist first class.

In the 1961 *Reader's Digest* article reprinted below, Haley recounts the origin of his writing career—his penning love letters for his shipmates while serving on the USS *Murzim,* a Navy ship manned by Coast Guard personnel. Haley pays special tribute in this piece to an illiterate first class steward's mate under whom he had served, a man who always attempted to do his best for his fellow black servicemen (including Haley) in whatever way he could. Haley's recollection not only vividly portrays the "Unforgettable Character" who is its main subject, but it also glances at the unfortunate situation of black sailors of the era. On the other hand, one notices here the informal power that a leading petty officer often wielded—especially a leading petty officer like this one, who had the ear of the ship's captain.

"THE MOST UNFORGETTABLE CHARACTER I'VE MET"

In our quarters on the USS *Murzim,* I glimpsed on the steward's bunk an incomplete letter to his wife, and saw my name: "Haley he the steward second-class, suposed to be my asistant. Ben to colege and can tiperite but schur is stoopid. Can't boil water."

This was World War II, and the *Murzim* was a Coast Guard cargo-ammunition ship newly arrived in the South Pacific. Scotty, with twenty-five years' service, had been a hostile old sea dog from the day I entered his galley. A huge, jowled Negro, his sail-like apron bulging over his washtub belly, he would glare down at me sourly: "Us bein' the same race ain't gon' get you by. Damn civilians done ruint the service!"

Scotty was the darling of the captain, who loved old-timers. He lumbered about the ship, poking into everyone's business, and the young boots trailed in his wake with open-mouthed awe and admiration. *The Seafarer,* the ship's mimeographed newspaper, ran such Scotty quotes as, "I wrung more seawater out of my socks than you ever sailed over."

My ambition was to be a writer. Nights, off duty, I typed stories in the officers' wardroom pantry. Scotty, after haranguing me all day, was irresistibly lured to watch me "tiperite." I'd make the portable rattle, certain it angered him that a subordinate had a skill he hadn't. I didn't know Scotty.

One night his deep voice interrupted me. "Looker here, boy, you ever seen the Cap'n talk letters to his yeoman?" I replied that the yeoman took shorthand. "Don't need all that chicken-scratchin'!" Scotty exclaimed. "Fast as you run that thing, you might make a yeoman. I'll help you practice, I'll talk you some letters." The idea of this ungrammatical clown hijacking my off-time to dictate to me was hilarious, and I laughed in his face. "You *real* wise, ain't you?" he rasped. "Opportunity ain't every night!"

The next morning a messboy shook me awake. "Man, Scotty wants you on the double!" I hurried to the galley. "I meant on the *double!*" Scotty roared. "This ain't no cruise ship!" He lobbed a big steel pot into midair. "*Scour that!*" He flung a sweat-popping succession of more pots and abusive orders. I shined steam kettles, scrubbed garbage cans and bulkheads. Finally I realized that I could revolt—and land in the brig—or I could type Scotty's letters. "You got the message?" he asked. Choked with rage, I could only nod. "You a smart boy." Derisive laughter was in his eyes. "Take off— see you tonight!"

After 8 P.M. muster, Scotty, scowling around a new cigar, followed me to the pantry. Angrily I zipped paper into the typewriter as he overflowed an armchair he had swiped from the wardroom.

"This here letter's to Pop Robinson. He's a first-class cook on the *Pamlico.*" I smacked out the heading, and Scotty smiled approvingly. "Hello—it is a long time since we was in touch. . . ." I typed

Alex Haley enlisted in the Coast Guard in 1939.
He was assigned duties as a messboy.
COURTESY OF GEORGE W. HALEY

that. I typed one garbled, ungrammatical cliché after another for half a page. Abruptly Scotty ended: "Forever always your ex-shipmate." I added, in caps, "PERCIVAL L. SCOTT, STEWARD FIRST-CLASS, USCG," and thrust the page and my fountain pen at Scotty. He signed as though it were the Emancipation Proclamation.

In the galley next morning, Scotty assembled the five messboys. "You better wish *you* had some brains! Don't never forget, Haley give orders, it's the same as me!" All morning he excluded me from any real work. After dinner he growled, "Chow's in the stove. See you tonight." Again, I got the message. That night I typed half-pages to three former shipmates of his.

After a week of fifteen stilted letters, Scotty began to relax. Fat elbows on aproned knees, jowled chin in hands, he paced his sentences to the moving typewriter at about thirty words a minute, and his letters lengthened with "good old days" reminiscings: "Never will forget the time I hired that civilian to come busting in that woman's place and scared you half to death." "Remember when I raffled champagne and let you win and we drunk it?" The stories portrayed a hard-drinking, hard-loving Scotty, always exploiting the gullible.

As the *Murzim* shuttled between islands, Scotty happily showed me replies to his letters. The laborious scrawlings expressed joy at hearing from him and incredulity that he had learned to type. Meanwhile, U.S. magazine editors rejected my love stories. "You help me with my mail," Scotty gruffed, "maybe I can help you with them stories."

The stories obviously impressed him. Nightly, after dictating, Scotty would leaf through my dictionary. Soon new words cropped up in his talk. "Can't *tribulate* no ninety-day ensigns," I heard him tell a chief. "They ain't got no *significance*."

Scotty demonstrated *my* significance by letting me spend whole afternoons with the friendly signalmen on the bridge, who were teaching me to read flags and blinker lights. "Signalin' takes brains," Scotty approved. When I could read blinker, Scotty, while dictating, kept alert to hear any clicking of the bridge signal light. I would dash on deck, read the message, and then Scotty would go forward and "predict" news sometimes hours before it was broadcast on the public address system. His fo'c'sle followers soon whispered that Scotty had second sight.

Every night, after dictating and studying new words, Scotty left me to write stories while he made his circuit of the ship. One night he returned towing a big, rawboned youngster from Ohio, who was red-eyed and upset. "Go 'head, show *him!*" Scotty barked. Nervously, the seaman handed me a pink envelope. The first few lines revealed a "Dear John" letter. Appalled at Scotty's indelicacy, I handed it back.

"I'm gon' set her straight!" Scotty exploded.

"Scotty, you can't do that!"

But wild horses couldn't have stopped him. Scowling over the letter, he dictated: "It's a cryin' shame you think bein' out here is some good time. Here I set on a ship full of five-hundred-pound bombs in a ocean full of subs and sharks. You don't even wait to see if I get back. I bet you grabbed some disanimated 4-F. It ought to be him out here doin' your fightin' and dyin'. . . ." While the shaken seaman signed, Scotty raked me with a black look.

For my Alma Mater
U.S. Coast Guard,
and all of The
shipmates —
Semper Paratus!
Alex Haley
(212-548)
JOC, USCG (Ret.)

Even as a successful author, Haley always spoke
with pride of his Coast Guard heritage.

U.S. COAST GUARD MUSEUM

When the *Murzim* put into Brisbane, mail call was held. Scotty
and I were shelling peas when his "Dean John" client burst into
the galley. We read an astounding reply from the boy's girl, beg-
ging forgiveness. "See, dammit, you wouldn't of wrote!" Scotty
trumpeted.

This triumph made Scotty a strutting Cupid among the admir-
ing kids in the fo'c'sle. Back at sea, he confronted me: "Looker here,
few kids want me to cor'spond to some Brisbane gals they just met."
His face struggled with delight, but his voice conveyed menace if
I balked.

Each night now, Scotty brought two to four young clients into the pantry. "I'll dictate later—dictatin' oughter be private," he instructed me. "I'll just ask stuff I need—you keep notes."

Seating a youngster in his appropriated officer's chair, he would ask, "Anything special you want to say?" "What's her hair and eyes like?" "How'd she act?" When a client was reticent, Scotty blazed, "You ain't got nothin' to write *about!*"

To my astonishment, he had marked lyric passages from my rejected love stories. "Ready-made stuff! Take right here—'the enchantin' moon studdin' the night ocean with diamon's as he think about her. . . .'" We began to produce love letters. Scotty gave me a ream of the captain's bond and a box of carbon paper which the captain's yeoman had traded for a surreptitious steak. "Make a copy of every letter," he directed. "No reason we can't use the same ones over."

Soon mail calls brought gushing responses from Brisbane girls and Scotty's young clients exulted. But I began to grow concerned: clearly the girls would now expect Scotty's distinctive letters. "Scotty," I said, "what happens when some of these kids get transferred? What will they do without your letters?"

All morning he worried. In the afternoon he asked, "Them copies you been makin'—how many you got now?"

"About three hundred."

"Tell you what. Bind up different copies in folders. Them kids can pick stuff they like and write in they own hands."

It worked fine. Nightly, clients clustered about mess-hall tables, shuffling through twelve binders. Selecting passages they liked, they wrote furiously. Scotty steamed around inspecting them as he once had my typing. "Han' writin's more better!" he sang out, encouraging independence. "Stick in some of your own words—twis' stuff around!"

Finally orders came for our second stop in Brisbane. In the wee hours of the first night, one after another of Scotty's clients wobbled back, describing fabulous romantic triumphs. Scotty, painfully incapacitated with varicose veins, presided in the fo'c'sle. Three cheers for the old sea dog rang out regularly. Scotty was fit to split with bliss.

The next afternoon, a messboy telephoned me on the bridge where I spent all my spare time with the signalmen. "Scotty wants you in the pantry—on the double!" It was my first "On the double!" in a year. I rushed below, wondering. Scotty and the messboys stood around a white-frosted cake. On it, chocolate-chip Morse code spelled "HALEY." Scotty, shuffling his feet, spoke gruffly. "I tol' the Cap'n you could stand watch as signalman. He say go 'head." Suddenly glowering, he whirled on the messboys. "Looker here, don't it rate a hand when one of our race can better hisself?"

They clapped as my tears blurred them all. And it was in that humbling instant that the massive old sailor spun into brilliant focus. I saw with crystal clarity the enormous soul and heart seasoned through a quarter-century of fo'c'sles into barnacled wisdom. He cultivated being rough to mask even from himself his benevolent, patriarchal affection for shipmates. I had resented his vicarious attachment to the education I had been luckier than he to have—and now he had helped me to leave him behind.

Scotty often visited me on the signal bridge. Once he came when we had anchored off an island and "Mail Call!" was being piped. Naming two men, he said, "Watch 'em down there and see what you see."

We looked down on the forward main deck as yeomen barked names and passed thousands of letters from a dozen bulging mail sacks to the jubilant sailors. But the two men we were watching got nothing. "Poor guys don't never get no mail," Scotty said. "Looker here—fix up this thing." He gave me a Pen Pal Club ad, torn from a magazine. I filled in the two men's names, and in time the two astounded men received their first letters.

The poignant "Mail-Call" scene kept bothering me. One night in the pantry, I wrote it as I felt it, and it was printed in *The Seafarer,* which many men enclosed in letters home. Someone's home-town newspaper reprinted my story. A press wire service picked it up; [my article] "Mail Call" was printed widely over the United States. From across America, letters came addressed: "Lonely Sailors, c/o *The Seafarer,* U.S.S. *Murzim.*" Before long, a message was relayed to me, too—from U.S. Coast Guard Headquarters. Ordered back to the States, I wound up assigned in Third (New York) District public relations. There, in 1950, I was named the U.S. Coast Guard's first chief journalist, and my stories, too, began to click.

But my letters to Scotty went unanswered. Then, in 1954, some reader mail resulting from a *Reader's Digest* article included an envelope addressed in a wavering, unruly script that I joyously recognized. Scotty told me that he had made chief steward on the *Murzim.* But in 1945 his varicose veins forced him to retire and he had settled in Norfolk, Virginia, where he was a night watchman at the Brook Avenue Navy Men's Y.M.C.A. "Reeding your name folowed by story a grate thril," Scotty ended his letter. "Knowed you'd make good was how come I help you out."

JAMES A. MICHENER

JAMES A. MICHENER, a popular author with an enormous
audience, was almost forty when he wrote his first novel. Born
about 1907, he grew up in Pennsylvania, graduated summa cum
laude from Swarthmore in 1929, and later got an MA from what is
now Northern Colorado University, where he became an associate
professor of education. Upon the success of several articles he wrote
about teaching social studies, he became a visiting professor at
Harvard. Then (in 1941) he took an editorship at Macmillan.

But this basic "résumé" account doesn't do justice to the spirit
of Michener's life up until then. At age fourteen he hitchhiked
through forty-five states. He traveled with a Chautauqua tent show
one summer while at Swarthmore, and upon graduating he enrolled
at St. Andrews University in Scotland on a scholarship. While overseas he toured throughout Europe, studied subjects ranging from
folklore to art history, and even worked as a merchant seaman on
a cargo vessel in the Mediterranean.

In 1942 Michener was commissioned in the Navy, and his zest
for travel and his general inquisitiveness returned. Originally
assigned duty to check the availability of publications in Pacific aviation units, he used a forged travel pass—along with some legiti-
mate orders—to visit forty-nine South Pacific islands, and since he

seemed to know what he was doing, he was made a naval trouble-shooter in bizarre situations. Desiring a second tour of duty, he got himself assigned as the official naval historian for the South Pacific region—but naval officials say he didn't write much history. Instead, he decided to write a novel; he wrote most of it during the war.

The results of this decision are well-known. *Tales of the South Pacific,* a set of loosely connected stories, won the Pulitzer Prize for fiction in 1948, was made into a hit musical by Rodgers and Hammerstein, and was adapted for the movies as well. Over the next forty-five years a steady stream of long novels (*Sayonara, Hawaii, Chesapeake, The Covenant,* and *Texas,* etc.) plus some nonfiction works have followed. Incidentally, one of Michener's novels, *The Bridges at Toko-Ri,* tells the story of American naval jet fighters in the Korean War.

In 1992 Michener wrote an autobiography, some ninety pages of which deal with his naval service. The author recounts the moral origin for his first novel—and for his whole writing career—in the passage reproduced below.

from

THE WORLD IS MY HOME: A MEMOIR

Had I been a devout man, I would surely have interpreted my experience on the Tontouta airstrip as a theophany.

In the latter days of World War II I flew back to my headquarters in French New Caledonia in the southwestern Pacific after exciting duty in the Fiji Islands and a tumultuous exploration of Bora Bora. I had been so inspired by my adventures and so eager to get back to my typewriter to report upon them that my senses were very alert. As our plane approached big Tontouta Air Base for a sunset landing, the sky darkened ominously and I had a premonition that this landing was going to be somewhat more dangerous than normal.

My fears were realized when, just as we approached the long strip enclosed at the far end by a range of low mountains, we lost visibility. I remember saying to myself: 'He'd better go up and

James Michener as a newly minted naval officer.
COURTESY OF JAMES A. MICHENER

around for another shot!' and to my relief he did just that. The plane dipped its left wing, the engines roared, the nose went high in the air, and we shot upward through the menacing clouds, took a wide sweep to the left to avoid the mountains and went back out to sea to make a second attempt, hoping that in the meantime the clouds would have dissipated.

While we were executing these routine maneuvers for avoiding a hazardous landing, twilight had darkened, and as we made our approach in minimum visibility my nerves tensed, my muscles tightened. No go! Visibility nil! Again the roar of the engines, the sickening swing to the left with the wing dipping almost vertically, and the swerving away from the mountains ahead. Then back out to sea and another wide swing over waves barely visible below for a third approach.

I cannot now recall whether Tontouta had night-landing radar at that time—probably not, but if it did it was undoubtedly insufficient. During the third approach I was extremely tense but not panicked because I had flown thousands of dangerous miles in small planes in the Pacific and had learned to trust Navy pilots. I remember telling myself: It's got to be this time or we don't make it, and I did not care to speculate on whether we would have enough fuel to carry us back to Fiji or north to Espíritu Santo.

With skill, nerve and determination our pilot brought his heavy plane into perfect alignment with the barely visible runway and eased it down in a flawless landing. We applauded, but he gave no sign of acknowledgment, because he, better than we, appreciated what a near thing it had been.

That night I had no appetite, for the tenseness in my stomach banished any interest in food, but neither was I ready for bed. In what was to become the turning point of my life, I left the transient quarters where travelers like me stayed until they could get back to their home base, and unaware of where I was wandering, I found myself back on the long, dark airstrip with the mountains at the far end visible whenever the low, scudding clouds separated momentarily to reveal them.

For some hours I walked back and forth on that Tontouta strip without any purpose other than to calm my nerves, but as I did so I began to think about my future life and to face certain problems: What do I want to do with the remainder of my life? What do I stand for? What do I hope to accomplish with the years that will be allowed me? Do I really want to go back to what I was doing before? I spent at least two hours kicking these ideas about.

At this critical point I was by no means alone in this forthright evaluation of myself and my life goals; thousands of men I knew in the South Pacific were asking themselves identical questions on the lonely islands and during the long night watches on ships or airfields. An astonishing number would decide: I will not be satisfied just to plod along in what I was doing. I'm a better man than that. I can do better. And they resolved when they returned home to become ministers, or go back to law school, or run for public office, or strike out on their own in some daring venture, or become college professors, or work in hospitals. On those remote islands lives changed, visions enlarged, directions shifted dramatically, and it is to the eternal credit of those leaders then running our nation that they anticipated such frames of mind and provided financial assistance after the war to the young men who were determined to alter their lives for the better.

As one who has earnestly contemplated American history and the various acts of Congress, I have concluded that in two instances Congress has indeed helped to improve the quality of our national life. Interestingly but not surprisingly, each was passed during a war, as if the legislators as well as young soldiers and sailors were eager to brighten the future, and each act helped redirect lives.

In 1862, during the darkest days of the Civil War, Congress passed a pair of interrelated bills that I think of as one: the Homestead Act, which gave free land to settlers in the West, and the Morrill Act, authorizing the establishment of land-grant colleges in which tuition would be either minimal or free. These were acts of genius, for they ensured a free, active society in which citizens of good purpose could receive both land for homes and education to strengthen themselves and their nation.

The second laudable act of Congress was passed during World War II. What would become known as the G.I. Bill promised all men and women who had served in the war funds toward the completion of their education after the war ended. Millions of young people availed themselves of this opportunity, and I judge it to have been one of the best expenditures of public money made in my lifetime, for it helped an entire generation of bright young people improve themselves and make an effort to accomplish something meaningful. The burst of achievements in all fields that the United States saw in the decades following the end of World War II stemmed in large part from the flood of energy released by the G.I. Bill.

So I was not alone, there on the Tontouta airstrip that night, in deciding that I was ready for something better than I had been able to accomplish previously. But in another way I was unique, for I had never been ambitious in the usual sense of that word. I had not dreamed, as a boy, of becoming this or that; I had never aspired to wealth or acclaim; and the best description I ever heard of myself was one given by a college classmate: 'Jim wanders down the road picking his nose and looking for the stars.'

Therefore, my evaluations that night did not resemble those of other men who had a clearer vision of themselves. I did not aspire to be a clergyman, although I believe I would have made a good one, nor did I want to go into a different type of business, for I was happy as an editor at the fine Macmillan publishing company. I had not the kind of profound belief in my own destiny that would have propelled me into politics or public service, and I could see in myself no dormant talent that was waiting to spring into life if I gave it encouragement. Since I had already attended half a dozen of the finest educational institutions in the world I did not feel the need to go to yet another school.

As I walked in the darkness I concluded that I was not dissatisfied with my employment; I was dissatisfied with myself. And I am embarrassed at the decision I reached that night, because when it is verbalized without the qualifications I gave it as soon as I uttered it, the impression it leaves is almost ludicrous. But as the stars came out and I could see the low mountains I had escaped, I swore: I'm going to live the rest of my life as if I were a great man. And despite the terrible braggadocio of those words, I understood precisely what I meant: I'm going to erase envy and cheap thoughts. I'm going to concentrate my life on the biggest ideals and ideas I can handle. I'm going to associate myself with people who know more than I do. I'm going to tackle objectives of moment.

On and on I went, laying out the things I would and would not do, but always I came back to one overriding resolve: I will constantly support the things I believe in. And in the nearly fifty years since that night, I have steadfastly borne testimony to all my deeply held beliefs.

Before the night was out I modified my initial conviction; I would not act as if I were a great man, for that was too pompous; but I would act as if I knew what greatness was, and I have so ordered my life.

Was this powerful experience on the dark airstrip a theophany in the literal sense of the word, an appearance of God to a human being? As I said earlier, had I been devoutly religious I could have avowed that it was, and I might even have claimed that voices spoke to me in the hallowed darkness after the miracle of our safe landing. But that was not the case. I heard no voices other than the inward ones that warned me that I had come to the end of the line in the direction I had been heading and that I sorely required a new path. I had observed that certain men and women lived as if they had shorn away the inconsequentials and reserved their energies for serious matters, and I decided to pattern my life after theirs.

Lest the reader suspect that I am overdramatizing the perils of that difficult airstrip, let me report that some weeks later my successor in my work at Navy headquarters in Nouméa wangled an aircraft for unauthorized use and, coming back to Tontouta after a jolly escapade, flew smack into the hills I had eluded earlier, killing himself and all my former staff.

*   *   *

How did I behave after my soul-searching experience? In no visible way differently from before. I returned to my home base on Espíritu Santo, resumed control of a vast warehouse filled with papers needed to prosecute the air war against the Japanese, and tried to continue to treat my six enlisted men with special consideration, especially Jim, the shoemaker from Tennessee, and Garcia, the wild-eyed poet from Texas. I flew to all corners of the Pacific carrying my precious wares; and I approached my fortieth birthday without having accomplished anything special.

There was one minor change. As I rode about my own island and the forty-eight others I serviced using the [forged] travel orders Bill Collins had provided, I began to listen with attention as men told stories at night in the various Hotels de Gink in which transients lived when on travel orders. I sought out men who'd had unusual experiences or more likely had usual ones that they understood with unusual clarity, and from this mélange of information and observation I acquired a good perception of what the great Pacific adventure meant in human terms. Clearly, almost clinically, I concluded that if you ordered all the young men of a generation to climb Mount Everest, you would expect the climb to have a major significance in their lives. And while they were climbing the damned mountain they would bitch like hell and condemn the assignment, but years later, as they looked back, they'd see it as the supreme adventure it was and they'd want to read about it to reexperience it.

These thoughts led to a clear-cut conviction: Years from now the men who complain most loudly out here will want to explain to others what it was like. I'm sure of it, so I'm going to write down as simply and honestly as I can what it was really like. And then I reassured myself: No one knows the Pacific better than I do; no one can tell the story more accurately. This was not a boast; it was true and relevant to the task I planned to set myself.

Loving movies as I do, and never having come upon one that was so bad I walked out before I saw how it ended, I enjoyed going to see the show each night at seven, when we sat on coconut logs under the stars to see Betty Grable and Ann Sothern and Rita Hayworth and Dick Powell and John Payne go through their paces. I found entertaining even the dreadful Republic Pictures productions shot on a shoestring in the back lots.

But at nine-thirty each night I would repair to my darkened Quonset hut, light a smelly lantern, which helped keep away the mosquitoes, and sit at my typewriter, pecking out with two fingers the stories I had accumulated as I traveled the Pacific. Sitting there in the darkness, illuminated only by the flickering lamplight—the electricity was cut off in the big sheds—I visualized the aviation scenes in which I had participated, the landing beaches I'd seen, the remote outposts, the exquisite islands with bending palms, and especially the valiant people I'd known: the French planters, the Australian coast watchers, the Navy nurses, the Tonkinese laborers, the ordinary sailors and soldiers who were doing the work, and the primitive natives to whose jungle fastnesses I had traveled.

Rigorously I adhered to my commitment: to report the South Pacific as it actually was. By nature I stayed away from heroics and I was certainly not addicted to bombast; I had seen warfare but I shied away from talking much about it, and I had none of the excessive romanticism that had colored the works of my predecessors in writing about the Pacific: Pierre Loti, Robert Louis Stevenson, James Norman Hall and especially the very popular Frederick O'Brien, author of *White Shadows in the South Seas.* In familiarity with the various islands I probably exceeded them all, but in narrative skill I was no doubt inferior.

What I did was what I would do in all my later books: create an ambience that would both entertain and instruct the reader, invent characters who were as real as I could make them, and give them only such heroics as I myself had experienced or found credible. I felt then, as I feel now, nearly half a century later, that if I could follow my plan I would fulfill my aim of refreshing the wartime memories of my colleagues in years ahead. For whom did I write as I sat night after night fighting the mosquitoes with those little bombs of insecticide the Navy gave us and pecking out my stories on the typewriter? Not the general public, whom I did not care to impress; not the custodians of literature, about whom I knew little; and certainly not posterity, a concept that simply never entered my mind. I wrote primarily for myself, to record the reality of World War II, and for the young men and women who had lived it.

I concluded after six or seven chapters that my work was achieving more or less what I desired, but I had no assurance that it was and certainly I never cried at the end of a long night—at three or four in the morning because I rewrote a great deal—'Hey, this is pretty good!' Since I was figuratively as well as actually working in the dark I decided to seek other opinions, but to whom could I turn?

In the huge building next to mine there was a young enlisted man with a sardonic nature, a fellow drafted into the Navy much against his will, who spent his time collecting cowries, those beautifully formed little shells of lovely colors. He stuffed them with a mixture of cotton and aviation glue and strung them together on strands of silver wire to make delicate necklaces, which other sailors bought for fifteen dollars a strand to send home to their wives and girlfriends. His name was Fred, and if he is still living I hope he will get in touch with me, for I owe him much and would like to repay the courtesy he extended to me.

I could see from watching the lines of sailors who came to his building next to mine that since he was raking in a fortune with his necklaces he must be a rather sharp item. I was about to approach him about reading one of my chapters when he surprised me by saying one morning as we opened our Quonsets: 'Lieutenant Michener, when I'm working at night making my necklaces I see that you're over there working at something. What's your racket?' And when I told him that I was trying to write an account of what war was like in the South Pacific he said, 'I'd like to see how you find it.' Within a minute I had handed him a chapter, then suffered agonies wondering if I had done the right thing.

The next morning he appeared in my building with the chapter: 'This isn't at all bad' was all he said, and later as I fed him one chapter after another he repeated his comment: 'Not bad, not bad at all.' He never spoke about story line or character development or style or even the general coherence of the material, but morning after morning he told me, 'Not bad,' and once he said about a battle scene, 'You know what you're doing.'

His support was invaluable, for only he knew what I was trying to do there in the dark while he was making his necklaces. I never bought any and he never tried to sell me one, but had he ever asked I believe I would have inspected the necklace, admired it, and said as I handed it back, 'Not bad, not bad at all.'

He never wrote to me after the book, which was called *Tales of the South Pacific,* was published. I'm sure he felt no need to, for when I needed his assistance most he had generously given it. I cannot express how much I valued his support, for writing in an empty shed darkened with mighty shadows and infested with mosquitoes is a task that cries out for moral support, and he provided it.

ATLANTIC WAR

DANIEL V. GALLERY

NAVAL ACADEMY graduate Daniel V. Gallery spent more than
forty years in the Navy, becoming a pilot in 1926 and retiring
as a rear admiral in 1960. Professionally, he is best known for boarding and capturing the German submarine *U-505* in the mid-Atlantic
in 1944, an operation conceived by Gallery and planned and carried out by his antisubmarine task group. It was the first enemy warship to be captured by the U.S. Navy in 129 years. Gallery was, in
fact, an outstanding officer, aided by a powerful imagination and
lively sense of humor. Always known as an engaging raconteur, in
the middle of his naval career Gallery began to write for the public.

Gallery wrote in excess of forty articles and short stories in national magazines (with twenty in the *Saturday Evening Post* alone); in
addition, he wrote motion picture and television scripts on naval
subjects. The success of his short stories led him to write humorous novels—*Now Hear This, Away Boarders, Cap'n Fatso*—and he
wrote several other books as well: *The Pueblo Incident* and an autobiography, *Eight Bells and All's Well*. Gallery had an eye for other
good fiction too. For instance, he wrote Herman Wouk praising *The
Caine Mutiny* before any other naval official would do so. As a con-
sequence, he and Wouk became good friends, and Wouk introduced
one of Gallery's novels, calling its author a "true original."

Gallery certainly was. We get a feeling for his sense of humor and engaging style of leadership in the following description of his 1941–1943 command of an antisubmarine air base in Iceland. This account is drawn from an article he published in 1949 in the *Saturday Evening Post*.

from

"OUR HOT WAR FOR ICELAND"

I arrived in Reykjavik late in December 1941, and found the situation grim. Our Navy fliers, eking out a miserable existence knee-deep in mud, were waiting for their supply ship to come in. All that came in was me!

The Navy's Iceland contingent had taken refuge in dilapidated Nissen huts abandoned by the British, through which the Arctic winds howled with glee. The well-dressed young man about camp wore long flannel drawers and at night he closed himself up in an eiderdown sleeping bag.

The galley was equipped with salvaged junk and the food was terrible. The principal plumbing necessities were of the Chic Sale variety, and you couldn't take a bath even if you wanted to. While struggling to stay alive under these conditions, we also had the little problem of flying the North Atlantic convoy lanes in the world's worst weather.

My first job obviously was to keep the planes flying and help get the convoys through; next, to get decent living conditions established; and third, I thought, to prevent the boys from blowing their tops after six months in that godforsaken hole.

It seemed as if the top brass in Washington had forgotten us. But soon the long-awaited supply ship arrived. From her holds she discharged one naval air base complete with spare parts.

We turned to with a will to set it up. Everybody helped build the new camp. One day I caught the dentist, paymaster and chaplain dynamiting rocks out of the frozen ground. They were making a foundation trench. From that day I knew the United States couldn't lose. This was really total war.

Quonset huts go up fast and, while there is nothing luxurious about them, they do provide adequate shelter, even in Iceland. Our planners back in Washington sent us a lot more than the bare walls and frames—every hut had electric lights, automatic phonograph and radio.

We made our own electricity with Diesel generators designed to run at a constant speed. At first, the boys who stood watch in the generator hut suspected me of being either a mind reader or a magician, because I often called up from my hut to bawl them out for running the generators a little too fast or too slow. Sometimes the machines differed so little from the correct speed that you couldn't tell it by looking at the lights, but the dials on the control panel always showed that my beef was justified. The secret was my electric record player and an album of records by Toscanini. When the music sounded sweet, I knew the generators were exactly on the right speed. When it came out sour, I knew it wasn't Toscanini who was off the beam.

Each hut had fourteen bunks and lockers, a card and checker table near the stove, and writing desks near the door. As time went on, easy chairs made out of discarded shipping crates, homemade lamp shades and rugs began to appear. One hut even had a make-believe grandfather's clock standing by the stove. Of course, every square inch of wall and locker space was inevitably plastered with lurid reminders, clipped from magazines, of the one missing comfort of home.

Complaints about the lack of home cooking soon stopped. I wish you could have seen the galley equipment they sent us—excellent ranges, ovens and steam kettles, automatic dishwashers and driers, freezing lockers and fine butcher-shop equipment. When I brought the British air commodore over to inspect it, his eyes bugged out like a tromped-on toad's. He went away muttering to himself about the hardships the poor colonials have to put up with.

After our new ovens began roasting, we received daily tribute to the excellent work of our cooks. Every day at noon and supper time a dozen or so British and U.S. Army truck drivers found excuses for stopping at the Fleet Air Base and bumming a meal off us. I never objected, because as long as all those vehicles lined up on our main street at chow time, I knew without going any further that our cooks were doing all right.

Our Navy chow attracted visitors from all over Iceland—after we got our camp built, rats overran the place. Although we welcomed our hungry brothers-in-arms in the Air Force and the Army and our Allies in the RAF and British Navy, we had to draw the line some-place. I put a bounty of one dollar a head on rats. Catching and shoot-ing rodents became a profitable and exciting pastime. Large boun-ties were collected at first, and after a couple of weeks I saw no more rats nosing around our streets. However, our "game warden's" office continued to do a brisk business, and it took me some time to find out that I was paying bounties on rats killed all over Iceland. My boys paid two bits apiece to their friends in the adjacent RAF, Norwegian and U.S. Army camps for dead rats, and smuggled them in to collect a nice profit. However, our soda fountain made money for the welfare fund so fast that we decided to ignore the rat racket. By cleaning out the surrounding camps we were helping ourselves anyway.

During the long Arctic nights we held grave discussions about the name for our camp. We finally adopted one with an Icelandic or Eskimo air about it, which on close inspection contains some good American advice to all hands: KWITCHERBELLIAKIN.

One thing our logistic planners back home forgot was the need for a recreation hall and gymnasium. They sent us plenty of recre-ational gear, but no place to use it. We remedied this oversight by "misappropriating" two of the supply officer's big storehouses. I fig-ured that, if necessary, I would rather try to justify leaving some of our equipment out in the weather than to explain why the boys were going nuts. Admiral King put a terse "Okay" on that decision when he stopped in at our place some months later, on his way home from a conference in London.

The arrival of our first shipment of recreational equipment from the United States led to an incident which helped us bypass pro-

Comdr. Dan Gallery stands nonchalantly at the hearth
of his well-outfitted Quonset hut in Iceland.
U.S. NAVAL ACADEMY/NIMITZ LIBRARY SPECIAL COLLECTIONS

tocol, break the ice and get acquainted with the British. Opening
up the boxes in this consignment like a bunch of kids on Christmas morning, we found, among other things, a pushball, which we
promptly blew up to its full five-foot diameter. Exploring the boxes
for more loot, we left the pushball sitting outside the gymnasium
unattended.

You should never leave anything as big and light as a pushball
unattended in Iceland, because the wind comes along and blows it
away. I came out of the gym just in time to see our pushball bounce
down the hill, over the bluff and into the water. It sailed rapidly
across the inlet and grounded on the opposite shore, where a British
antiaircraft battery had its camp.

We wanted that pushball, so I picked up my field telephone to
call the commanding officer of the antiaircraft battery and ask his
help. Strange things often happened on the labyrinth of wires form-

ing our field-telephone system. Very often connections got crossed—as they did this time. I heard my friend across the way calling British Admiralty Headquarters and reporting, "The biggest bloody mine you've ever seen in your life has just washed ashore at our camp, and will you please send a bomb-disposal party over to deal with it?"

I hung up without saying a word. A few minutes later I called Admiralty Headquarters and reported that we, too, had seen this mine wash ashore, that we had a qualified bomb-disposal squad, and if the Admiralty wished us to do so, we would be glad to deal with this situation. Of course, the Admiralty wished nothing in the world more than to have somebody else take this nasty job off their hands. They promptly replied that this would be "quite satisfactory."

So I rushed around to the adjoining huts, rounded up about a dozen helpers, explained the pitch to them, and we organized a bomb-disposal squad on the spot. We all knew enough about bomb disposal to have a pretty good idea as to what equipment we needed and how to go through the proper motions. We commandeered a half-dozen rifles, scrambled around the camp and grabbed a portable field-telephone set, a couple of voltmeters, a stethoscope and some small toolboxes. Dumping this equipment into jeeps, we roared over to the British camp, where we found a crowd of our Allies all standing back at a respectful distance, casting nervous glances at the "mine."

The arrival of our businesslike group of American experts obviously relieved the tension. We immediately stationed our sentries and pushed the crowd back to a safer distance. Leading out our field telephones, we placed one of them at the "mine" and the other about a hundred yards back, so that our mine-disposal boys could phone back every move they made—to be recorded in a notebook—for the guidance of future mine-disposal squads, in case we made the wrong move and blew ourselves up.

After a few minutes of hocus-pocus with the stethoscope and voltmeters and much telephoning back and forth, we finally gave the signal that the big moment was at hand. As the crowd watched in awed silence, we unscrewed the valve, let the air out, and with our deflated mine, got the hell out of that camp as fast as we could.

Although there was plenty of this kind of horseplay and monkey business on the ground, we were playing for keeps out over the convoy lanes. Flying through stinking weather, at night and in fog, when the low-lying clouds around your airdrome have centers of solid rock and your wings load up with ice, is bad for your blood pressure. To keep enthusiasm for this kind of flying at a proper level, the skipper has to take his regular turn out over the convoy lanes too. I often wondered, during some of my all-night hops, whether there was any worthwhile future in the business.

We worked hand in glove with the British covering the convoys, and Air Commodore Lloyd of the RAF turned out to be a grand teammate. He and I saw eye to eye on every operational question, though at first inclined to be somewhat skeptical of each other. After we became close friends, he confessed he had feared that anyone whose ancestry was as obviously Gaelic as mine would necessarily make things as difficult as possible for His Majesty's representatives.

I assured him that I bore no ill will whatever toward the British. "In fact," I said, "I am eternally grateful to your ancestors for persecuting my ancestors, so that I was born in the U.S.A."

Through association with the air commodore I acquired a unique honorary title, the Order of the D.D.L.M. I am the only officer in the U.S. military services to be so honored. As a matter of fact, I created the title and bestowed it on myself. This came about as follows:

Cooperating with the British on a common job, I naturally had frequent exchanges of official memoranda with the air commodore and the British admiral. Whenever a high-ranking British officer signs a letter, he puts a long string of initials after his signature— DSO, KCB, CBE, and so on—indicating the orders and decorations which he holds. When I replied to such letters, I had nothing to put behind my name except "junior," and that made no impression whatever upon our gallant Allies.

So, after I got to know my correspondents pretty well, and found that they were regular fellows with twinkles in their eyes, I began putting DDLM after my signature, knowing full well that sooner or later they would ask me what it meant. Sure enough, one morning

I met the air commodore in RAF Headquarters, and after saying "Good morning, Dan, old man" and discussing various matters, he asked, "I say, old boy, what does that DDLM that you put after your name mean?"

"Why," I said," that's the American equivalent of your KCB."

Of course, KCB—Knight Commander of the Bath—is one of the highest and best decorations the British have. So the air commodore was duly impressed. He said: "That's splendid. That's fine. I didn't know you Americans had any such thing." I could see the wheels going round inside his head as he tried to puzzle out the meaning of the cryptic initials.

Finally he gave up and asked, "Just what does it stand for?"

I said, "It means Dan Dan the Lavatory Man."

Concurrently with the international leg pulling, our camp construction moved along, the Seabees performing their usual miracles. The last thing to go up was the officers' club. By this time we proudly exhibited our place to sightseers.

Showing some American nurses around the camp, one of our boys gloatingly pointed out what we had already done and described future plans. Having seen our ultramodern galley, well-equipped recreation hall and gymnasium, the gals were about ready to believe that anything was possible for the Navy. Going through the nearly finished officers' club, my gallant young gentleman pointed out the window at the forbidding rocky beach in front and said, "The next convoy is bringing us a shipload of white sand from Miami, and we'll have a regular beach out there by summer." The nurses believed this story and spread it through all the Army camps on the island, causing great indignation and some threats to write to congressmen.

Even though we never got our beach, we did have some almost equally improbable things. Our proudest possession was a pair of palm trees near the main entrance of the camp. Trees do not grow in Iceland. So when the leading chief from our metalsmith shop came into my office one day and said, "Captain, we ought to have some palm trees around this place," I thought to myself, *Now it begins—here's the first man we have to ship home in a straitjacket.*

However, I humored him and listened to his proposal. When he got through outlining his plan, I quoted Joyce Kilmer—"Only God can make a tree."

The chief replied, "Yeah, we know that, Captain, but we'd like to have a shot at it anyway."

Within a week, two authentic-looking palm trees had grown on our main street. The trunks were steel pipes about six inches in diameter which we wrapped with burlap to give them a tapering and rough appearance. The stems of the leaves were reinforcing rods for concrete runways, bent to the proper curvature, and we cut the leaves from tin obtained by flattening out five-gallon kerosene cans. A coat of green paint plus worn-out softballs for coconuts completed the horticultural wonder.

More monkey business by our versatile metalsmiths produced fire hydrants on every street corner and in front of every hut in the camp. Casual visitors thought we had overdone things a bit on fire protection. However, the hydrants were phonies, manufactured from an oversupply of one-hundred-pound, water-fillable practice bombs. In their spare time the metalsmiths welded two short lengths of pipe on the side of each bomb to simulate hose connections, stuck a large nut on top, painted everything a brilliant red, and planted them around all over the camp with the tail fins buried in the ground. The result was a perfect facsimile of a fireplug, and the camp was a puppy dog's paradise.

For the official opening of our recreation hall we put on a gala event and we invited all the top brass in Iceland. There were three Army hospitals with nurses in Iceland, and it was obviously my duty as commanding officer to stand in well with the chief nurses, so they would be favorably inclined to date my boys from the Fleet Air Base. I invited the three chief nurses to the grand opening, sent my car to pick them up and instructed my driver to stand by at the OOD's shack to take the ladies home after the show.

When the *première* was over, all the official guests adjourned to my hut for coffee, sandwiches and "one for the road." At this gathering, one of the generals graciously offered to take the nurses home. In the midst of all the social activity, I forgot to pass this word along

Adm. Ernest J. King (then chief of naval of operations) and other
dignitaries visit the Fleet Air Base in Reykjavik; King is fifth from
the right and base commander Gallery is third from the right.
According to Gallery, even the normally austere King relaxed a bit
and grinned when he saw the "palm trees."

to my driver. So, after speeding the last departing guest into the
night, I crawled into my sack and slept soundly until seven o'clock
the next morning. On the way to breakfast I stopped in at the OOD's
shack, and there sat my driver, heavy-eyed and sleepy, but with an
accusing smirk on his sassy face.

He was carrying out my orders and waiting to take the three chief
nurses home! He had spent an all-night vigil in a place where everybody who happened to be up and around in the camp saw him and
wondered what he was doing. Every four hours during the night a
new duty section of about thirty men mustered in the OOD's office
before relieving the watch. Naturally, they all wanted to know why
the captain's driver was up so late. All night long he spread the
happy word, "I'm waiting to take the Captain's gal friends home—
he's got three of 'em down in his hut."

I noted a marked increase in the deference with which I was treated by all hands from then on.

In the meantime we hunted Nazi submarines amid icebergs, sleet and Arctic gales. I encouraged my crews to relax at our recreation centers. I had no trouble getting this order obeyed. Soon after the opening of our officers' club we fumbled our first three opportunities to sink subs, due to buck fever, bad luck and inattention to seemingly minor details. I read the riot act to the boys and announced that our recently opened club was hereby closed until we got our first kill. This was cruel and unusual punishment. But my platform was that I would rather be a Son of Brotherhood and help win the war, than help lose it and be thought a swell guy.

During the era of the closed club, one of our pilots, Lieutenant Hopgood, caught a sub surfaced about fifty miles from a convoy. He crippled her so she couldn't submerge, but could still limp along on the surface. All his depth charges expended, Hoppy circled and watched the sub go alongside a nearby Icelandic fishing trawler and commandeer her. The Nazis abandoned and scuttled the U-boat, and laid a course toward Germany.

Hoppy duly reported all this by radio and spent the next couple of hours shuttling back and forth, coaching an oncoming British destroyer which broke off from the convoy. This was an exciting three hours in all the RAF and Royal Navy operations rooms in England, as well as in ours up in Iceland. Hoppy's first electrifying message that he had a cripple on his hands, but couldn't finish it off, brought everybody in England to the operations rooms. For the rest of the morning vice-admirals, air marshals and their staffs sat with their ears glued to the radio, following the dramatic developments at sea.

All Hoppy's radio reports up to the final one were masterpieces of correct official phraseology, giving a terse, clear and complete picture of events in the North Atlantic. Finally he came through with the big punch line that we were all waiting for: "Destroyer is alongside trawler and has taken off fifty-two prisoners." Then shifting from code to plain English, he continued: "Personal message for Commander Gallery. Sank sub, open club!"

We opened the club all right. We damned near blew the roof off the joint. But Coast Command Headquarters and the Admiralty were a bit puzzled over that final message, and even after the Air Commodore, Iceland, explained it to them, they considered it "most extraordinary."

*   *   *

Until May 1943 we were losing the Battle of the Atlantic. Submarines sank more than 500,000 tons per month, England's plight became desperate, and the only faint ray of hope was the fantastic shipbuilding program just getting into high gear in the United States. We kept our heads above water by the ghastly expedient of launching ships faster than the Nazis sank them.

In May 1943, very-long-range land planes and small aircraft carriers finally extended our air umbrella to cover the whole North Atlantic and we broke the back of the U-boat fleet by making a hundred kills in May, June and July. The Nazis never recovered from that crippling slaughter. From that time on, the avalanche of ships going down our building ways exceeded the sinkings by a constantly increasing margin.

We sealed the fate of the Axis in the summer of 1943, off the shores of Newfoundland, Greenland, Iceland and England, by winning the Battle of the Atlantic. After we gained control of the seas, the mass bombing of Germany and the invasion of Normandy became possible.

I hope the last Battle of the Atlantic has been fought, but if there should ever be another, it will again be the crucial battle of the war, and you will need seafaring aviators to win it. But I'll let the drugstore strategists take on from here.

However, before I mush off into the Arctic night, I have one last word to say. The Navy's Camp Kwitcherbelliakin was a good spot. We had plenty of fun while doing deadly serious work. But a year and half was enough for me. From now on, my foreign policy is "Iceland for the Icelanders."

GORDON FORBES

G ORDON FORBES had extensive combat experience flying a variety of seaplanes and bombers during World War II. He entered flight training in Pensacola in 1939 and then saw brief duty as an instructor. When the war came he received orders to a PBY-5 ("Catalina") seaplane squadron as a head pilot and hunted U-boats in the Caribbean and off the coasts of South America. Forbes recalled in a letter he sent in the summer of 1995 that he attacked twenty-six subs in the first eight months of the war (when "the U-boats were everywhere") but got only one because the plane was so slow. "[T]he depth charges were set for twenty-five foot and if the sub saw *you* when you saw *it*, it would be down around a hundred feet by the time you arrived."

Forbes went on to operational training in the PV-1 (the "Ventura") and flew it for about a year; he also flew the B-25 (the Navy designation of the PBJ-1, or "Mitchell") near Nova Scotia, laying aerial mines. In 1944 and 1945 he flew the Navy version of the B-24 (the PB4Y-1, or "Liberator") in England, North Africa, the Mediterranean, and for about ten months in the Pacific—from bases like Tinian, Leyte, Iwo Jima, Morotai, and Palawan.

The latter service is described in Forbes's exceptional 1961 novel, *Goodbye to Some,* an account of a naval bombing squadron in the

Pacific in 1944–1945. Like some of the novel's characters, Forbes sank many small Japanese freighters, was in numerous air combat engagements, blew up blockhouses, shot up phosphorus mines, engaged hidden shore batteries and destroyers, and flew countless thousands of miles in the searches and campaigns of the last several months of the war.

Forbes left the Navy in 1946 and flew commercially for some ten years, the last five or so with American Airlines. He has written many magazine stories, another novel, *Too Near the Sun,* and several television and movie scripts. He teaches and tutors in a private school near Aspen, Colorado, where he has lived since the 1960s.

Forbes's account of a supposedly simple training flight suggests that disorientation, stress, and trauma are not solely coincident to combat.

"TRAINING FLIGHT"

Every page of the 1940 *Flight Jacket,* the naval aviation yearbook from Pensacola, Florida, has a pair of Navy wings. It is a seductive emblem. The Navy put it on every page so we wouldn't forget for a single moment why we were there. Going to flight school at Pensacola was the biggest thing that had ever happened to any of us. The place was tough but honest. One in three cadets would leave without the gold wings.

Roommates came and went. A new class arrived every two weeks, and in my room were guys from all over the country—Cricket Hill, Virginia; Lenni Hills, Pennsylvania; Flatonia, Texas. I was from Summerland, California. Flatonia didn't stay long and Lenni Hills was killed almost as soon as he graduated. Cricket Hill was in a PBY amphibian that somehow managed to land on top of a Greenland glacier in thick fog. Another roommate disappeared on a flight to Hawaii, and yet another was killed when the Japanese hit Cavite in the Philippines.

In the year and a half before Pearl Harbor I morbidly kept track of calamities by circling the photos of the dead in *Flight Jacket.* The first to be circled, alphabetically, was Paul Alter; the last, Marv Zimmerman. In between these two were an awful lot of black circles—guys who had spun in making night landings on carriers, flown into high-tension lines, hit each other in formation, or simply disappeared at sea. After Pearl Harbor I stopped keeping track.

My own records noted that I had pranged a number of airplanes—one took down a set of high-tension lines, two I ditched, and one I landed in downtown Jacksonville. One of my aircraft had caught fire, one had been hit in a midair collision, and several had been shot at. I had also flown over eighty missions, sunk some ships in low-level bombing, battled fighters, flown through typhoons, and seen so many airplanes crash, burn, explode, or collide in midair that I could no longer keep track of them. Eventually I seemed to be in a constant state of fear, in an airplane or out of it.

By the winter of 1943 I had logged some two thousand hours, most of it in twin-engine land- and seaplanes. When the Navy got its version of the B-24 Liberator, the PB4Y-1, I began to train in it at Chincoteague Island in Virginia.

The Navy did a funny thing with the Liberator: they installed a non-pilot navigator. Every Navy pilot shot the sun and stars, used plotting boards, did dead reckoning, flew wind stars—and here came a navigator who would do nothing else. My crew was mildly disdainful of the arrangement. A long, dumb training flight—three legs, eighteen hundred miles, ten hours, all over water—would be made just for his sake, accompanied by a navigation instructor.

Except for myself, as pilot, the crew was green. The six gunners and radiomen averaged nineteen years old. Buzz, the crew chief, was twenty-one; the copilot, Todd, twenty-two. Our training flights had the atmosphere of a bus en route to a high school football game. The tail gunner was convinced that he sang like Dick Haymes and occasionally tried to convince the rest of us by singing over the intercom. The bow turret gunner did splendid imitations of Donald and Daffy Duck. Joe, the non-pilot navigator, was a famous softball pitcher. Buzz and I, the least talented of the crew, fell back on the fact that Buzz had been based at a refueling station a hundred miles up the Essequibo River in British Guiana and I had flown there often in a patrol squadron. We began our stories with, "Well, down in B.G. one time, I remember this guy fell into the river"; then would come the piranha part. We were all stars of some sort, but none of us could compare with Todd the copilot.

Todd had gotten out of half the training flights in a medical *tour de force* that had included problems with his eyes and ears and various inner sanctums where symptoms were harder for the flight surgeon to judge. Todd talked about valvulae conniventes and the receptacle of the chyle and organic weakness in these areas and got away with it. The other ensigns disliked him because one of them constantly had to take his place and fly an extra hop.

The truth was that Todd was afraid to fly, or had become so after marrying his seventeen-year-old sweetheart. He couldn't bear to be away from her for even a few hours. When he did fly he brought along some talisman—a letter or picture or her charm bracelet. Todd could not take off or land a B-24, and what's more, since he got married, he said he never intended to learn how.

After this flight, we would be finished with the operational training program and would leave for a hotel at Old Point Comfort on the Chesapeake Bay for a few days before flying to England. We knew that if we didn't finish up, anything left undone, including perhaps this ten-hour flight, would have to be completed at the possible cost of time at Old Point Comfort.

The morning of the flight the aerology man told me there was a big cold front out to sea. It should be well north of our sector, he said, and it shouldn't be very violent if we did get into it. We took off at noon, flew a wind star, and set off on the course given us somewhat pompously by the navigation instructor, who was one of those guys who wore everything wrong. He wore his overseas cap, for instance, under his earphones, all puffed up like a tea cozy.

Buzz made his daily announcement about the fuel gauges, which were notoriously unreliable glass tube sight gauges. According to them, we had fuel for twelve hours at normal consumption, and

Pilot Gordon Forbes *(center)* stands with his crew
before a B-25 bomber that had been borrowed from the Marines
for laying aerial mines off Nova Scotia.

COURTESY OF GORDON FORBES

Buzz planned to compute consumption by taking fuel flow meter
readings every hour. I put the airplane on autopilot and we began
the eating, coffee drinking, and smoking that would go on all afternoon. After a while Todd pulled out a letter, unfolded it tenderly,
and began to read. At the nav table Joe was busy under the instructor's eye. A little after four we finished the outbound leg and turned
north. The instructor pointed out that Joe was doing compass deviation, drift, and magnetic variation corrections. (A month later Joe
took us over the middle of Spain by cranking the magnetic variation backwards.)

Far to the north we began to see huge masses of cumulus clouds.
The radioman decoded a message that said two other airplanes from
our base had canceled their flights in sectors to our north and had
reported a big cold front with cloud tops at thirty thousand feet. If
we had not had an instructor on board I would have faked it, cruis-
ing around not too far from land and sending phony position reports
until our estimated time of arrival came up.

We went on, bending our track to the west to distance ourselves from the largest clouds to the east. But late in the afternoon we came right up on the face of the front. It was indeed a big one. The clouds were solid and boiling and reached way up, far higher than we could climb. Below them was the typical ugly roll cloud—black, full of rain, and sagging almost to the sea. Over our earphones came the crackle of electricity.

No matter—we would pick our way back and re-plot a course to the base. But it was soon obvious that neither Joe nor the instructor was able to plot the course changes fast enough. They kept poking their heads in the cockpit to ask for the heading we had been on a couple of minutes earlier.

I looked up at the big cauliflowers and knew we would have to fly through them. I told the crew to ready themselves and told the navigators to watch the course changes, time them, and just do the best they could. I snapped off the autopilot and headed into the roll cloud at eight hundred feet.

We began to bounce—hard. Lightning flashed ahead and then starboard. A gust of rain hit the skin, then violent hail. The roll cloud swallowed us. I looked over at Todd. He was staring ahead, letter in hand. "A real washer biter," I yelled, which meant your behind was biting the washers out of the seat.

The altimeter said six hundred feet when we broke out about eighty feet above the water. Spume flew downwind in streams like fire hose torrents and the wingtips seemed to be lower than the huge waves rolling under us. I reset the altimeter. A few minutes later it said we were two hundred feet *under* water (barometric pressure changes radically in cold fronts).

We were back in clouds. Now came a steady barrage of hail. We started climbing at two thousand feet per minute, the airframe creaking and snapping. I pulled back the power, lowered the landing gear, and added twenty degrees of flaps in an effort to slow our ascent. We went up even faster.

I pounded on the pedestal to get Todd to help me wrestle the yoke. At that moment Buzz appeared between the seats. "Get him out of there and come help me," I shouted.

We went on up, pressed into our seats, in the midst of a fearful racket of surging propellers, thrashing hail, electrical discharges, and vague cries and yells from aft. The wings were whipping like balsa. At nineteen thousand feet, according to the unreliable altimeter, we stopped climbing. We had a second or two of calm, then started down. Instead of being pinned in our seats we were drawn upward against the seat harnesses. All kinds of things were plastered against the ceiling, including the new cordovan shoes I had taken off to keep from scuffing them on the rudder pedals. Coffee cups, pencils, maps, and cigarette butts clung up there as if drawn to a magnet. We had by now retracted the gear and flaps and applied full power, and still we dove.

We broke out of the clouds at one thousand feet and went skidding across the waves in a tremendous yaw. The wind had swung around sixty degrees. We seemed to be heading south and drifting to port. I forced the airplane around into what might be a westerly heading, but I really couldn't tell. I could no longer think.

I looked into the nav compartment. The instructor was on the floor, braced under the nav table. His puffy hat was on sid6ways, sort of a Napoleon look. I called the radioman on the intercom, but he talked so fast I couldn't follow him. I waved for him to come up.

"Get a bearing from the base," I shouted.

"Like I was telling you, I can't get the base no more."

"Why the hell not?"

His head swayed back and forth near my ear. "I dunno. Just the conditions, I guess."

We staggered on. The airplane was light now and even climbed a little under reduced power. It was now 10 P.M. The allotted time for the flight had elapsed, and I hadn't a clue where we were—over land, over water, north or south of the base, east or west of the Allegheny mountains.

In my earphones I heard someone say faintly, "Negative, not able any approach." Whoever he was talking to on the ground demurred. A moment later the voice said angrily: "The hell with that! We're leaving the ship."

No one answered my calls on the same channel. I thought about all of us jumping out. Perhaps we were a hundred miles out to sea. On the other hand, perhaps we were about to run into a mountain.

Buzz told me that the fuel levels in the sight gauges had disappeared. I knew he didn't trust them even when he could see them. "What do you figure?" I asked.

He shrugged in the dim light. "We got maybe an hour set up like this. If you need power to climb or something, then I don't know."

It was midnight. We had to be over land. I didn't bother to reason why, I just decided we had to be. I announced on the intercom that we were going to climb and then jump out in exactly ten minutes.

Buzz had opened the bomb bay doors. Their strong lights shone down on scudding mist and rain. The people in the nav compartment started aft and disappeared in the catwalk. But the nose didn't come down as it would have if people were exiting from the rear.

Buzz and I got up. Just ahead of me as I started to squeeze through the nav compartment, he grabbed my arm and pointed down the catwalk. Way aft we saw legs—lots of them. No one had jumped.

I looked down through the bomb bay doors. I wasn't going to jump either. Not yet, not into that dark void, not while all four engines were running. We sat down again.

"Okay, you won't do it," I croaked over an intercom. "We'll just let down until we see something—or hit something."

One thousand feet. How far off could the altimeter be? Now five hundred. We broke out almost lined up with a long row of lights. An airfield! No, the lights were on the masts of fishing boats moored in a line. Dead ahead, a hazy glow spread through the clouds. We ducked in and out of the low ceiling, which was maybe three hundred feet.

Almost crying with excitement I cranked the handle of the automatic direction finder. Suddenly the needle twittered and began to swing in an arc of about twenty degrees. As we followed its uncertain waving I could hear the beginning of a signal. In minutes I knew it was the Washington, D.C., low-frequency range. Lights, again in a long row! It must be Washington National Airport!

I let down, lined up with the lights, and lowered some flaps. I had my hand on the landing gear lever when Buzz yelled, "The arsenal! Aberdeen Proving Ground!" We flew down the long street of ammo bunkers. The needle, steadier now, still pointed dead ahead.

Fifteen minutes later, there it was, off to the left, just a glimpse of an airport. The runways were lit by red lights, and there was a big red X in the middle that began to disappear off the left wing. I banked the airplane to port, worrying about stalling at our low speed, but damned if I was going to lose that red X. Down came the gear and some flaps. At that moment a huge white shaft flashed by on the right, very close. I had just missed hitting the Washington Monument.

The airport looked like it was under water. At the last moment Todd poked his head in and shouted, "You dumb bastard, you're landing in the river!"

It certainly looked like it. When we hit, a thick sheet of spray flew over us. We bobbled along, went off the runway, and skidded to a stop on the grass. I grabbed my new cordovans for some reason and piled out with the others, who were rolling in the water, crying and laughing and hugging each other. Some of them grabbed me, kissing me, and pounding my back. They either didn't know or didn't care that I had nearly killed them all.

A jeep with masked headlights arrived and a man with a white brassard on his arm shone his flashlight on us. "Didn't they tell you?" he shouted. "The field is closed. You can't land here. Who is in command of this airplane?" Prone in the grass I held up one arm. The man pointed at the huge red X. "See that?"

"It was an emergency," I said. "We were lost. Out of gas."

"You're under arrest until we see the duty officer," he said.

There were hoots and howls of derision. "Shoot us! Kill us! Tell the duty officer he can insert this B-24 sideways, and by the numbers!"

It was 2:45 A.M. We had been flying for fifteen hours. The duty officer said we had been reported missing two hours ago. Two inches of rain had fallen in one hour. We spent the rest of the night in big lounge chairs in the airport waiting room.

Back at Chincoteague the Navy convened the usual board, this one to see why a training flight had been sent out when the biggest cold front of the year was hanging off the coast. They didn't go into the confusion and mistakes that had characterized my performance but blamed the people in charge of training. Todd turned in his wings.

Also at the hearing was a captain who came down to inquire into another matter. An aircraft, presumably military and almost certainly ours, had flown twice over the White House between 2:00 A.M. and 2:30 A.M. at "a dangerously low altitude." The occupants of the White House had been terrified.

I wrote to Franklin D. from North Africa, explaining what had happened and apologizing for scaring him. Perhaps he and Eleanor had been frightened, I wrote, but believe me, Mr. President, no one was more frightened that night than the crew in the airplane that went over your house. I never got an answer.

WILLIAM J. LEDERER

W ILLIAM J. LEDERER, coauthor of *The Ugly American*
(1958), and author of *A Nation of Sheep* (1961), as well as
many other books, tells the following story about why he joined the
Navy. At age fifteen, with skills in dictation his only real asset, he
got a job working for Heywood Broun, one of the prominent journalists of the day. Most of the important writers of the country
passed through Broun's office, and when they did, Lederer would
ask each of them what he needed to do to become a writer. One day
the eminent journalist and essayist Alexander Woollcott came by.
Upon Lederer posing this question to him, Woollcott responded by
saying: "(1) You have to learn manners—you're not properly
dressed. (2) You need to be healthy (you have to have vigor to be a
writer)—you're always coughing. (3) You have to get an education—
have you been through high school?" Lederer hadn't; in fact he had
been kicked out of two.

Lederer took Woollcott seriously—but how could he get an education? Walking along, he saw a recruiting poster that proclaimed
if a young man joined the Navy, he would have an opportunity
to attend the Naval Academy. So Lederer immediately joined up.
As Lederer recounted in a phone conversation in October 1995, it
took five years of service as an enlisted man before someone gave

him the chance, but he finally was allowed to test into the Naval Academy.

Lederer graduated from the academy in 1936 and quickly saw duty on the USS *Indianapolis* (CL-35), USS *Hovey* (DD-208), and USS *Bulmer* (DD-222). In 1940 he was ordered to the Asiatic Station and assigned as executive officer of a gunboat based at Chungking, the USS *Tutuila,* where he saw his most arduous duty. Although a noncombatant, the ship was straddled many times during the many weeks of the Japanese bombardment of the Chinese in the city, and over half the crew became physical or emotional casualties. In December 1941, Lederer reported for duty aboard the destroyer USS *Bristol* (DD-453). He was serving as her executive officer in October 1943 when it was sunk by a German submarine in the Mediterranean.

Lederer told many colorful stories of his naval career in his first book, *All the Ship's at Sea* (1950), including the story of a collision that eventually caused him to change his designator from unrestricted line to public affairs. Lederer retired in 1958 as a captain and soon thereafter began a full-time career as a writer. Reprinted below is the story of the sinking of the USS *Bristol* (called the USS *Litch* in this excerpt). For the most part, this account was researched and written down soon after the event.

from

ALL THE SHIP'S AT SEA

At four o'clock in the morning, in the autumn of 1943, an almost full moon lighted the Mediterranean. The USS *Litch* steamed from Salerno en route to Oran. Our destination lay only a few hundred miles away. In a matter of hours the lookouts on the morning watch expected to sight the cliffs of Mers el-Kébir.

All hands, for the first time in months, relaxed in their sleep. The danger area had been passed and two weeks of recreation started tomorrow. It had been a rugged year—invasions, air attacks, and patrols off enemy shores had come one after another without relief. The cruisers had rests between action, but the indispensable little destroyers went out night after night. Six destroyers in the area had been sunk by the Germans in the last few months. Almost all of them had gone down in about a minute after the torpedo or bomb struck.

Now, starting tomorrow, good times beckoned; two weeks of wine, music, and dancing girls in Oran, which looked to us like Paris in North Africa. At 0400, having just completed an inspection of the ship, I went to my cabin. After undressing (going to bed with clothes off was a luxury I hadn't enjoyed for several months), I lighted a pipe and sat on the edge of the bunk considering methods of handling liberty for the crew. Should we start it immediately upon docking, or should we wait until regular liberty hours? Which section rated liberty the first day . . . ?

Up on the bridge the members of the morning watch checked on the telephone circuits. At 0401 the officer of the deck, Ensign Farnum, started a new zigzag pattern.

He said to the helmsman, "Right fifteen degrees rudder."

"Right fifteen, aye, aye, sir."

The ship turned.

In the chart house Baylor, the sonarman, trained his sound unit from one bearing to another, listening for submarines. It threw out a directional sound beam, a series of "pings." These pings, if they hit a solid object like a submarine, reflected back to the operator. The instrument also reacted to turbulences such as those made by a school of fish or the wake of a propeller.

Baylor did his job automatically; his ears listened for telltale sounds, but his mind computed how much money he'd have on the book if the *Litch* stayed in the Mediterranean for another six months.

0402—a faint rumbling noise came out of the sound unit. Baylor tensed. Switching the mechanism from automatic to manual, he trained it to the point of loudest rumbling. He hunched over his equipment, now concentrating on what he heard. It sounded like water noises caused by the wake of a ship. But why should there be water noises? There were no other ships in company. He notified the Bridge and Radar.

"Bridge, Radar, this is Sound. Water noises at 210. Please check."

Comdr. William J. Lederer at a desk job after World War II's end.

"Radar, aye, aye."

"Bridge, aye, aye."

All battle-station telephone talkers heard the conversation. Personnel all over the ship acted. The officer of the deck put his glasses out to 210 and examined the area visually. The radar operator swung his radar antenna there. The main battery trained to that bearing. The junior officer of the watch energized the dead reckoning tracer and broke out his mooring board. Depth-charge personnel stood by their racks.

At 0403 the Bridge made its report first.

"Sound, Bridge, bearing 210 is clear."

Radar came next.

"Sound, Radar, bearing clear here."

But Baylor still heard the noise. The bearing remained at 210. And now the noise assumed a cadence, a definite chut-chut-chut-chut-chut. A propeller! Maybe it's our own propeller—the ship had just turned. It may be the kickback of our own wake.

He trained the sound unit aft to check the *Litch*'s propeller. He wanted to compare its pitch and cadence with the other noise. The ship's propeller sounded a slow, deep beat; arump . . . arump . . . arump . . . arump. The noise at 210 whined fast and high-pitched.

At 0403-½ Baylor moved his gear to the bow again. The noise came louder, increasing with each second. CHUT-CHUT-CHUT-CHUT-CHUT-CHUT-CHUT!

Baylor screamed into the voice tube leading to the bridge, "Torpedo! Starboard bow, close aboard! Torpedo . . ."

The explosion of six hundred pounds of TNT interrupted his warning; it knocked Baylor to the deck. Lights flickered out. The whip of the bridge structure flung equipment about the compartment. The heavy recording apparatus, toppling off its base, struck the back of Baylor's head. Unconsciously, by instinct alone, he pulled himself to his hands and knees and crawled in the direction of the bridge.

Blood from the back of his neck spurted over the ship's log which lay on the deck, blotting out the last entry, the one made by the quartermaster four minutes ago: "0400—CONDITIONS NORMAL."

* * *

Ensign Farnum, standing behind the helmsman, heard Baylor's warning scream. Before he could move, the explosion threw him to the overhead and then to the deck. He got up, frantically tried to ring the general alarm. It was dead; no power. Rushing to the wing of the bridge, which shook violently, Farnum looked aft to find out what had happened. The torpedo had exploded amidships, in the number one fireroom. Number two stack broke at the base, toppling overboard with a hiss. Steam came up from the engineering spaces. Both bow and stern were high; the ship had split in two amidships. The after part of the bridge stove in and the deck plates on the main deck buckled. Farnum observed that some of the life rafts had been released.

The captain staggered out the rear door of the emergency cabin, his head, face, and chest bloody. Groping, he felt his way by holding on to the wind break.

"Officer of the Deck!"

"Yes, Captain."

"Officer of the Deck! Where the hell are you?"

"Here, Captain. This is Farnum, the officer of the deck."

The captain fell to the deck.

* * *

The torpedo had exploded under the forward fireroom. During the moment of time the boiler and steam pipes were in a state of physical change—from boilers and steam pipes to rubble and steam and burning oil—the fireroom personnel still lived.

"Mary and Jesus . . ." said Napolito.

"Hey, Chief . . ." said Kelly.

Gustophsky opened his mouth to shout, "Get out of . . ." But the detonated TNT was too swift, too strong. The personnel in number one fireroom became nothing; like the boilers and steam pipes they became rubble and ashes. Only Kackett survived, miraculously blown up through the deck hatch and into the water. . . .

* * *

Miflin, the man in charge of the depth-charge watch on the fantail, was shifting his men from one station to another when the torpedo hit. The full jolt of the explosion did not reach the fantail; there was a muffled roar followed by a shaking. A second later, Miflin saw the stack fall over, heard the hissing of steam, and felt the stern rise out of the water.

He shouted to the men on watch. "Put the depth charges on safe! Willy, you and Jones take the port side. Johnson, you and Comp take the starboard side. I'll get the racks."

Willy and Jones ran to the port depth-charge throwers. Johnson and Comp hesitated. Miflin barked at them. "For Christ's sake, shake a leg!"

"I know the charges are on safe," said Comp. "We're going to stand by the rafts."

"I said put them on safe, you son of a bitch! Now, God damn you, check them or I'll bash your ——— head in." Miflin rushed at the two men, waving a wrench.

They began checking the depth charges. Miflin ran aft to the racks. He examined each depth charge carefully, using a light. The stern angled about forty degrees to the horizontal. Miflin held on to the racks to keep from slipping. He glanced over the side, it looked like a mile to the water. He thought of the suction the ship would make when she went under.

The depth charges in the racks were okay. He looked forward and saw the life rafts floating in the water; men were abandoning the ship. The stern lurched up to an angle of about seventy degrees. Miflin lost his grip, slid, almost dropped, twenty feet down, smashed heavily into number five depth-charge thrower. A flash of pain jabbed in his loins. He tried to abandon ship, but couldn't move. His frantic efforts brought pain throughout his lower body. Try as he would he could not get up. From the hips down he was paralyzed.

The stern settled. Miflin knew that if he didn't pull out he'd be lost. From where he lay he couldn't even float free as the ship sank; he'd tangle in the deckhouse netting. Grabbing the snaking and using the muscles in his arms and shoulders he tugged on the life line. But the lower part of his body remained paralyzed. Sweat poured out all over him. His hands shook; he could barely keep his grip on the snaking, let alone pull himself over it. The pain in his groin spread upward to his stomach.

He remembered his knife. Slipping it out of the sheath, he cut the snaking. Then, by wriggling his shoulders, he rolled over the scupper and dropped from the main deck into the water below. Using his arms he sculled away from the wreck. About fifteen minutes later, a shipmate pulled him onto a raft.

* * *

The explosion lifted me from my sitting position on the bunk and threw me violently against the bulkhead on the opposite side of the cabin. The lights went out and I couldn't find myself. I had no idea what had happened and couldn't associate myself with anything, either in place or time. I lay suspended in a bundle of whirling darkness.

For an undetermined length of time, I didn't know whether I was having a bad dream, or if I were in bed at home, or if maybe I had been walking in my sleep and had fallen down a ladder.

I stood up; my groping hand felt the dogged-down port. I was aboard the *Litch*. Under me the ship shuddered like a flag in a gale. I heard the groaning of steel mashing on steel, and the whining hiss of berserk steam shrieking out of the engineering spaces.

This is it, I thought, we've been hit and we're sinking fast! Get the hell out of here! I fumbled around in the dark, feeling for my life jacket. The nauseating odor of oil and smoke drifted into the cabin. I couldn't locate the life jacket, nor did I search long.

Stumbling over debris, I rushed into the dark passageway. Dimly, I heard many voices shouting.

"The door's stuck!" the voices screamed. "We can't get out!"

At the end of the passageway, barely discernible, I saw a dozen men huddled in front of the door which led topside to freedom— to air and a chance to live. The explosion apparently had jammed the door. I ran to the end of the passageway. One thought dominated me, Get topside! The *Buck* and the *Rowen* sank in less then a minute after being torpedoed.

I found the door open about a foot. Looking out through the crack I saw that the main deck and the water still were in proper relation to each other. The *Litch* wasn't sinking yet. That relieved me and I felt like the executive officer again. I shouted, "All right, men, now let's all push on the door together. One, two, three . . . go!"

The steel door swung open. We all crowded out and made our way to the fo'c'sle. Me, too. Approximately forty men gathered near the wildcat. The ship seemed normal except that the bow was at an angle of ten degrees to the horizon. I thought perhaps we'd passed over a mine and had only been jarred. Maybe I was only imagining the ten-degree angle. I decided to go aft to investigate.

When I reached frame 60 the ship heaved violently; the after part of the ship angled to about forty degrees, in a direction opposite to the slant of the fo'c'sle. The ship formed a "V" with its bottom at the forward stack.

The agony of the *Litch* lay in front of me. Both stacks had tumbled over; flames and sparks mixed with steam shot upward from cavities in the main deck. The stubby remains of the after stack lay askew like a broken nose.

Only the main deck platings and the power cables held the bow and stern together. The sea's motion grated the raw ends, making the ship shiver and screech. The midship section, where the *Litch*'s back had been broken, settled in the water. The main deck plating parted with a clang.

I went back to the forward part of the ship, up to the extreme bow. Because of the steep incline of the deck I had to stoop and crawl like an animal. I knew she was sinking quickly. I wondered if the depth charges were set on safe.

Picking up a sound power telephone I tried the bridge, hoping that perhaps communication might miraculously still be had. No luck. My mind raced. Were those depth charges on safe? Depth-charge explosions killed most of the men in the *Ingraham*. Would the boilers set off the forward magazines? That's what murdered them in the *Buck*.

The ship gave a grunt, and I saw the stern float off. I smelled a peculiar odor, like urine on hot coals. The stern stood on end, sinking, sliding under, and I noticed in a detached way how gigantic and ugly the propellers looked sticking up in the air. Now our end twisted on its longitudinal axis. Far away from the bridge I heard someone shout, "Abandon ship! Abandon ship!"

Number two turret swung around as if it might tumble out of its trunnions.

"Abandon ship!" I shouted.

A few sailors jumped, but most of them hesitated. The distance to the water from the bow increased as the angle got larger. It was now forty or fifty feet down. The men apparently were afraid to make such a high leap. I thought, We better get the hell off here before the magazine explodes.

I shouted, "Let's go, boys, let's go! Get the hell off as quickly as you can. Then swim like hell!"

Not many of them moved.

They don't recognize me, I thought, I have nothing on but skivvy pants. They're excited and I'm just another voice hollering.

"Abandon ship! Abandon ship!" I ordered, almost screaming. "This is the exec, and I'm shoving off." I climbed over the lifeline.

"This is the exec," I hollered again, "and I'm going over the side." My mouth then opened on its own account and out came something I hadn't intended to say, "The last bastard over is a pig's ass!"

Looking down to make certain I wasn't jumping on top of something, I held my nose between my thumb and forefinger. . . . I heard a babble behind me, of men repeating, "The last bastard over is a pig's ass," and from the corner of my eye I saw men scrambling for the lifelines. Then I jumped.

I landed in the water with less shock than I had expected. The water felt warm, but the plunge took my breath away. Looking back at the ship I saw that she had a twisting motion, and noticed that bubbles gurgled and belched from the submerged section.

Swimming away from the dying *Litch* I felt like a rabbit trying to escape the hounds. My breath came hard, my legs hurt, my lungs burned, my arms dragged . . . yet I swam fast, using every muscle, all of my will and my instinct, to get away from the ship.

When I stopped to rest I was about a hundred and twenty yards from the bow. The partially submerged stern drifted toward me. I started swimming again, away from the stern which had nine tons of TNT on it. When I could swim no more I looked at the ship again. The bow still stood on end. The stern had disappeared. If the depth charges aren't on safe, I thought, the explosion will come any moment now. I floated on my back, placing my hand tightly over my rectum, to prevent the water pressure caused by the explosion from rupturing my intestines. I started counting for a time estimate. About a minute went by.

No explosion.

In my awkward position, I accidentally rolled over and breathed in a lungful of water. Despite the pain and coughing, I managed to stay on my back with my hand firmly in place.

Two minutes.

Three minutes.

Except for the swish-swish of the waves, the ocean was silent. Although I couldn't see them, all of the men who had got off the ship probably lay on their backs doing the same thing I was—most likely not more than a few hundred yards away.

Four minutes.

Well, I thought, that's that. She's not going to explode. The next thing is to get organized until we're picked up. The immediate fear of dying left me and the secondary instinct of taking charge of my men returned.

I shouted, "Hey, hello!" but no one answered. I probably had drifted off from the main group. I shouted more, but received no answer. An empty ammunition can and a piece of timber floated by. I grabbed them. Resting my shoulders on the can and my feet on the wood, I made myself comfortable and concentrated on relaxing. I knew I had to hoard my energy—in case they didn't find me at first. It would be light in about two hours. But I might be out there for days.

I closed my eyes and tried to go into a quasi-sleep.

I heard someone mumbling; I "got up" and looked around. About fifteen feet away I saw Davis, a seaman. He was the last person I wanted to see. Davis didn't know how to swim. During the two years he had been in the *Litch* I had tried to teach him to swim, but he had been afraid of the water and wouldn't even get in and try.

"Davis!" I said.

"Who's that?"

"Commander Lederer."

"Jesus, I'm glad to see you. Nobody else's around."

I saw that Davis had a life jacket, which relieved me considerably.

"Sir?" said Davis.

"Yes?"

"I wish t'hell I could swim."

"You'll be all right, you've got a life jacket."

"These kapoks get soggy after a while."

"They'll last for days. We'll get picked up after daylight."

"Sir?"

"Shut up, Davis. Save your energy, you may need it later."

"You think they'll come after us?"

"YES! Now goddamn it, shut up."

"I can't swim. You'll stay near me, in case this kapok gets soggy?"

"Yes."

"Commander?"

I didn't answer.

"Commander—I think I see a ship!"

There was a ship! A couple of hundred yards away stood the black outline of a destroyer—or maybe it was the enemy submarine looking for prisoners. No, it had too much superstructure for a submarine. It was a destroyer, lying still in the water, obviously looking for the *Litch*'s survivors.

For two or three minutes we shouted "Help" as loud as we could. No one replied.

Davis whined, "They'll never see us. They'll go away and leave us . . ."

I was thinking about the same thing, trying to come to a decision. If I swam to the ship and got there in time, everything'd be fine. But if she departed after I'd started to her, then I'd be stranded in the Mediterranean without a thing to keep me afloat. And Davis would be alone too. Ocean currents separate people quickly.

Davis said, "I'm going to make a try for it!"

I tried to make up my mind if I should swim toward the ship, pushing the ammunition can in front of me, or just swim alone as fast as I could. An empty life jacket floated by me; I was about to grab it when I saw that Davis had cast it off and was dog paddling furiously toward the destroyer. Pushing my ammunition can in front of me, I swam alongside Davis. In what seemed months, we finally got alongside the destroyer. Rescue ladders were over the side and I climbed aboard. Davis had to be carried up.

As soon as he had his breath he babbled, "I swam here! I swam—for the first time in my life I swam—at least a mile—I swam!"

We were the first survivors from the *Litch* to be rescued. I pointed where I thought the others were and the destroyer started after them.

In the meanwhile (as soon as the medical officer treated the wound on my leg—which I hadn't known I had, and still don't know how I acquired), I went to the radio shack and quickly wrote down the events while they still remained fresh in my mind.

* * *

I learned later that the rest of the *Litch*'s survivors had had experiences similar to mine. As soon as the stern went under, hundreds of men floated on their backs, holding their hands over their rectums. Farnum told me that after about five minutes he looked around and saw life rafts (some with men on them), wooden shores, and powder cans as they bobbed on wave crests. The smell of oil upset him. But it was the quietness which particularly caught his notice.

He swam to a raft. Standing on it, he saw the men still on their backs.

"Hey! Hey! Men!" he shouted, "climb on the rafts before they drift away."

This was what they wanted; a voice of authority to inform them that the danger of explosion was over. All hands started to sing, talk, shout.

"Hey, Joe! You all right?"

"Yeh. Say did Kelly get off?"

"Dunno. C'mon pal, let's get on the same life raft."

"God, we're lucky the oil didn't catch fire."

"Or that the depth charges didn't go off."

"Thirty days survivor's leave, hot damn!"

"Hey, I hadn't thought of that . . . thirty days . . . I almost don't mind getting sunk."

Within a half-hour the group had been organized. There were eight balsa rafts and two ball nets, adequate room for all the survivors. After tying the rafts together, the officers held a rough muster. There were forty-three men and two officers missing. Eleven of the 251 survivors suffered injuries. This included the captain, who had a serious head wound. The casualties were all placed on a raft with the hospital corpsman, and the officers spread out so that there was at least one to a raft.

The commissary officer started calculating methods of rationing the emergency food and water. An hour later the rescue destroyer arrived.

* * *

Men's memories of themselves aren't accurate. One month after the sinking of the *Litch* I questioned the survivors for the second time. The stories had altered—in some cases radically. When the ship blew up it was honorable and acceptable to save one's own skin. Later, as we got closer to civilization and normal society, many men remembered something new—how they had struggled to save others at the risk of their own lives.

My notes on a signalman, made ten minutes after he was rescued, read: "After I jumped over, I swam as fast as I could. I swam upwind like you always told us. I had no life jacket and got scared. I saw someone floating with his head under the water. It was Mr. ———. His back was broken; I could tell by the funny way it angled just below the neck. I said to myself if he's dead there's no use in his wasting the life jacket. I took the jacket from him and held on to it. I don't know what happened to Mr. ———'s body."

When I interviewed the same man a month later he told me this: "I swam from the ship as fast as I could. I swam upwind just like you always told us. I saw someone floating with his head under water. It was Mr. ———. Although his back was broken and his head had been submerged, I figured maybe the doctor could do something for him. I pulled his head out of the water and tied the jacket tie-tie under his chin so that his head'd stay in the air. I tread water for about an hour, just holding on to Mr. ———'s life jacket for rest occasionally. I saw a raft about five hundred yards away. I thought maybe the doctor or a hospital corpsman might be on it. I swam over to it. The doctor wasn't there. We paddled over to where Mr. ——— had been, but there was no sign of him."

I met the signalman on the street in Washington a couple of months ago—five years after the *Litch* sank. His story had changed more. Now it was he, the signalman, who had the life jacket. When he saw that Mr. ——— had a broken back, the signalman removed his life jacket and gave it to the injured officer. "I knew he was dead, but figured maybe there was a chance in a thousand he might be saved. It was my duty to try to help him, so I gave him my jacket."

*   *   *

While we were in the rest camp at Oran, our commanding officer recommended Miflin, the torpedoman who had saved us all by putting the depth charges on safe, for the Bronze Star.

Later, the awards section in Washington didn't agree. They cut Miflin's reward down to a letter of commendation. I was in Washington the day he received his letter of commendation. On that morning an Air Force colonel and a Navy captain received Bronze Stars. Neither of them had been in combat!

LOUIS AUCHINCLOSS

WHILE LOUIS AUCHINCLOSS was an undergraduate at Yale he wrote stories and published them in college magazines, but the rejection of his first novel by Scribner's dejected him so much that he left Yale without a degree. Nevertheless, he proceeded (even without a BA) to get a law degree from the University of Virginia, and he was admitted to the bar and joined a first-rate law firm in New York State in 1941.

Then the war loomed, and Auchincloss applied for a commission in naval intelligence, a decision he was later to regret. After Pearl Harbor he was assigned duty in the Panama Canal Zone. He was sickened by the smug and conceited naval bureaucrats he encountered in this theater, and repeatedly applied for sea duty. After fifteen months in Balboa, he finally did get to sea—if only as a gunnery officer on a converted yacht, the USS *Moonstone* (PYc-9). On 15 October 1943, while Auchincloss was temporarily detached to obtain sounding gear, the *Moonstone* sank in a collision with the U.S. destroyer *Greer* (DD-145) in New York harbor. He then applied for amphibious training and was assigned as executive officer of a Landing Ship, Tank (*LST 980*), newly commissioning in Boston and bound for Normandy.

Late in the war, Auchincloss applied for and was given command

of another such ship (the *LST 130*) in the Pacific. While on this relatively peaceful assignment, he finished the first draft of a novel.
When *The Indifferent Children* (based on Auchincloss's Canal Zone
experience) was put forth in 1947 under the pseudonym Andrew
Lee, it became his first published work. So began a long career as a
writer, which Auchincloss has successfully alternated with prac-
ticing law. He is the author of well over twenty works of fiction,
many of them highly respected "novels of manners" about what
remains of American high society, novels such as *Portrait in Brown-
stone* and *The Rector of Justin.* He has also written biographical
works and respected literary criticism on such figures as Shakespeare, Henry James, and Edith Wharton.

In the selection below from his 1974 autobiography, Auchincloss
describes how he confronted both the danger and the vacant hours
of LST duty during and right after the Normandy invasion.

from

A WRITER'S CAPITAL

After a course of amphibious training at Camp Bradford, I went, as
executive officer, with the captain and crew of the *LST 980,* to join
our ship which was to be commissioned in Boston. The captain was
an ex-chief quartermaster of the regular Navy, and his dislike and
distrust of his junior officers, mostly college graduates and "ninoty-
day wonders," can be imagined. Although in some ways a decent
and oddly charming man, he was riddled with a sense of social inferiority which he took out on us in abuse, in petty persecutions, in
constant unreasonable demands and orders. In time the mutual dislike between him and us, exacerbated by a hundred *Caine Mutiny*
incidents, flared into something closer to hate. Our revenge was the
only one available to juniors: to isolate him. One young ensign who
joined the ship some months later came to my cabin to ask me why
nobody would speak to him in the wardroom. "I believe you went
on liberty with the captain," was my terse reply. It was all very
small, but men get small, penned up together for months on end.

The perennial problem of the Navy is much more Captain Queeg than Captain Bligh.

* * *

In the Chesapeake [Bay] we practiced beaching the ship. To a reserve officer, heading at flank speed toward the shore and feeling the rich, surging impact of the bow on sand was great fun, but to the few Annapolis graduates engaged in the exercises it was acutely painful. The approaching shoreline must have represented to them the ultimate nightmare, and I remember how our group commander would avert his eyes in instinctive recoil as we struck the beach. But then his relegation to the amphibious navy must in itself have been a partial disgrace. We were definitely a second-class fleet, and the battleship *New York,* proceeding down the Chesapeake, signaled to him: "Get your trash out of my way."

The *LST 980* arrived in Plymouth, England, in the late winter [of 1943–44], and after some weeks of exercises in the Channel, we proceeded through the Strait of Dover and north to the Thames where we anchored near Tilbury Docks. London in that preinvasion spring seemed full of color and gaiety. Uniforms of different nations abounded, and the air was charged with excitement and a tense anticipation. I felt smug with some of the old friends that I met, for, unlike them, I knew all the plans for the invasion. With what still seems to me incredible folly the Navy believed that every officer of an amphibious vessel had to be apprised of every detail of the operation, instead of being told simply to "follow the leader," as the similar British units were. After one of our flotilla conferences in Tilbury, an old janitor at the base came hobbling after the departing officers with some papers which had been left on the table. They contained the entire plan for the Normandy landings! How this was kept secret from German intelligence agents must remain one of the mysteries of the war. I imagine that it never occurred to the spies that they could find what they wanted simply by hanging around the docks. They may have been too subtle for their job.

Loaded with British and Canadian troops we sailed for Southampton whence we departed for France on June 6. To me the whole thing had rather the air of a regatta. The long lines of unmolested

Ens. Louis Auchincloss is shown on the deck of the converted yacht
USS *Moonstone*. This vessel sank when she collided with a destroyer
while Auchincloss was temporarily detached to obtain sounding gear.
He then was ordered to duty as executive officer of the *LST 980*.

COURTESY OF LOUIS AUCHINCLOSS

ships seemed formidable, handsome, valiant; the waves were crisp
and blue, the men eager. We saw no enemy craft, no enemy planes.
And there was an electric sense of the whole world being there. Two
days after the landings King George VI arrived on the *Aresthusa,* and
Mr. Churchill flew overhead in a bomber with a large fighter escort.
One of our crew looking up was heard to say: "It must be Clark Gable,
on one of his missions." Surely, the enthusiasm of so many hundreds

of thousands had to prevail against a Germany gorged with plunder and weakened by sin!

But soon after the invasion the bright colors in which I had fatuously conceived it were all blown away. One night, while the *LST 980* was anchored off Gold Beach, waiting to disembark troops, she was struck by three bombs dropped from a low-flying German plane. Two crashed through bulkheads into the water; the third lodged in an ammunition truck, one of several such on the tank deck. Obviously, since I live to tell the tale, it did not go off. We were lucky enough to have a British demolition squad among our passengers, the officer in charge of which said to me, with scrupulous good manners, as I was gloomily inspecting the protruding end of the shell: "I realize it's your bomb, sir, but considering how closely we're all concerned, I wonder if you would allow me to take care of it." I never surrendered title to anything more willingly. The bomb was removed with infinite skill and lowered in the sea, but it took with it the last element of my "regatta" atmosphere.

We now operated a shuttle ferry. We crossed and recrossed the Channel, docking in Portland, Southampton, or London, picking up troops, medical units, and even, as the front moved away from the beaches, entertainment groups, and bringing back the wounded and prisoners—thousands of prisoners. Most pathetic among the latter were the Russians, captured by the Germans on the Eastern Front and forced into their western armies. These poor creatures sometimes spoke no dialect known to us and had no idea where or whom they were supposed to be fighting. After loading the tank deck on a Normandy beach we would have to wait for high tide to retract. Sometimes in these delays, when the fighting was still close enough, officers who had come over with us would return for a quick cleanup. I remember one angry British captain, his face caked with mud, pulling open the curtain of the wardroom where I was playing bridge and screaming "Jesus!" as he heard me bid: "Four no trump." He had come out of hell, only a few miles inland.

I think it was this incident which made me and another officer reconsider how we would occupy the long hours of waiting on beaches, at docks, at anchor. My friend was Chauncey Medberry, now chairman of the board of the Bank of America, then an ensign and communications officer of the *LST 980.* I had two copies of a "Complete Plays of Shakespeare," and I suggested that we read *Macbeth* aloud. Chauncey had a surprising answer. He said that he hated doing things in part and that he would read with me only on condition that I undertook to read all thirty-seven plays, including *Titus Andronicus* and the three parts of Henry VI. I was quite willing, and we started, reading in turn, not according to role but speech by speech. We would do this any time we had a few minutes, on the bridge, in the wardroom, in our cabins. At first I was a bit self-conscious when other officers or passengers would peer over our shoulders to find out what the hell we were up to, but Chauncey never was. He had purchased a third Shakespeare in Southampton, and he would simply hand it, open at the correct page, to anyone who lingered beyond a few minutes, asking him to join in. Indeed, one of our officers, who read very slowly and inarticulately, became something of a problem to our sessions.

We read all of Shakespeare, all of Marlowe, and a good deal of Beaumont and Fletcher in the course of the next nine months. Despite the Battle of the Bulge and the buzz bombs, the cold, foggy winter of 1944–45 still echoes in my mind with iambic pentameter. Chauncey and I were keen enough about our aesthetic solution to the ennui of war to try to proselytize others. He organized discussion groups with the crew; I took volunteers to visit landmarks near our home ports, such as Salisbury Cathedral or Stonehenge. Neither of us had much success. But I remember the charming courtesy of the verger of Salisbury Cathedral, a gas victim from the first war, who, in a valiant attempt to explain a second visit to the cathedral made by two rather Philistine young officers from my ship, offered this suggestion:

"You see, Salisbury is unique among English cathedrals in that it was entirely constructed within a period of twenty-five years. This gives it a purity of Gothic form which the natural good taste of your American boys at once picked up."

I wondered. But I was to think of his kindness a bit ruefully, a year later, when the entire crew of another LST signed up for a tour

of the ruins of Nagasaki. There is something about total destruction
that is intriguing to American youth.

The *LST 980* sustained damage to her hull from a rocky beach in
Le Havre which kept her out of the invasion of southern France and
ultimately led to her being ordered home. The captain thought that
we might now be eligible for shore duty. For me, even after two
years, the memory of Panama was sufficiently vivid to make any
war zone preferable to any desk job. It was not bravery; it was simply blind horror of the idea of being even ostensibly one of those
atrocious bureaucrats who pared their fingernails and read *Life* and
Time while men died. In much the same way, when I read accounts
during the Nuremberg trials of Nazi atrocities in concentration
camps, my nightmare was always of being a guard, not a victim. So
I applied for command of an LST in the Pacific, and before we had
even arrived in Norfolk, I received a message, relayed in blinking
lights from the escort commander, that I was to be detached on
arrival and to proceed to San Francisco for further orders.

My joy at being relieved at last from my carping, bickering skipper was intensified by a last-minute triumph. Later I was to incor-
porate it into a short story for the *New Yorker,* ironically entitled
"Loyalty Up and Loyalty Down," but I shall tell it here, for it illus-
trates the pettiness of wartime obsessions. The convoy commodore,
a naval commander, rode the *LST 980* on the Atlantic crossing from
Plymouth to Norfolk, and I was designated his navigator. This gave
me a certain independence of my captain which I abused whenever
possible. Every time he sent for me, I would send back word that I
was engaged in navigation with the convoy commodore. Fortunately for the convoy, we checked our noon position each day with
the escort commander, and I would substitute his for mine. This
was only sensible, since he was operating on loran, and his position was exact.

The winter Atlantic was frightful, and our crossing took more than
thirty days, more than Columbus took on his fourth and final voyage. One morning in the chart room, as the ship rolled and pitched,
the commander steadied himself by catching hold of the side of an

open doorway. I saw that the heavy door was loose and swinging. I shouted at him, but he only looked at me, and as he did so, the door closed, shearing his thumb away as a razor might cut through a piece of rope. When his doctor came up and saw my green expression, he hurried to me. The commander growled:

"There's nothing wrong with *him*. See what you can do about my hand."

The commander was a very brave man, but when his wound had been bound and dressed, it throbbed agonizingly, and this, added to the tempestuous weather, put him in an ugly temper for the next few days. Our captain was so afraid of him that he hugged his cabin, which made life more agreeable for all. And now occurred the incident which gave me my chance. On a stormy night, coming up on the bridge to check our course during the mid-watch, I had a curious sense that something was wrong. Staring ahead through my binoculars, I thought I could make out a ship dead ahead. When I had checked the radar and compasses, it was at once clear what had happened. The gyrocompass had failed, and as it had spun, the helmsman had turned the ship slowly to a course 180 degrees from the convoy course. We were headed directly back toward the second ship in our column!

I relieved the officer of the deck and ordered the helmsman to come hard right. In that sea the turn broke every piece of crockery on the ship. It also flung the captain from his bunk to the deck, and he hurried up to the bridge in a fury. Why had I not requested permission to change course? I replied that there had not been time. In a tantrum he forbade me ever again to relieve the officer of the deck. If the officer of the deck saw fit to take my navigational advice, it would be up to *him* to request permission of the commanding officer to change course. The captain soon forgot his silly tantrum and sillier mandate. I did not.

In the early morning of our expected landfall I was on the bridge watching for the first sea buoy at Norfolk. We were not accustomed to loran, and to pick up a buoy, as I now did with my binoculars, after thirty days of tumultuous seas, at precisely the time and angle that our charted position led us to anticipate, struck me as nothing short of miraculous. But as we drew closer to that wailing buoy, a less exalted idea occurred to me.

There was a distinct set, and the officer of the deck was not compensating for it. On his present course he would probably hit the sea buoy. I called out a suggested course change in a deliberately snotty, superior tone. It was ignored. The officer knew that I had been disempowered, and he was inclined to be stubborn. My tone was just right to fix him in his determination. I now called out suggested course changes loudly every five minutes and insisted that they be entered in the log. The officer of the deck blandly ignored me. When he at last took in the effect of the set, it was too late. He turned desperately to the right, but we were borne down ineluctably on the buoy whose wail seemed to mock him.

Chauncey and I rushed delightedly to the radar as we heard the heavy booming of the buoy against our bottom. We saw the black dot reappear on the screen and then disappear under the bigger dot of the next LST in column. We were leading the whole convoy over it! On the bridge the captain, black-faced, was being gloriously bawled out by the irate convoy commodore. A year of petty persecutions had been revenged.

But even in false triumph, even in this fetid bottom of my swamp of wartime animosities, I was not quite so blind as to feel no shame. That buoy might easily have damaged the screws of the ships that passed over it. And I had had the gall to criticize the fools in the Panama Canal Zone for impeding the war effort! I saw now what the claustrophobic atmosphere of the LST had produced in me. All I can say in retrospect is that without Shakespeare it might have been even worse.

LOUIS R. HARLAN

L OUIS R. HARLAN, University Distinguished Professor Emeritus at the University of Maryland, is renowned for his scholarship on Booker T. Washington. His first biography, *Booker T. Washington: The Making of a Black Leader, 1856–1901* (1972) won the
Bancroft Prize, and his second biography on this same leader, *Booker
T. Washington: The Wizard of Tuskegee, 1901–1915* (1983), won the
Bancroft, Beveridge, and Pulitzer Prizes. Harlan also edited Washington's papers, and he has written other books on African American
history. A champion of civil rights, Harlan marched on Washington,
D.C., and Montgomery, Alabama, during the 1960s. But long before
that, he had taken part in a different campaign. After his academic
retirement, Harlan wrote a book he had long contemplated, a memoir about his "coming of age" in the Navy during World War II.

Harlan had reported aboard ship at the Solomons, Maryland,
amphibious training base on 2 March 1944 (his reporting was an
inauspicious occasion: as he saluted the petty officer on watch from
the gangway, Harlan simultaneously dropped one of his seabags into
the bay). The new ensign was a recent graduate of Emory University,
and he had been assigned as fourth officer of the newly commissioned *LCI(L) 555*, a small landing ship designed to carry infantry
to a beachhead.

Harlan's vessel quickly completed shakedown and general amphibious training and then crossed the Atlantic in time to carry troops to Omaha Beach on D-Day. A couple of months later, the ship played an active role in Operation Dragoon, the Allied amphibious landing in southern France. After several months of additional service in the Mediterranean, *LCI(L) 555* was redeployed to the Pacific. It would arrive too late to see further combat. In his memoir, however, the author's recollections of the ship's many port visits (in this period and earlier) and of his romantic entanglements add considerable color to the narrative of naval affairs, and they help to flesh out the portrait of a young man's experience.

Harlan (who had eventually fleeted up to executive officer) would leave his ship and the Navy in the spring of 1946. In the selection below, the author recollects the invasion of southern France, according to naval experts one of the most well-executed amphibious assaults of the war.

from

ALL AT SEA: COMING OF AGE IN WORLD WAR II

We got underway about sunset on August 14, saw flashes of heavy gunfire around 0300, and by dawn next morning were in sight of the French coast. Our charts for this invasion were not as detailed as those for the Normandy landings, perhaps a reflection of the haste with which this strategic maneuver was improvised. The American forces in northern France, having broken through the German defenses, were racing toward Paris and the southern France invasion was intended to create a diversion that would prevent German occupation troops there from moving north to help stem the Allied drive.

Lying offshore, we sounded General Quarters in the early morning and took our beaching stations. We waited all morning, however, for our call into the beach. The weather was warm and the sea smooth, in sharp contrast to our Normandy experience. All around us were ships of many kinds, sizes, and nationalities. We saw the battleship *Nevada* on our right, firing broadsides from its 16-inch guns into the beach, and on our left the battleship *Texas* was doing the same. Rocket ships hurled a tremendous amount of flak against the shore defenders, who offered little apparent resistance. The whole shoreline seemed to be going up in smoke.

At noon our ship received its call into the beach as part of a second wave of landing craft, and we touched bottom at the beach at 1243, a little distance to the east of the small resort town of St. Maxime. It was then that I came as close as I would ever get to qualifying for a Purple Heart, for my teeth! As we approached the beach, which seemed to be uncontested except for occasional shell-bursts and the rattle and pop of small arms, I stood at my beaching station on the starboard side of the gun deck. Several enlisted men, the gun crew assigned to the 20-millimeter gun nearby, crouched behind the semicircle of quarter-inch steel plate sheltering the gun, while I stood foolhardily erect, protected only by my Mae West. A member of the gun crew grabbed me by the back of my belt and pulled me down with them, saying apologetically something like, "Excuse me, sir, but you don't want to be a dead hero, do you?" My front teeth were full of porcelain fillings, and when the gun crew pulled me down, my upper lip and teeth struck the edge of the gun turret. A numbness set in, hardly noticeable at that moment of high adrenaline. A few hours later, however, when during a moment of respite I popped some dried-out caramel Walnettos from our ship's store into my mouth, the fillings began to come loose in the candy. I wondered whether this combat wound would qualify me for a Purple Heart. The thought brought a crooked grin to my sore lips, but I was too busy to pursue it. For the next year I was too busy and too isolated even to see a Navy dentist about my decaying teeth. Otherwise, our beaching was uneventful. "A piece of cake," the British would say. "A piece of candy," I could have replied.

The water was calm, without real surf. We touched bottom in waist-deep water only fifteen yards from dry land, and our troops filed ashore in good order, unmolested by gunfire. We spotted a few German dead on the beach and about thirty German prisoners, but only four American casualties. Retracting from the beach, we

Ens. Louis Harlan *(bottom left)* poses with members of his
"ship's company" at Plymouth, England, on May 24, 1944.
Ens. Harold W. "Cotton" Clark, then *LCI(L) 555*'s executive officer
—and soon to be its captain—stands in blues in the second row.
COURTESY OF LOUIS HARLAN

returned to the staging area, tied up alongside a transport, the SS
Marine Robin, and took aboard a second load of troops, some three
hundred men from a headquarters company.

We made a dry beaching at a new spot. Since this group had
much gear to unload and kept us on the beach for quite a while, we
took turns wandering along the beach. To our right was a machine-
gun nest, possibly the most heavily fortified spot on the beach. Dead
Germans lay in pathetic attitudes all around the gun like rag dolls
carelessly thrown by a child. They had probably been hit by naval
gunfire before any Americans had set foot on the beach. We were
stunned by this and other signs of violent death, but that did not
stop members of our crew from looting rings and other souvenirs
from the bodies of the dead. A few days later I wrote Diana: "When
we went ashore to collect souvenirs I'll have to confess the only
souvenir I took back to the ship was a white pebble from the beach.
This business of looting the dead enemy who died fighting, who

died a hero's death no matter what cause they may have fought for—
that's a little too much for me. Nevertheless, scavengers on the ship
did a pretty good job of it and brought back some mighty interesting things." A few days later, however, I stooped to taking a souvenir, a cloth patch. At least it was from a live German, a prisoner.
"You can still see the outlines of the imperial eagle, but the swastika
got torn off," I wrote. "The prisoner who gave it to me tore it off in
a hurry as he was going over the side. It's for combat infantrymen
only, and is worn above the left breast pocket. You probably don't
want it, which reaction I can fully appreciate. If you don't, save it
for me, though."

An air alert sounded that first afternoon, and we laid a smoke
screen over our area of beach. We dropped a floating smoke pot for
good measure. We worked all night and all the next day, unloading
transports and carrying their human cargo to the beach. On one
occasion we were sent to the beach to take wounded to a hospital
ship, but when we got there we could find none to transport. They
had probably been picked up by another ship. We went ashore and
gawked at the forlorn German prisoners herded in large numbers
into a barbed-wire enclosure on the beach. The majority were said
to be Poles and Czechs forced into German army service, mostly
middle-aged men and young boys, a sign that the Germans were
scraping the bottom of the manpower barrel. They had probably
sent these questionable troops to the south to free more combat-
ready troops for the struggle in northern France. At any rate, the
prisoners we saw didn't show much fight, and were probably not
sorry to be captured.

That night, we tied up alongside a French transport to take a load
of Free French troops into shore, and had great difficulty getting its
crew to understand the phrase "take our lines." Just at that moment
an air raid siren sounded, and we could see ten German bombers,
flying low, dropping their bombs on the newly arrived transport
ships. Ships all around us opened up with antiaircraft fire, and
bombs exploded around us in great numbers. A ship about a hundred yards away received a direct hit, and bombs landed in the
water about fifty yards from us, sending up a column of water. After

two bombers went down in flames the others flew away. We and other ships with fog generators somewhat tardily laid such a thick smoke screen that we could see nothing whatever, neither the enemy planes nor our own ships nor the beaches. The smoke screen was probably unnecessary, for the Germans were running out of planes.

During and after the air raid we took about three hundred troops aboard, mostly Moroccans or West Africans, "the roughest, toughest looking group of humans I've ever seen," as Cotton Clark described them. "They were almost wild looking creatures, each armed with a bayoneted Springfield rifle. From head to foot their clothes & equipment were U. S. Most all were dark skinned, tall and big boned." Included in our troop load and more or less in charge was an irascible American brigadier general named Swain, and also a detachment of fifty French WACs—petite, feminine, and stylish in their perfectly fitted uniforms. We summoned up what little French we knew to give the WACs our solicitous attention. One of the French WACs was out of her head, screaming insanely every time she heard a gun or a bomb. We wondered whether she could safely be taken into a war zone, but her comrades told us they would take good care of her. They said she had gone crazy when her entire family was killed in the war, but was determined to return to French soil.

We settled General Swain comfortably in the officers' wardroom, while we undertook in the thick smoke screen we had laid to find our landing spot. At this point we committed one of the errors by which our ship earned its nickname of USS *Dopey*. While we were alongside the French transport, Commander Warburton, our flotilla commander, ordered us by blinker to "Go to the head of the bay," where a beachmaster would guide us into shore with signal lights. The skipper called me to the conn. After all my humiliation at his hands, I was flattered to learn that the skipper wanted my advice. "Harlan, you are supposed to be so smart," he said with a sarcastic twist, "what does he mean by 'the head of the bay'?" A pun sprang to my lips, bypassing my brain. "Well, skipper," I answered, "where the head is, there will the mouth be also. I'm not sure what he means, but it logically follows that he must mean the mouth of the bay, the outer end, like a river mouth." "I guess you're right," the skipper said with his best imitation of a chuckle. He set our course toward the outer edge of the bay.

We wandered off through darkness and smoke screen to one side of the mouth of the bay and, seeing no light signal waving us in, then crossed to the other side. We muddled thus for an hour or two. Meanwhile, it was my duty to keep the general happy. Every few minutes he would put his cigar down on his coffee saucer and ask when we were going to land. "Any time now, General," I would say, pointing out the difficulty of piloting through a dense smoke screen, trying to pacify him as one would a restless child. Finally, exasperated at my evasive answers, he demanded to break radio silence. I took him to the radio shack across from the wardroom, and we reached the flotilla commander on the voice radio. The general impatiently grabbed the mike from my hands and shouted, "This is General Swain! I want to speak to the Commander personally. . . . Commander, we've been wandering around in the dark for hours and none of these god-damn incompetents know their ass from their elbow. Can you get us ashore and out of the hands of these morons?"

The commander called me to the mike, explained testily that the head of the bay was at the opposite end from the mouth, and demanded to know who my commanding officer was. I told him, "Lieutenant Flinn, sir." I could hear an explosion at the other end. He demanded to speak to the commanding officer. I told him the skipper couldn't come right then, that he was in the conn trying to find his way through the smoke screen. The commander said, "Tell your commanding officer to report to me in person as soon as you have unloaded your troops." I had to relay this message to the skipper, but fortunately he was too crestfallen to shoot the messenger. Now that we knew where the head of the bay was, we quickly found our beach.

Clark's attention meanwhile was focused on the French babes. "One thing which made me stop and think," he told his diary later, "was the sight of those 50 French gals, carrying a pack of some 60 pounds, walking down those ramps in the darkest of nights, and knowing exactly nothing of what was waiting for them. I guess I'll never forget the funny feeling I had when a little gal took me by the arm and she and I made a hand chain for the other gals coming down the ramps. She clung to my arm as though she didn't intend to turn it loose. The Wacs were afraid of a wet beaching which would have been very difficult for them considering their packs. When I told her that we had hit dry land and there was 'no water' she smiled and said 'Oh bonne,' snapped her shoulders back and left the ramps like a real beachjumper, ready indeed to take her place among the French soldiers. We all had much admiration for these gals, certainly a wonderful example of fighting spirit. I couldn't help wondering how American gals would react to these conditions and I dismissed the thought from my mind with the hopes that they would never have to face such circumstances as these. This beach was in good order, the shouting of French officers offering the only confusing elements."

As soon as we had unloaded our restless passengers, we tied up to the commander's flagship and informed the officer on watch that our skipper was now ready to report to the commander. The commander had apparently hit the sack by then, because we got no reply. After waiting for a humiliating hour, we tried again. The commander finally sent us a curt order, "Get on back to work," as though in carrying out his earlier order we were simply malingering. "Me and my big mouth," I thought, blaming myself for my bad advice to the skipper. Hanging our heads at the head of the bay, we did get back to work. We worked all that night and all the next day. This made three days since we had been to bed, and the entire ship's company were half-dozing at their beaching stations. In all, we carried seven troop loads into the beach in a twenty-four-hour period. Red alerts sounded nearly all day, and planes were frequently overhead. To make matters worse, the wind whipped up and a driving rain pelted us. The lightning of a severe electrical storm made everybody uncomfortable by setting about thirty barrage balloons afire. War was turning out to be purgatory, if not quite hell.

CARL ROWAN

CARL ROWAN, one of the most well-known black journalists in the country, has had a highly successful and varied career. He has authored a nationally syndicated newspaper column for decades, has appeared regularly as a commentator on television and radio, and has written books on the troubles of blacks in the South, the life of Jackie Robinson, and the career of Thurgood Marshall. In addition, under different presidents he was a State Department spokesman, the U.S. ambassador to Finland, and the director of the U.S. Information Agency.

Rowan grew up in poverty in McMinnville, Tennessee. As a freshman attending Tennessee State (a black college), he was called into the dean's office one day in the spring of 1943 and informed he was volunteering to join the Navy. The Navy had asked the college to have students take an exam for admission into the V-12 program, and the dean decided someone had to pass it. One of Rowan's professors chose him. Despite many shortcomings in his education, Rowan passed the test, and later he successfully completed the various phases of his naval training.

Rowan looks back at "those marvelous Navy days" in his 1991 memoir. He describes his V-12 training at Washburn University (where he was 1 black among 334 white sailors), followed by further V-12 training at Oberlin College (where he returned for a BA after the war), and eventually midshipman's school at Fort Schuyler in the Bronx, where the selected excerpt begins. While Rowan encountered some bigotry, the typical discovery of the naval groups in which he served is that if blacks were fully integrated with whites (not set apart by themselves), they could learn a great deal about each other.

from

BREAKING BARRIERS: A MEMOIR

I was greatly relieved to learn that I had done well enough at Oberlin to receive orders to the Naval Reserve Midshipman School at Fort Schuyler in the Bronx. There I met two more black "guinea pigs"— Theodore Chambers and Clarence P. McIntosh. We were pleased that no one tried to put us together, either out of racial animosity or of a misguided notion that we had to be kept from feeling lonely. Everything was strictly alphabetical in the billeting at Fort Schuyler, with the result that the midshipman in the bunk above mine was a white fellow from Pascagoula, Mississippi.

My bunkmate and I commiserated with each other throughout the early, tension-filled days of close order drills, meticulous bunk inspections, almost inhuman tests of our physical endurance, *running* from one class to the next, and frantic cramming for tests in navigation, gunnery, aircraft recognition, and more. Fort Schuyler was tough—so difficult that midshipmen at other schools called it "The Laundry," a reference to the high percentage of commission candidates who were washed out.

It soon became obvious to me that my Mississippi bunkmate was about to flunk out. He had virtually given up studying and sat around munching on Hershey bars during periods when the rest of us were cramming for an important exam. One night, as my company studied gunnery problems, he offered me half a candy bar. I shook my head to decline, then a sixth sense told me that the Mississippian was making a sort of parting gesture.

"Rowan, you know—*hell, everybody knows*—that I'm flunking out of this heah goddamned rat race," he said. "But there's one thing I gotta git off my chest, just sort of one southern boy to another."

Nearby midshipmen stopped studying to roll their eyes uneasily in our direction.

"Just wanna tell you," he continued, "that a little while back, down yonder in Pascagoula, if somebody had told me I'd be sitting beside a Nigra tonight I'da called him a damn liar. If they'da told me I'd be sitting beside one and not minding it—I mean *liking* it, *appreciating* it—I'da knocked somebody's teeth out. But here I am, and before I go I just wanna tell you that, and wish you luck."

As my bunkmate left, so did some of my bitterest feelings about my native South.

My qualifications ratings at Fort Schuyler were all better than "good," and I got scores of 3.5 for general attitude and 3.4 for maturity out of a possible 4.0. I thought it wasn't too bad. Especially considering the competition in my battalion from guys like Howard Baker of Tennessee, who would become Senate majority leader and White House chief of staff. It still ranks as one of the glorious moments of my life when, at age nineteen, I was commissioned as an officer and a gentleman in the United States Navy.

*   *   *

John Stuart Mill wrote that "The despotism of custom is everywhere a standing hindrance to human advancement." Never could this have been more obvious than during the World War II efforts to take racism out of the American military. Blacks had fought with valor in the American Revolution, even though they were less than wanted at first. When George Washington took command of the Continental Army in 1775, he ordered recruiters not to enlist "any stroller, negro, or vagabond." But when Lord Dunmore, the governor of Virginia, started recruiting both free and slave Negroes to fight on the British side, Washington changed his tune. Some five thousand of the three hundred thousand men who fought for United States independence were black, and two were with Washington when he crossed the Delaware on Christmas Day of 1776.

Carl Rowan was made an ensign at age nineteen.
Upon his commissioning, he became one of the first twenty
black Navy officers in American history.

COURTESY OF CARL ROWAN

Still, America's fighting men were racially segregated at this stage
of World War II. Dwight D. Eisenhower had expressed fears about
integrating the Army. One admiral had warned that if black officers
were sent aboard ships, "Race conflict will greatly impair morale
and hurt our war effort."

But by 1944 the National Association for the Advancement of
Colored People (NAACP), the National Urban League, Eleanor
Roosevelt, and a lot of other groups and individuals had laid on
such pressure that the U.S. Air Force could not go on with a segregated group of fighter pilots at Tuskegee, Alabama, the U.S. Army
with a segregated division at Fort Huachuca, Arizona, and the U.S.
Navy with nothing but a bunch of black cooks and mess attendants.
So, under intense pressure, the Navy commissioned directly thirteen Negroes at the Great Lakes Naval Training Center. But the three
of us from Fort Schuyler, along with Ensign Samuel L. Gravely from
the reserve midshipman school at Columbia University, were the

first Negro Navy officers with the training that qualified us for duty anywhere, including on oceangoing vessels.

As we blacks graduated, we had no doubt what the next phase of "Operation Integration" would be. Yet the despotism of custom caused the Navy to move with great caution. I overheard one officer at Fort Schuyler say, "This integration scheme will blow up the first day a Negro officer walks into a ship's wardroom or into an officer's club." So many people doubted the ability of a democracy to change.

So the people in Washington who sensed that integration was inevitable, who believed that it had to come if there was real justification for fighting Hitler, mostly yielded to the cowards. For the first experiments with integration at sea, they picked auxiliary craft—fleet tankers, troop transports—for mixing black signalmen, electricians, boatswain's mates, with white counterparts. The fighting ships were declared off-limits for "social experimentation."

The Navy wanted to be sure, and I now think correctly so, that every Negro officer sent aboard ship where he might be commanding whites would carry with him the best of training and credentials. So I was sent to Great Lakes for fire fighter training, and then to Miami for intense training in antisubmarine warfare, the usages of the latest radar and sonar, the actuality of commanding a vessel at sea.

After almost two years of training, the Navy finally assigned me to a seagoing vessel, an old tanker, the USS *Mattole*, where I was, in less than two months, named assistant first division officer, assistant cargo officer, assistant communications officer, third division officer, and then communications officer. The ship's commanding officer, Commander George H. Chapman Jr., said in my first fitness report, "The officer's services have been satisfactory." To the questions of what duties he recommended me for, he said that ashore I should be "administrator of colored personnel" and that at sea I should be on a "ship manned by colored personnel."

Considering Chapman's mentality, I was gleeful that, after only two months under his command, the Navy transferred me to a newer, faster, bigger tanker, AO-30, the USS *Chemung*. I was given deputy command of the communications division, a group of about thirty-five men of whom only two were Negroes. Several of my white men, including the chief petty officer, were southerners.

What the Navy obviously wanted to know was whether white southerners would take orders from a Negro officer. They did, and they executed them without protest or even the slightest hesitation; but most of the credit here must go to the two commanding officers of the *Chemung*.

As a communications officer, I saw every message coming aboard that ship before the captain saw it. I also rummaged back through the files to read messages from the Bureau of Personnel advising the captain that a Negro officer was coming aboard. There were suggestions that he might want to "prepare the crew." Yet there were no indications that the skipper had done any preparing.

One icy, windy night in the North Atlantic as I stood the midnight to 4:00 A.M. watch, the skipper came to the bridge. For some reason, he uttered the first and last sentence about race that I ever heard him say.

"I guess you've wondered why I never called a meeting of the crew to explain that you were coming, or anything like that," he said. "Well, I'm a Navy man, and we're in a war. To me, it's that stripe that counts—and the training and leadership that it's supposed to symbolize. I didn't want any member of my crew to think you were any different from any other officer coming aboard; therefore I figured I'd better not call any meetings about you that I didn't call for other officers."

I appreciated that remark, for without any do-gooder lectures, the skipper had shown an acute understanding of what I—and other Negroes—wanted: no special restrictions and no special favors; just the right to rise or fall on merit.

I felt that I had run for six touchdowns and been named to the all-American team when Commander C. K. Holzer showed me his report to Washington saying: "This officer is colored, but has been outstanding in preventing any adverse criticism of this fact, by his performance of duty. . . . This officer has demonstrated a marked willingness to learn his assigned duties, and a good perception of his particular tasks. With more experience he will be an able communications officer. Recommend promotion."

Having heard other crew members (white) bitch vehemently about Holzer, I felt this was high praise. Weeks later they told me with glee that Holzer was leaving and that we were getting "a real Navy man" as a skipper. I wasn't rejoicing, because I learned that the new commanding officer was to be Philip H. Ross, an old-line graduate of the Naval Academy. I had serious misgivings about what he would think of having a racial "experiment" taking place on his ship.

But as far as I could determine, Ross never paid official, public, or private notice of the fact that I was a Negro. We were carrying high-octane gasoline for the refueling of aircraft carriers, and he simply took it for granted that I knew what I was doing during refueling and that I would know what I was doing while standing watch as officer of the deck. It occurred to me that he probably lost a hell of a lot more sleep over the fact that I was only nineteen than he did over the color of my skin. I was happy to see that in his report to Washington he said he would be "pleased" to have me under his command anywhere, and if only 30 percent of those under him were to be promoted, I should be one of them. He commented: "This officer has performed his assigned duties diligently and efficiently. He has manifested a marked willingness to learn."

It would be nice if I could report here some heroic roles in naval battles that earned me a chestful of ribbons. But policy decided at the presidential level still dictated that blacks were not to be assigned to combat ships until it became clear that their presence did not endanger the morale of white fighting men. So the closest I came to getting killed was during those days near the end of the war in Europe when we were hauling gasoline into the North Atlantic. I was always wary of slipping and tumbling into the sea during the very delicate operations of refueling a huge aircraft carrier, and we worried like hell about being hit by a torpedo from a German submarine, but I have since concluded that by the time of my most dangerous seagoing, the Nazi subs had mostly been chased away. . . .

*   *   *

I have not told the full story of those marvelous Navy days. I have slipped over some things and people that were very important to my growing up. A man is not made by algebra tests, calisthenics, and North Atlantic deck watches alone. Racial slurs, commendations for ignoring them, perfect refuelings at sea—these are at the fringes of life.

Boys of eighteen become men-going-on-twenty-eight according to the women they meet. Because of my unique spot in the Navy, I met more than my share. I had not understood why the girls in McMinnville were soldier crazy when the GIs from Camp Forrest rolled into town in their jeeps. But I learned the magic of having one Topeka girl pass the word to others that "There's a colored guy in that V-12 unit at Washburn!" In New York, that midshipman's uniform attracted women more than a Swiss bank account ever could. Lord, how the gold braid of an ensign wowed girls!

I was a male chauvinist in those days, exploiting my midshipman's and ensign's uniforms from the Stagedoor Canteen to Chicago, to Miami, to Norfolk. I knew that most Americans had never seen a black Navy officer, so I strutted in my uniforms like a peacock. I met some women who wanted to pluck me feather-by-feather.

My game produced no serious fumbles until the *Chemung* pulled into Norfolk on a summer day in 1944. I didn't know anyone in Norfolk, so I hired a taxi and asked the driver to "take me to a neighborhood where I can meet some nice people."

We reached an area that I remember as very nice. I asked the driver to let me out, paid him, and began to stroll in a black neighborhood of houses that were most imposing by the standard of my daddy's domicile—houses with neat lawns and pretty shrubs and flowers around them.

I was wearing my Navy whites on which that stripe of gold braid was matched only by the splendiferous cap of a Navy officer. I walked along until I spotted a marvelously sculptured young woman trimming a hedge. I went over and introduced myself.

We chatted, and I got the sense for the first time since I joined the Navy that it was not my uniform that impressed a woman. This woman acted as though she had not seen the Navy whites, the gold braid, the cap, but that she was interested only in me. She had just gotten a math degree and planned to do postgraduate study.

She went inside and cleared it with her parents, then invited me to join them for dinner. I went in and came to know a part of the rising black middle class that did not exist in the McMinnvilles of America. Her daddy worked at the Norfolk Navy Yard, so he in his way, like me, was a beneficiary of a god-awful war.

After dinner, I learned that my accidental date played the piano and sang beautifully. We joined in a couple of tunes to her parents' delight. I relished doing a little teaser that I now sing to my grand-daughters:

Aw, gimme a little kiss, Will ya, huh?
And I'll give it right back to you.

Thus began a torrid and beautiful romance—so hot that it wouldn't cool down even when at age twenty, with no college degree and no certain notion of a future, I asked her to marry me. And, still impoverished, bought her a costly engagement ring.

NAVAL HISTORY
AND RESEARCH

SAMUEL ELIOT MORISON

S AMUEL ELIOT MORISON was a military veteran and distinguished historian long before he saw naval duty. Born in
1887, Morison was an infantryman in the U.S. Army in World War
I and a professor at Harvard by 1922. In 1942 he applied for a commission in the Navy, but he was initially rejected on account of his
age. Morison then changed tack, writing Secretary of the Navy Frank
Knox to propose that he be brought on active duty as the Navy's wartime historian. Finding Knox unconvinced, Morison went over his
head to the president. President Franklin Roosevelt may already
have been considering Morison, for he had reportedly just finished
Morison's biography of Christopher Columbus, *Admiral of the
Ocean Sea* (which Morison had sent him months earlier), and was
impressed by Morison's sailing Columbus's routes as a part of his
historical method. Upon Roosevelt expressing his wishes to Frank
Knox, the Navy's objections evaporated, and Morison was brought
on active duty in the Naval Reserve as a lieutenant commander.

Although no one has yet written the full, rich history of Morison
and the Navy, Morison tells a bit of that story and outlines a part of
his own approach to "participatory history" in the attached essay.
Basically, the Navy gave him license to go where he thought best,
serve with combat forces or retire to write, and make his own judg-

ments about the major actions of the war. Assisted in his task by many naval authorities (Admiral Nimitz was especially helpful), Morison was present during a wide variety of combat operations in both the Atlantic and the Pacific. He formed his own opinions of all the major naval combat decisions of the war, applauding some and blaming others, and naturally offending some senior naval figures (like Bull Halsey) in the process. He also had to defend himself against newspaper editors and professional historians, some of whom regarded him as taking the official Navy position (about Pearl Harbor, for example), rather than remaining an objective historian. Morison weathered all these attacks. It took twenty years, but the result of his project was the extensive, authoritative, and highly readable *History of United States Naval Operations in World War II.*

Morison died in 1976. On 11 October 1980, the Navy christened its newest guided missile frigate the USS *Samuel Eliot Morison* (FFG-13).

The attached piece is a major portion of an address Morison delivered upon receiving the Balzan Award at the Quirinal (in Rome) in 1963.

from

VISTAS OF HISTORY

From earliest youth I have been an amateur sailor. My love of the sea, possibly inherited from remote ancestors in the old China trade, more likely acquired in the cool waters off the coast of New England, is so deep, almost passionate, that after my doctoral dissertation I turned to writing on aspects of history in which the ocean provides both basis and background. Hence my *Maritime History of Massachusetts,* my biographies of Columbus and John Paul Jones, and, above all, my history of the United States Navy in World War II.

In this choice I have enjoyed a certain advantage over historians such as Fortescue and Churchill, even over Ferrero and Parkman, who have written about land battles, forest forays, and military campaigns. For they, when visiting scenes of conflict, find the terrain so changed as to be almost unrecognizable; the battlefields of Waterloo and Gettysburg are so covered with monuments as to resemble great cemeteries; and those who would write on the development of the American Far West find the open cattle range cut up into farms, crisscrossed by railways and the American equivalent of the Italian *autostrada*. Imperial Rome, too, is o'erlaid by medieval Rome, Renaissance Rome, and now confused by the steel, concrete, and glass of modern Rome. (But I must say a word of praise to the city fathers who have made stringent regulations against altering the façades of ancient buildings, so that the essential appearance of Renaissance Rome is preserved.) In the last fifty years the bulldozer has done more to change the face of that part of the world inhabited by Europeans than any earlier device of man; and the bulldozer, followed by the skyscraper, has even invaded Asia and Africa. Henry Thoreau's Walden, the lake where he sojourned in Concord, Massachusetts, was little affected by the railway that traversed one of its shores in his day; then in 1960 a stupid, insensitive government, by sending bulldozers to create a recreation area, had almost ruined the scenery that Emerson and Thoreau loved, when a cry of anguish from America, Europe, and India halted the desecration.

But the ocean, like the starry firmament that hangs over it, changeth not. Thus, when I came to write a biography of Christopher Columbus, I dealt with elements of sea, sky, and stars unchanged since his day. My knowledge of sailing enabled me to appreciate Columbus's problems and to evaluate his navigation. By following his voyages in a sailing vessel, I could accurately identify his landfalls, and the islands, bays, and promontories that he "discovered for Castile and for León," as his motto reads. Columbus was not only a great sailor; he enjoyed every moment of his voyages except when there was foul weather or threatened mutiny. On one occasion in his sea journal he remarks: *Que era plazer grande el gusto de las mañanas*—"What a great delight was the savor of the mornings!" That rings a bell in the heart of every sailor. For there is no beauty like that of dawn at sea, running before a trade wind; the paling stars, the rising sun kindling both clouds and sails rose color, the smell of dew drying on a wooden deck. Columbus was unique

Samuel Eliot Morison and his small staff relax aboard
Morison's boat the Navaho in Seal Cove, Maine, in August 1943.
Behind the skipper is Donald R. Martin, a yeoman second class; in front
of him sits Henry Salomon Jr., then a lieutenant (junior grade).
COURTESY OF ROGER B. SALOMON

among early navigators in appreciating the beauty of seascapes and
landscapes. The atmosphere on his first ocean crossing, he said, was
"like April in Andalusia—the only thing wanting was the song of
the nightingale."

"Romantic history!" some readers will exclaim, to which I reply:
"No tags, please; read me first!" As in the world of poetry, so in the
world of history, "romantic" has become a pejorative word. In several dull books about history and historians that have appeared of
late, Parkman has been dismissed as a romantic, one who saw nothing in history but drama. Now, if Parkman be a romantic, I shall be

proud to be painted with the same brush; but Parkman saw plenty of things in history besides drama. In his *Old Regime in Canada* he had chapters on Marriage and Population, Trade and Industry, Priests and People, Morals and Manners, that are models of social and economic history. The story of Columbus is dramatic indeed; but besides relating the story of his voyages I made a point of describing how a ship was sailed and navigated, and how people spent their time at sea on voyages that might extend into months. Romance is a part of life, and it will be a sorry era that yields no drama to the questing historian. . . .

* * *

My *Admiral of the Ocean Sea,* the product of several voyages under sail, and of years of study in the documentary sources, led directly into writing the history of the United States Navy in World War II. President Franklin D. Roosevelt, after reading possibly a few pages of the *Admiral,* accepted my proposal to be the Navy's historian, based on actual participation. This naval history, *une oeuvre de longue haleine,* of which the fifteenth and last volume was completed twenty years later, and a one-volume epitome in 1963, is generally regarded as my most important work. It was certainly the greatest challenge to me as an historian. It required not only a background in modern naval technique, but knowledge of infinite detail and the necessity to make a clear and coherent narrative out of a multitude of conflicting sources. It comprised a number of very controversial subjects, charged with emotion, such as responsibility for the calamitous surprise at Pearl Harbor, the Navy's unpreparedness to meet the assault of enemy submarines, and its bad thrashing at the hands of the Japanese off Savo Island.

At the beginning of my work on naval history, I laid down certain conditions which the Navy accepted and has loyally respected: (1) I was not to be censored, or denied free criticism of officers; but on my part I agreed to respect security regulations, such as not divulging the nature of secret weapons, or printing coded messages literally. (2) I should not be required to publish until after the war was over, when I would have opportunity to study naval records on the enemy side, since military history written from one side only is worthless—the British Admiralty had to recall Sir Julian Corbett's volume on the Battle of Jutland, and employ Henry Newbolt to write another, because Sir Julian had ignored the German sources. (3) I could rove the seven seas in U.S. naval vessels, or work at naval bases, as seemed best. The secretary of the Navy urged me to build up a staff, as most people in government service feel they must do, to make themselves important—"Parkinson's Law." But this offer I declined, having observed what happened to one of my masters, Robert M. Johnston. Appointed U.S. Army Historian in World War I, Johnston exhausted his strength and energy bucking the Army to build up a staff, and died at the age of fifty-three without accomplishing his mission. But I did have attached to me for short periods during the war several of my former pupils who were already in the Navy; and they, being familiar with my methods, participated in operations on one side of the world while I was on the other, and made extensive notes of their observations that were most helpful.

As my position in the Navy was unprecedented, I had to move warily and gingerly in order to obtain cooperation from those who were doing the fighting. Amusingly enough, their initial suspicions of a "long-haired professor in uniform" were dissolved by perusal of my *Admiral of the Ocean Sea,* which told them that I was a sailor before I became a professor, and thus exorcised the academic curse. So, thanks to Columbus, the Navy accepted me; and with many of its members I made warm friendships, which even survived what I felt obliged to write about some of their mistakes. But there were not many mistakes to chronicle. In general, our naval officers were highly competent, both in planning an amphibious operation which, if properly done, goes like clockwork, and in making quick decisions in a fluid tactical situation, the test of a great commander by land or by sea. Most of the mistakes made during the war by American naval officers were due to excess of zeal in coming to grips with the enemy, which, as Lord Nelson once remarked, is a pardonable kind of error.

In general, my method was to participate in an operation, then settle down at some naval base, read all the action reports I could obtain, write a preliminary draft, file it for future use, and then shove off on another operation. For instance, I first went to sea in the summer of 1942 in a destroyer, escorting a fast convoy from New York to the Clyde and back. After that firsthand view of this highly specialized branch of naval warfare, I joined the antisubmarine warfare unit of the Atlantic Fleet, studied the subject intensively, visited the principal training centers for antisubmarine officers and vessels, sailed on a patrol off the Atlantic coast, sent my first assistant on an air antisubmarine patrol, talked to hundreds of officers, and before the end of 1943 had written the first draft of what later became my Volume I, *The Battle of the Atlantic.* Next, cruiser *Brooklyn* took me into Operation "Torch," the invasion of North Africa by Anglo-American forces in November 1942, and returned me to Amphibious Forces headquarters at Norfolk to write about it; this eventually became Volume II. In the spring of 1943 I went to the Pacific, in time to see the last phases of the Guadalcanal campaign; and so on, to the end.

One thing learned from this experience was the importance of oral testimony and visual observation. My history teachers tended to discount these and to put the document above everything as an historical source. In remote periods of history one naturally has to depend on inscriptions, coins, ruins, potsherds, and other artifacts for one's sources, and is lucky to have a papyrus by a contemporary. But the academic discipline of modern history has, I believe, placed too much stress on the very numerous—in most cases too numerous—documents that exist, forgetting that they are not facts in themselves but symbols of facts; that everything in a document has passed through a human brain. So why is a document superior to evidence from the eyes, ears, and mind of an actual participant? A human trait which naval officers share with others is to rationalize decisions and maneuvers when they write action reports; to imagine that they anticipated all probable contingencies and directed the battle just as it had been planned. But for a participating historian, it often became clear that things did not run as smoothly as they appeared in the official account, and that a victorious issue of an operation owed more to the mistakes of the enemy than to our own cleverness.

On the other hand, I learned that visual impressions must be checked by documents. A good instance may be adduced by the night Battle of Kolombangara in the Solomons in July 1943. On the bridge with Admiral Ainsworth, I distinctly saw three Japanese warships exploding and burning. So we reported it; and the admiral was awarded with the Navy Cross for his victory. But, after the war, checking from Japanese records, we were disappointed to find that we sank only one enemy ship. Our eyes had deceived us. Our gunfire had whipsawed the Japanese flagship so that her two halves looked like two vessels; and what the third was, we cannot explain, unless it was another Japanese ship firing so fast and furiously that in the darkness her gun flashes looked like explosions.

After the war was over, I concentrated on rewriting my initial drafts in the light of more oral testimony, the numerous documents from our side, and those of the enemy. It took seventeen more years to complete the job. For some actions like the Battle of the Philippine Sea in June 1944 and the Battle for Leyte Gulf in October, there were six-foot stacks of reports by captains, admirals, air group commanders on carriers, and others; together with an enormous footage of documents from enemy sources that had to be translated for me and worked through carefully, in order to ascertain what actually did happen. In this work I was greatly assisted by two professional naval officers, Capt. James C. Shaw and Rear Adm. Bern Anderson, who made up my staff after the war; and by two others, Lt. Roger Pineau and Lt. Philip Lundeberg, who were, respectively, my Japanese and German language experts. Lundeberg had to work through all the patrol reports of the German U-boats to discover who sank what, when, and why. Expert assistance also came from Rear Adm. Richard W. Bates, who wrote, for circulation only in the Navy, blow-by-blow accounts of three great naval battles in the Pacific.

At the same time, I visited every scene of action in which I had not personally participated; and in these visits enjoyed the full cooperation of foreign navies, and of my beloved wife. During the summer of 1953, numerous Sicilians dwelling near the coast were puzzled by the movements of a certain U.S. Navy motorcar driven by a stalwart chief petty officer, with an Italian-speaking naval lieutenant next to him. In the rear they observed a young, beautiful, and auburn-haired American lady, and her historian husband dimly visible behind enormous binoculars. Mrs. Morison and the lieutenant, who between them could cope with any Sicilian dialect, frequently inquired the way to obscure beaches in which no tourist had ever shown interest. Whenever a crowd gathered, as it did at every stop, we interrogated all and sundry about the events of 1943. There was great excitement when our party debouched on a quay where Commandante Boido's smart *motosilurante* took us on board and put to sea in order to enable the historian to approach landing beaches from the proper direction. A few natives indicated by the Communist closed fist that they suspected something sinister; but the greater part were satisfied with the explanation that we were working for a navy that seems to have left only pleasant memories in Sicily. We shall never forget the kindness and courtesy with which we were everywhere received on Italian soil.

Besides helping me in this investigation, one of many that we made together, my wife has contributed to the quality of my work by listening to my presentation and criticizing it from the viewpoint of the nonmilitary reader. You may be amused to learn that she has even played censor. When describing the tense, hushed mystery of a night amphibious assault on a darkened enemy shore, not knowing what might happen next, I proposed to quote that beautiful line from *La Traviata:*

Misterioso, misterioso altero.

But she wouldn't let me; for, said she: "That means the mystery of love—don't desecrate it by applying it to war!"

HENRY SALOMON JR.

WHEN SAMUEL Eliot Morison began his "participatory history" of World War II for the Navy, he purposely took no assistants—but soon he found he needed one or two. Henry Salomon Jr. (universally known as "Peter"), who had been a student of Morison's at Harvard in the late 1930s, enlisted in the Navy as a yeoman in 1942 and was assigned to public affairs work in Washington, D.C. One day he spoke to Morison on the street, and Morison asked if Salomon would like to work for him. Morison got the Navy to send Salomon to the officer training program in Newport, and Salomon began work as Morison's "principal assistant" in 1943. He continued working with Morison well after the war.

Salomon eventually conceived an idea for an extensive television documentary of World War II using genuine war films from Allied and former enemy sources (especially U.S. Navy footage), the script for which he would write himself, basing it upon his extensive naval history work. Supported by his one-time Harvard roommate, Robert W. Sarnoff (then NBC's manager of unit operations), Salomon approached NBC with this idea. Although NBC was dubious that the American public would be interested in the project, Salomon by sheer determination eventually convinced the network to take it on. Salomon was to become the producer and cowriter (with Richard Hanser) of one of the most successful film documentary series ever: the award-winning *Victory at Sea.* The twenty-six half-hour segments first appeared on Sunday afternoons in 1952.

Salomon went on to produce the successful *Project Twenty* for the same network. In 1957 he was made head of NBC's special projects unit, which was to create a wide variety of special interest programs; Salomon died, however, in February 1958.

A rift eventually grew between Morison and Salomon, partly because Morison did not believe he had been given sufficient credit in the introduction to *Victory at Sea*—though one should note that some of Morison's naval assistants believed they had not been given enough credit for their own contributions to his naval history. In 1947, however, when Salomon wrote his account of the Morison history project for the *Harvard Alumni Bulletin* (from which the following excerpt is taken), he was still moved by the wonder and novelty of the experience.

from

"HISTORIAN AT WAR: CHRONICLING AMERICAN NAVAL OPERATIONS IN WORLD WAR II"

"Some men enter the Navy through the hawse hole, as enlisted men, but I entered through the cabin window," says Morison. He first wet his feet in the Navy in USS *Guinevere,* one of the former yachts that were trying so hard to catch up with German submarines around our Atlantic ports. Finding that the *Guinevere* had frequently sighted Mount Desert on her Bay of Fundy patrol but never touched at a port, Morison "sold" her skipper the idea of showing the flag in Maine waters. They were given a great reception at Matinicus Island, and were furnished with enough lobsters for all hands. Morison himself timed the bilin' of 'em, and good fun was had by all—except the pharmacist's mate from Missouri who had never tasted lobster and discovered the hard way that he was allergic to it.

Lt. Comdr. Henry Salomon Jr. *(seated)* sorts through photographs for
Morison's history project with Lt. Albert Harkness Jr.
at the Naval War College in January 1947.
COURTESY OF *THE PROVIDENCE JOURNAL* (PHOTO BY EDWARD C. HANSON)

Although this trip afforded Morison a little Navy indoctrination,
he was no stranger to the sea. He had spent many summers sailing
off the New England coast, had cruised in the Aegean with Alexander Forbes and crossed the Atlantic twice under sail with Paul
Hammond and others, when retracing the track of Christopher Columbus, Admiral of the Ocean Sea. So it did not take him long to
milk the Ship Lane Patrol of all it had to offer, especially since no
U-boat was so obliging as to show itself.

His next voyage was right in the groove of regular Navy work.
He shoved off on convoy duty with Capt. John B. Heffernan, commander Destroyer Squadron 13, and commodore of one of the escort
groups that convoyed American troops to the United Kingdom. On

board Captain Heffernan's flagship, USS *Buck,* Morison had his first real look at the war. In the captain's conversations in his tiny cabin he learned more about the Navy than any indoctrination course could possibly have afforded; and in the operation itself he had ample opportunity to acquire firsthand knowledge of antisubmarine warfare. The *Buck* spent five days in Scottish waters before starting home, time enough for Morison to make valuable contacts at the Admiralty in London.

*   *   *

Now that his feet were really wet, Morison was eager to get out into a slugging match. He did not have to wait long. On the invitation of Capt. Francis C. Denebrink, he joined the ship's company in the light cruiser *Brooklyn* at Norfolk in October 1942. A few days later she set sail for Casablanca to participate in Operation "Torch," the greatest amphibious expedition in history up to that time. Although subsequent campaigns overshadowed the North African landings, this was the first major operation in which Professor Morison or any of his staff participated, for the ultimate benefit of the naval history. For this followed Morison's theory that if one is to write history, one must relive it (as he did on the Harvard Columbus Expedition) or, still better, live it, as in this war. He is fond of a quotation that an English poet puts into the mouth of Ovid:

> Dream dreams, then write them. Aye!
>   but live them, too.

Hence he always tried to have one of us participate in every operation of major importance. There is, so far as I know, only one precedent for writing a history of warfare in this manner. But even Thucydides did not obtain an Athenian naval commission in the Peloponnesian War with the idea of writing the history of it. Anyway, Morison did just that and it was his great admiration for Thucydides that gave him the original thought of writing the naval history of World War II that way.

On Operation "Torch," Morison had his baptism of fire, in the naval battle off Casablanca; and while he admits he was plenty scared as the French shells began dropping all around, he insists that he enjoyed every minute. And he made more naval friends on board the *Brooklyn*. Captain Denebrink wrote this commendation of him after the action:

> By his alert, active, analytical work in recording the events of the action; by his keen fighting spirit which manifested itself throughout; and by his calm manner he contributed to the general and overall performance of the vessel. He volunteered for the trip when he learned there might be action. His desire to be in the fighting was gratified. He contributed to the success. He was as much a member of the *Brooklyn* crew as any officer or man regularly assigned.

Morison returned to Washington at the end of 1942, repaired to the headquarters of Admiral Hewitt's Amphibious Force Atlantic Fleet at the Hotel Nansemond, Norfolk, and immediately started writing the first draft of the volume which has just been published. Meanwhile, I had joined the Navy and had been assigned to the Office of Public Relations in Washington. Having known the skipper since my undergraduate days at Harvard, I saw him occasionally during his fleeting trips to the capital. He needed an assistant and offered me the job, an opportunity I accepted almost before the words were out of his mouth. So, early in 1943 I became "the staff," and shortly we were able to give that term further substance by acquiring the services of Donald R. Martin, who had distinguished himself as the only yeoman in Norfolk able to read Morison's handwriting. He is still working with us, as chief yeoman; and I am certain that no two officers in the Navy were as fortunate as we in having such a man assigned to them.

In the spring of 1943 Morison tossed "Torch" (as we called *Operations in North African Waters*) to me, while he sought new fields to study. There were plenty of them in those days, especially in the Solomon Islands. That is just where the skipper headed. This voyage took him first to Adm. C. W. Nimitz's headquarters in Pearl Harbor. This was the beginning of a friendship which for Morison, and later for me, has lasted right up to the present. From then on we always had a berth to anchor in. For all intents and purposes

"Cincpac-Cincpoa" at Makalapa, Oahu, was our headquarters through the rest of the war. No matter where else we went, we always returned to Pearl Harbor. Admiral Nimitz's interest in the history and his genuine hospitality during the toughest days of the war are things that an historian is likely to remember long after he has forgotten many of the facts about which he is writing.

Morison's journeyings during the spring and summer of 1943 took him through all combat areas of the South and Southwest Pacific, and as far afield as Australia. Much of his time was spent at Admiral Halsey's headquarters in Nouméa; a couple of weeks were spent at Guadalcanal, still under Japanese air attack; and a week or two at the headquarters of genial Vice Adm. A. W. Fitch in Espíritu Santo. There he met Rear Adm. W. L. Ainsworth. Common membership in the Society of the Cincinnati emboldened Morison to ask Ainsworth to take him "for a ride up The Slot," as that body of water between the two lines of Solomon [Islands] from Guadalcanal to Bougainville was called by the Navy. In fact, he made three trips up The Slot with Adm. "Pug" Ainsworth in the light cruiser *Honolulu*. During the third, on the night of July 12–13, a full-fledged night action developed with a Japanese surface force, which Morison later persuaded the Navy Department to call the Battle of Kolombangara. That night the *Honolulu* caught a fish in her bows, which inflicted no casualties but was close enough to satisfy even the most inquisitive historian.

By the time Morison had returned to Washington, "Torch" had been put on ice; not much more could be done to it for the moment. We turned our attention to antisubmarine warfare, and the next few months saw the first draft of that complex subject down in black and white. During this period we worked at the Antisubmarine Warfare Unit in Boston, then the nerve center of our fight against the U-boats.

One October day in 1943, as we were poring over reports on submarine activity in the Atlantic, Morison received a letter from Admiral Ainsworth, then at San Diego. The skipper inferred from the contents that it might be a smart thing to pack his duffle bag and shove off for California. So it turned out. "Pug" Ainsworth had him transferred to the heavy cruiser *Baltimore,* outward bound on her first war cruise, and this voyage landed him right in the middle of the Gilbert Islands operation. The *Baltimore* supported the landing on Makin, but she was alongside the *Liscome Bay* when that gallant flattop was torpedoed, and she took part in the famous early December carrier strike on Kwajalein.

When Morison went to the Gilberts, he arranged for me to visit our Atlantic bases of importance in antisubmarine warfare. This voyage took me all the way from Halifax south through the Caribbean to Recife and Rio, enabling me to bring our account of "Batlant" up to date, including the activities of Vice Adm. J. H. Ingram's Fourth Fleet in the South Atlantic.

During the Gilbert Islands operation, Morison met Capt. D. W. Loomis, a transport division commodore. The Marshalls were on the books for the end of January, and although it was not possible for Morison to participate in that campaign, he arranged with Commodore Loomis that I should go instead. Morison and I met in Boston at Christmas time and he broke the news of my impending initiation into the Pacific phase of the war. There was just enough time to have my laundry done, and wish my family a Happy New Year, before I had to leave for Pearl Harbor.

When I departed, *The Battle of the Atlantic* was carefully placed in Morison's hands; it was his turn to bat on that volume. So during the first three months of 1944 he completed the first draft of that volume, while I participated first in the landing at Kwajalein and then Eniwetok. With these operations under my belt, I rushed back to Pearl Harbor to get them down on paper. The skipper joined me there late in March, and for the next two months we ground out first drafts of the Gilberts and the Marshall Islands campaigns, setting forth our impressions, talking with as many people as we could lay our hands on, and grabbing off the hundreds of action reports as they poured into Admiral Nimitz's headquarters.

* * *

The spring of 1944 was our most active time so far as covering the war was concerned. Morison prepared to participate in the Marianas campaign; I headed for Bougainville, the Admiralty Islands,

New Guinea, and Australia, "breaking the Bismarcks barrier"; and there were some big operations scheduled to come off in Europe. In February we were fortunate in acquiring the aid of Lt. (jg) Henry D. Reck, USNR, a Dartmouth graduate who had studied under Morison in the Harvard Graduate School and had taken his MA in 1936. He had been in the Navy since 1940 and came to the naval history from staff duty with a destroyer squadron. Captain Morison immediately sent him over to the Mediterranean, where he reported for duty on the staff of Vice Adm. H. K. Hewitt, commander Eighth Fleet. From Admiral Hewitt's headquarters in Algiers, Reck went to Anzio and participated in the buildup of that famous, bloody beachhead. He then visited all U.S. naval bases in Corsica, Sardinia, and Sicily, besides studying the scenes of amphibious operations at Salerno, Oran, and Arzeu. When the long-delayed invasion of southern France took place on 15 August 1944, Reck was on the staff of Rear Adm. L. A. Davidson on the heavy cruiser *Augusta,* which participated in gunfire-support missions of the assault and follow-up. Reck joined the shore party that took the famous Chateau d'If off Marseille, and owing to his knowledge of German, he was detailed by the commanding officer to interrogate German prisoners.

It will be recalled that it was in June 1944 that the Normandy operation finally came off. Morison, Reck, and I had already stretched ourselves as far as three men could be stretched, and yet Normandy had to be covered for the naval history. This problem was solved by "borrowing" Lt. George M. Elsey, USNR, from the White House, where he was on duty with the naval aide to the president. Elsey, a Princeton graduate who had also studied under Morison and had taken his Master's degree at Harvard, went to England a couple of months ahead of the invasion and not only participated in the final stages of the planning, but covered our naval bases and training camps throughout the United Kingdom. He joined Rear Adm. J. L. Hall's staff on board the amphibious command ship *Ancon,* and landed on Omaha Beach on D-Day, 6 June 1944. During the next six weeks he shuttled back and forth across the English Channel with the follow-up forces, and studied the scenes of the amphibious assault.

Both Elsey and Reck returned to the United States in the fall of 1944. Elsey had to return to his duties at the White House, but Reck started right in on the first draft of Volume VIII, *Mediterranean Operations.*

Meanwhile, Morison had taken part in the Saipan and Guam landings on board the USS *Honolulu,* again attached to the staff of his friend, Admiral Ainsworth; and in August we met once again in Pearl Harbor. While Morison returned to Washington to complete Volume VI, *Breaking the Bismarcks Barrier,* and to start Volume VIII, *New Guinea and the Marianas,* I joined the staff of Vice Adm. T. S. Wilkinson, commander Third Amphibious Force.

When I reported on board the admiral's flagship, the amphibious command ship *Mount Olympus,* in early September, all hands thought we were bound for the invasion of Yap: we did not know yet the results of the quickest, most radical change of plans made during the war. Next day I went ashore, and Admiral Nimitz said, "Salomon, this time you'll get all you bargained for," and his chief of staff added, "We'll see you in Manila." Yap had been canceled and "III Phib" was bound for Leyte.

It was fortunate indeed that circumstances made it possible for one of us to be there. The invasion of Leyte was important enough; but the Battle for Leyte Gulf (a name which we persuaded the Navy to adopt in place of the misleading "Second Battle of the Philippine Sea") was one of the highlights of the war; and, in my humble opinion, the greatest naval battle of all time. While Admiral Wilkinson's command ship did not participate in the shooting, it was one of the nerve centers of the battle, and my presence there enabled me to visit numerous combat ships before their guns were cold and obtain valuable first impressions from the participants.

Admiral Wilkinson, an old schoolmate of Morison's at St. Paul's, who twice won there the top classical scholarship, for which Morison was only a runner-up, took a great personal interest in the naval history; and when we returned to Hollandia in New Guinea after the Leyte operation, he took me with him to Seventh Fleet headquarters at Lake Sentani. There I not only began to write the first draft of the Leyte Operation as the reports came in, but sat in on the planning phase of the Luzon campaign. The high privilege of per-

sonal contact with the late Admiral Wilkinson and the other great
military and naval leaders responsible for liberating the Philippines
will be reflected in our Volumes XI and XII.

* * *

The following winter, 1944–45, Morison crossed the Atlantic again,
this time on the staff of Capt. W. A. P. Martin, commander of an escort
group in the famous Coast Guard cutter *Campbell,* in order to catch
up with antisubmarine warfare, and to study the landing beaches
in Italy and southern France. After a brief stay in Washington, he
headed for the Pacific once more, and I met him in Pearl Harbor
after returning from Lingayen Gulf. We took a couple of deep breaths,
spent a few days on those marvelous Hawaiian beaches, and set out
for Okinawa. We missed the fight for Iwo Jima, but we visited that
island while the Japs were still being mopped up, studied the terrain, and talked with many of the Marines who were responsible
for that signal if costly victory.

Like Harvard, the Navy becomes a small place if you stay around
long enough. During the Okinawa operation in 1945, Morison found
himself back with Capt. John B. Heffernan, this time on board a battleship, USS *Tennessee,* flagship of Rear Adm. M. L. Deyo, now
commandant of the First Naval District in Boston. Morison was able
to observe the fire-support phase of that important operation, while
I covered the amphibious aspect in Rear Adm. L. F. Reifsnider's flagship, USS *Panamint,* which was also the headquarters of Lt. Gen.
R. S. Geiger, USMC, commander Third Amphibious Corps. One of
the advantages of serving in an amphibious command ship is the
presence of an Army or Marine Corps general staff. This enables an
observer to get the complete story of an operation.

The Okinawa campaign was the only one in which both Morison
and I participated, and we made the most of it. We met frequently,
both afloat and ashore, comparing notes on the spot. A Jap suicide
plane connected with the *Tennessee,* missing Admiral Deyo, Captain Heffernan, and Morison by only a few feet. Many others were
not so lucky. It was a long, drawn-out, tense, and tough operation
for both Navy and ground forces, yet humor occasionally breaks
through the bleak hours of war.

Morison stands between the executive officer and the first lieutenant
of the Coast Guard cutter *Campbell* late in 1944.

HARVARD UNIVERSITY ARCHIVES/COURTESY OF EMILY M. BECK

About two days after the Okinawa D-Day, Morison, Capt. E. M.
("Judge") Eller, now director of Public Information for the Navy
Department, and I went ashore to observe the results of the preliminary bombardment. We were examining some houses in a deserted
village when Morison picked up an old teacup and, with a twinkle
in his eye, remarked, "This must be a bit of old Ming." "Sure," said
Captain Eller, "Ming left three days ago!"

On another occasion Eller, Morison, and I arranged to have a picnic on the beach. We thought we might liven up our lunch of thick
spam sandwiches with some cocktails. I got hold of some fruit juice,
Eller provided the sandwiches, and Morison contributed a pint of
Scotch, a parting present from the famous commodore "Scrappy"
Kessing at Ulithi. With this liquid, more precious than gold, "yea
than much fine gold, sweeter also than honey and the honeycomb,"
the picnic was a great success. We came to the conclusion that the
only material assets an historian needs in the field are a clean pair
of socks, a couple of notebooks and pencil, and a bottle of whiskey.

C. VANN WOODWARD

C. VANN WOODWARD is one of the twentieth century's preeminent scholars in the history of the American South; one of
his principal subjects has been race relations in the southern states
since the Civil War. Having begun his academic career in the early
1930s, he was still writing more than fifty years later, although he
had retired from Yale (as Sterling Professor of History) in 1977.
Important books of his include *Tom Watson: Agrarian Rebel,
Origins of the New South: 1877–1913,* and *The Strange Career of
Jim Crow.* His edition of the diaries of the Confederate figure Mary
Chestnut won the Pulitzer Prize for History in 1982.

Although Woodward's books have dealt primarily with the South,
he also has been the general editor for the *Oxford History of the
United States.* And for three years during World War II he found
himself dealing with a quite different subject.

At the Battle for Leyte Gulf, the aggressive American admiral Bull
Halsey was fooled into chasing after a decoy Japanese carrier force
with all his battleships and carriers, leaving the main American
amphibious force unprotected. A few hours later, a heavy Japanese
force under Adm. Takeo Kurita approached. But finding his heavy
battleship force being pestered by a few American jeep carriers and
destroyer escorts (like bees stinging a bull), Kurita inexplicably

turned his force back, though the unprotected American landing force was just over the horizon. Woodward describes in the following very brief account from his memoir *Thinking Back: The Perils of Writing History* how it was that he came to write the first book on this battle—and how he came to regard his unanticipated experience of writing naval history.

from

THINKING BACK: THE PERILS OF WRITING HISTORY

After getting a naval commission and training at Quonset Point that led to qualification as a combat naval air intelligence officer, I was discovered to have written a book and ordered to report to the Office of Naval Intelligence in Washington. There my duties for most of the next three years consisted largely of writing more books. This was not in connection with Samuel Eliot Morison's official history of the naval war, but in an outfit assigned the duty of getting out to the fleet brief classified accounts of battles in small books or booklets as quickly as feasible after the actions occurred. *Combat Narratives* the series was called. So it was that my second book was not the result of my choice at all, but of military orders—as were my third and fourth books. For as it turned out, I wrote three such books, two of them classified "Confidential," printed without attribution of authorship, with circulation strictly limited to qualified personnel within the Navy. Only one, the last written, was released for publication and brought out by the Macmillan Company, which had published my first book. This one was called *The Battle for Leyte Gulf* (1947). That was the official name covering four battles fought between dawn of one day and dusk of the next in three bodies of water covering five hundred miles, all waged in repulse of one huge final operation by the Japanese Navy. It was the greatest naval battle of the war and the largest and most complicated ever fought on the high seas.

Quite by coincidence, therefore, it happened that I was to write more naval history—a subject quite remote from my center of inter-

Lt. (jg) C. Vann Woodward looks pensive
during the wartime photograph.
COURTESY OF C. VANN WOODWARD

est—than any other single kind of history. The experience, however, could not be dismissed as lost time. I came to regard it, in fact, as an important part of my education as a historian. The strenuous exercise of mind in a completely strange and highly technical field of history induced a new respect for precise and reliable information, exact timing, and the infinite complexity of events with large consequences. This was history as pure action written almost entirely as narrative. Yet for all their technological complications, modern

Woodward as Sterling Professor Emeritus,
History, Yale University.
PACH BROS., NEW YORK

battles on the high seas are still human events. The historian soon
found himself dealing with such familiar categories as personality,
accident, luck, ambition, stupidity, and human error, even national
character—factors that often proved more important than
weaponry, firepower, and numbers. It is rare that a historian gets to
know so many of his protagonists. The two colossal failures at Leyte
Gulf are reasonably attributable to an American Hotspur and a
Japanese Hamlet. It was a gratifying part of the naval experience to
learn that the historian, with his old-fashioned compass, could find
his way in deep blue water— surface, subsurface, or air—as well as
on dry land.

LEWIS THOMAS

LEWIS THOMAS was a doctor whose avocation was observation of the natural world. He began writing a popular column for a prestigious medical journal in 1971, and in 1974 some of his essays were collected into *The Lives of a Cell: Notes of a Biology Watcher.* This book was hailed on all sides for its pellucid style and its success at manifesting some of the intimate marvels of biological phenomena.

Thomas was an officer in the Navy's Medical Corps from 1941 to 1946. He essentially did medical research all that time, both on the East Coast, at the start, and again when his unit was deployed to Guam in the fall of 1944, and then on to Okinawa. He recounts some of his naval experience in the essay reproduced below, which comes from one of his later books.

from

THE YOUNGEST SCIENCE: NOTES OF A MEDICINE-WATCHER

I had the guiltiest of wars, doing under orders one thing after another that I liked doing. The Rockefeller Institute (now University) had been signed up as a Navy medical research unit, and I was taken on to work in the laboratory of the Rockefeller Hospital director, Dr. Thomas M. Rivers, who had one of the most extensive collections of viruses in the world stored under dry ice.

The Rockefeller Institute Hospital, mobilized as a naval unit in 1942, went to work in New York on several disease problems that were causing concern in the armed forces at that time: streptococcal infections and rheumatic fever, an epidemic form of pneumonia then known as primary atypical pneumonia ("atypical" because of the absence of pneumococci or other recognizable pathogens), hepatitis, yellow fever, malaria, parasitic infections, and meningitis. The hospital wards were filled with Navy and Marine personnel sent in from local training bases, most of them with pneumonia. My quarters were in Rivers's laboratory, which up to then had been devoted entirely to the study of highly pathogenic and uncongenial viruses; I had for my own use a dry-ice box filled with frozen samples of most of the known virus species, including rabies, equine encephalitis, rift valley fever, choriomeningitis, ten different varieties of psittacosis, and several samples of typhus rickettsiae (not a virus but classed with the viruses because of its inability to grow unless contained in living cells). Scrub typhus, a highly lethal disease also known as Tsutsugamushi fever, was of interest to the Navy because of its occurrence in Japanese-occupied areas of the Pacific.

I was given four simultaneous assignments in the New York laboratory. The first was to try to isolate a virus from the patients with primary atypical pneumonia. The second was to learn what I could about typhus fever, in particular scrub typhus, and specifically to learn how to handle this agent without catching it; there had already been several deaths among laboratory workers in other institutions. The third was to continue some work on psittacosis among New York City pigeons, which had been in progress under Joseph Smadel in Rivers's laboratory for several years; this was not really a military problem but was thought to be of considerable public health importance for the city.

My fourth assignment was the only one in which I felt safe and unthreatened. Once a month I received a box filled with urine specimens from each of the naval bases in the Northeastern states, for Ascheim-Zondek tests. Pregnancy was something the Navy worried a lot about, and the top officials had decided that Dr. Rivers's laboratory could be relied on for the appropriate facilities (mice, really) and also for confidentiality. Each month I reported two or three positive tests, resulting presumably in a return to civilian life of that number of Waves.

I spent most of that summer in Washington as a visiting investigator in Norman Topping's laboratory at the National Institutes of Health. Topping was the ranking authority on typhus fever, and his laboratory was busy with efforts to develop an effective vaccine against scrub typhus. I was taught how to cultivate the agent in chick embryos, how to prepare concentrated suspensions of the live agent for serological tests, and, above all, how to keep it from contaminating the air of the laboratory. The Waring blender had just been introduced as a useful instrument for homogenizing various tissues in research laboratories, and was in routine use in Topping's laboratory for getting smooth suspensions of the scrub typhus organism. It was not until later that year, long after I'd left, that it was recognized that taking the cover off the blender too soon after homogenization could be hazardous; one of the senior staff members, who had been my personal teacher in that summer, died of scrub typhus picked up from the air around the Waring blender.

In 1943 we were told that the Rockefeller naval research unit was to be sent to the Pacific, and preparations for the move were begun. It took a year to get ready. By the autumn of 1944 the purchases of laboratory equipment had been completed, and the necessary additions to the professional staff of the unit had been negotiated. When we left for the West Coast on the transcontinental railroad, we had representatives of almost every biological discipline in uniform and on board: entomologists, mammalogists, malacologists (snails), ornithologists, biochemists, clinicians, microbiologists, immunologists, virologists, two rickettsiologists (Jerome Syverton and me),

Lt. (jg) Lewis Thomas, Medical Corps, U.S. Naval Reserve.
THE ROCKEFELLER ARCHIVE CENTER

and a large number of administrative officers and noncommissioned ranks who had been signed on as technicians. We ended up at San Bruno, just south of San Francisco, for a mandatory period of military training before shipping out.

I think we must have been one of the strangest lots of trainees ever to pass through San Bruno. We were all housed together in our own barracks, away from the thousands of other Navy and Marine people on their way to the Pacific. Early each morning we were assembled for drill, marching to the cadence of a full-throated

Marine sergeant who had little use for us; what he knew for sure about us was that we would be of little value in any hand-to-hand fight. Before drill, he called the roll, and it always went the same way, down through the alphabet; each of us was supposed to bark "Here!" the instant our name was called. Just before my name was Jerome Syverton, an extremely dignified professor from Rochester. Syverton's name was pronounced *Si*verton, but the first day of drill the sergeant called out *Sy*verton with the long *y;* Syverton's response was "*Si*verton—here!" This went on for four weeks—every morning the sergeant getting down to the *S*'s, all of us waiting, then the firmly and loudly mispronounced name, then Syverton's correction followed by "Here!" The moment had everything: the military versus the academic mind, a touch of class warfare, territoriality, human rights, pure fun. It lightened each day at its beginning.

Three days each week we were piled onto half-track trucks and driven west to the cliff overlooking the Pacific and taught to use the Browning Automatic Rifle—the BAR—the most terrifying and lethal weapon any of us had ever seen. One man in our group, an insect systematist and one of the country's major figures in taxonomy, but not quick on his feet and possessed of extremely thick eyeglass lenses, took up the instrument when it was his turn to fire and, his attention caught by something moving in the grass alongside, swung around in the direction of the drill sergeant with his finger on the trigger, almost but not quite firing, then waking up in surprise to see that everyone, the drill master and all his academic colleagues, were face down on the ground, yelling at him to put the damn thing down or point it toward the ocean.

We shipped out in early December, landing at Honolulu for a week or so, and then went on to Guam, a cluster of scientists and technicians in the midst of a huge convoy of Marines and Army infantry on their way to combat. We set up camp, living in tents while the construction work proceeded, and all of us—all ranks, from commander to Marine private—built as fine a set of research laboratories as ever existed on a Pacific Island. The metal panels for the roofs and sides were labeled and ready to be screwed together; it was the simplest task to fit them together, hard to get wrong, but we finished with a sense of immense pride in our workmanship while we watched a crew of Seabees, professional construction workers, on a neighboring plot of ground putting up the island's Navy hospital using the same materials. Later we learned that the Seabees had originally been scheduled to build our laboratories, but our commanding officer had decided that it would be better if we did it ourselves, thus preserving our political independence from other parts of the Guam establishment. This was believed to be important for the unit's future; we were supposed to be autonomous, capable of making our own selection of research problems to work on, not subject to orders from other authorities on the island who might, it was feared, be inclined to make a routine health department laboratory out of the unit.

The first call on our services came from Iwo Jima, where it was reported that tiny red mites had been encountered in the deep caves being taken from the Japanese. The invasion of that island had just started, and the casualties were beginning to arrive at the Marine hospital down the road, along with rumors that the invasion was becoming an impossibility. The presence of mites added to the disaster; an outbreak of scrub typhus on Iwo Jima would have been a catastrophe. A team of technicians were sent to obtain samples of the insects, returning with the news that they were the wrong sort of mites, not the vectors of Tsutsugamushi fever. Congratulations were exchanged all round. The unit, which was always at risk for seeming an academic frivolity, a Guam ivory tower, was acknowledged for its usefulness to the Navy, and our reputation was, at least for the time, solid.

At about the same time an outbreak of infectious hepatitis was reported from the Philippines, and a small group under Dr. George Mirick was flown off to pick up blood and fecal samples for study in the Guam laboratories. The disease was believed to be caused by a virus, but there was no information about the nature of the agent nor any experimental animal to which it could be transmitted. Beyond isolating the new cases and carrying out conventional epidemiological surveys in attempts to locate a source of the infection, there was nothing to be done about the problem. Nevertheless, it was a reassurance to the Navy to know that the Guam unit was available and working on the matter.

Richard Shope occupied the laboratory across the path from mine, and in the early months on Guam there were no direct assignments for his group. He was at the time one of the country's leading virologists, having discovered the viruses of swine influenza and rabbit papilloma. He had already been told that he would be leading a team scheduled to land in Okinawa when the invasion took place the following spring, but he now had time on his hands. I watched him with fascination every morning, stepping out the front door of his laboratory holding a petri dish containing blood agar in each hand. He performed the same ritual each day, arms outspread, holding the open dishes first to the north for a full minute, then in successive right turns, facing each compass point for whatever might land on his agar plates, then back inside to put the dishes in his incubator. He was looking for any wild microorganism which might possess antibiotic properties for the influenza virus being propagated in his mouse colony. Shope was not only persistent and careful, he had always been an extremely lucky investigator. Within a matter of weeks he had isolated a strain of *penicillium* with exactly the action he wanted: filtrates of broth cultures of the bug protected his mice against virus infections. It was, so far as I know, the first demonstration of an antiviral antibiotic. He named it, for his wife, Helen, "Helenin." It was effective against equine encephalitis viruses, not effective enough to be clinically useful, but an important clue for future work on antiviral agents.

While this was going on, Shope was organizing the contingent for Okinawa, ten officers and about twenty enlisted men, equipped with mobile laboratories for work on scrub typhus, insect and rodent studies, viruses, and a parasitology group with firsthand knowledge in schistosomiasis and the snails that transmit this disease. My assignment was to look for scrub typhus, and I had charge of a box containing fifty white mice for the purpose.

We left Guam for Okinawa on an Army transport vessel in March and cast anchor in the harbor just north of the town of Naha two days after D-Day. The battle for the southern end of the island had already begun, and we could hear the bombing from our carrier air-craft and the cannon and small-arms fire and, at night, see the flashes a mile or so inland. It looked like a dangerous place, but we were more anxious to land than to stay on board the transport, which seemed to us a lot more hazardous. The kamikaze raids had begun, and we were sitting targets, along with scores of other ships densely packed in the harbor. Several ships were hit in the first days of the battle, but not ours. After a few days—I forget how many—we went ashore, climbing down a rope net strung along the side of the ship and into small launches. I had to clamber my way down with one hand, using the other to clutch the rope around my box of white mice. During the voyage I had kept the box beneath my bunk, adding reams of toilet paper each day as bedding for the mice. This was, therefore, the first time the mice had come into public view, and I could see the astonished faces of the Marine troops lining the rail overhead, calling to each other and pointing at the box. All I remember, apart from the general sounds of wonderment, was one comment: "Now I've seen every fuckin' thing!"

We went ashore and settled down partway up the slope of a hill-side, and immediately found that we needed foxholes, not because of enemy fire, but to protect ourselves against the antiaircraft fire from our own ships, aimed at the occasional Japanese planes div-ing in just over our heads. Our first discovery was that Okinawa's earth was made of sweet potatoes. Everywhere we dug was culti-vated, also generously fertilized with night soil—a rich source, we later discovered, of typhoid and paratyphoid bacilli, which a month later produced a mild outbreak of fever among our troops (at first misdiagnosed as scrub typhus because of red spots over the abdomens of some of the patients).

There was, as it turned out, no scrub typhus in Okinawa, nor had there ever been. Nor was there any record of schistosomiasis on the island. This meant that Shope and I were effectively out of busi-ness from the outset; I would have to find other uses for the mice, and Shope, after a week or so of walking through island streams looking for the snail vectors without success, had to look for other interests.

Weeks later, in June, the real problem arrived, predicted by no one, a considerable shock to everyone in Island Command Headquarters. An outbreak of a malignant form of encephalitis occurred in several Okinawan villages at the northern end of the island, and three cases of a similar brain disease were reported in American soldiers. In its symptoms and clinical course, the illness was obviously some sort of viral infection of the central nervous system. The likeliest candidate was the agent known as Japanese B virus, which had long been recognized as the endemic disease on the Japanese mainland but was not anticipated by American epidemiologists as a hazard on Okinawa. Our unit set to work on it in a hurry. We obtained specimens of brain tissue from autopsies of several fatal cases, froze them in dry ice, and sent them back to the Guam laboratories by Marine air transport. Simultaneously, we inoculated some of our dwindling stock of white mice with brain tissue suspensions. Within a week we had the virus, reproducing the disease in mice, and the Guam serological laboratory reported that it was indeed Japanese B. The cases were isolated, mosquito control measures were taken by Island Command, and, although sporadic cases were seen each week during the rest of the summer, there were no new patients with encephalitis among the American troops. Our job then became the search for the source of the virus. Similar encephalitis viruses were familiar in America, called "equine" encephalitis, carried by horses and wild birds and transmitted to man by mosquitoes. We traveled in jeeps from one end of the island to the other, collecting blood specimens from various domestic animals and wild birds (we were staffed by ornithologists as well as mammalogists and entomologists, and equipped with shotguns), trapped mosquitoes, and driving twice each day to the Marine airstrip to load our specimens for quick shipment back to Guam.

Apart from the research, the main concern was security. We set up our laboratory in an abandoned teahouse at the edge of the village of Nago, lived on C rations, and placed bunks in a nearby barn. The day after we had everything in place, we were visited by the local Marine commandant and informed that we were on the perimeter of defense; indeed we *were* the perimeter. Just to the south of our encampment was a narrow road leading between two high hills, and for about a week we received each evening a scatter of machine-gun fire from isolated groups of Japanese soldiers who had made their way through the main line of battle in the southern part of the island. Nobody was hit, but we dug very deep foxholes outside our tents.

The Marines assigned a machine-gun post in the road just behind us. We felt the deepest affection for the gunners and, one evening, an even deeper respect. A trip wire had been placed across the road, a couple of hundred yards to the south, and late one evening its flares went off, revealing a group of people running toward us in silence. The young Marine posted at the machine gun held his fire and began calling on his radio to the other posts in the vicinity: "Hold your fire. Civilians." Then he climbed over his sandbag barrier and ran down the road in the dark, alone, unarmed, to escort the group—several old men and some women carrying children—up to our barn. I don't suppose anyone recorded this act, but if we had had the authority we would have voted him a gold medal. As it was, we clapped our hands and cheered and told him he was a great Marine.

PACIFIC WAR–II

HERMAN WOUK

HERMAN WOUK began his long professional writing career as a gag writer for radio comedians such as Fred Allen, for whom he wrote scripts from 1936 to 1941. Wouk's first novel, *Aurora Dawn,* which he began while serving aboard ship in the Pacific, was published in 1947, and another novel, *The City Boy,* followed shortly thereafter. But *The Caine Mutiny* was Wouk's first big hit. This 1951 novel led the best-seller lists for a year, won the 1952 Pulitzer Prize, and was made into a memorable movie by Stanley Kramer, starring Humphrey Bogart as the infamous Captain Queeg.

Wouk has published many other novels during his long career, as well as some nonfiction. For instance, recently he has chronicled the history of Israel in the novels *The Hope* (1993) and *The Glory* (1994). *This is My God,* written in 1959, describes his Jewish faith from a personal standpoint, and has become a standard reference of its kind. As for naval-related fiction, Wouk followed up his *Caine Mutiny* success by writing *The Winds of War* (1971) and *War and Remembrance* (1978). A pair of long, panoramic novels that trace the trials of one American naval officer's family in Europe, America, and the Pacific from 1939 to 1945, these books captured the American imagination. They both became best-sellers and later were made into television miniseries for which Wouk served as screenwriter.

The naval service, according to Wouk, is "as noble a calling as any that a man can follow," and the U.S. Navy has returned his admiration. The novelist has spoken at the Naval War College and the Naval Academy, and his 1995 address to the U.S. Naval Institute held its audience spellbound. Wouk's own naval career lasted from 1942 to 1946. His first application for a commission (submitted just before the war) was turned down because he had no engineering background; after Pearl Harbor, however, a second application was approved. Wouk underwent brief naval schooling at Columbia and the Naval Academy, and in February 1943 he reported aboard the destroyer-minesweeper USS *Zane* (DMS-14) as assistant communications officer. He fleeted up to communications officer, first lieutenant, and navigator on the *Zane*, and then transferred to the USS *Southard* (DMS-10) as executive officer. While Wouk was aboard, these ships swept ahead of or escorted eight of the great Central Pacific invasions. The episode outlined below (originally published in the Naval Academy Alumni magazine *Shipmate*) comes from his tour on the *Southard*. Wouk was slated to become commanding officer of this vessel when it was wrecked in a typhoon.

"THE BREAD OF OCHILTREE: A REMINISCENCE OF THE WAR"

Responsibility came fast in World War II. I was scarcely two years away from my old Broadway haunts (I had been a writer for Fred Allen) when I was promoted to "exec" of a three-hundred-foot ship of war, a destroyer-minesweeper very like the mythical CAINE, with a crew of 130, and millions of dollars worth of minesweeping gear. My competence was soon put to a severe test by the arrival on board ship of Seaman Second Class Ochiltree.

Ochiltree came aboard late in 1944, among the draftees. He was not one of the dejected married men dragged from the bosom of their families by the bad luck of number-pulling. He was young, he looked strong, though fat, and he appeared cheerful. He was about twenty, round-faced, thick-haired, blond, broad-shouldered, with an absent-minded, far-off little smile. He seemed ordinary enough, but it soon turned out that he had one distinctive trait: he could do absolutely nothing.

I tried him in the deck force. I tried him in the black gang. I tried him in the radio shack. I sent him to the shipfitters and to the gunners. In a day or two, perhaps in a week, the petty officer in charge would come to me in despair, asking me to relieve him of Ochiltree. With a blowtorch in his hand, Ochiltree was a greater menace to the ship than a kamikaze. Training or elevating a gun, Ochiltree could not help braining some other, more useful, sailor. He once snarled up a boat we were lowering during abandon-ship drill; the deck force was all day unsnarling it, and one man had his leg broken by the swinging boat. Not Ochiltree, of course.

It soon became evident to me that Ochiltree was a candidate for a replacement pool. The islands throughout the Pacific were dotted with these pools. Personnel policy was free and easy in those days. New ratings from the States were shipped out to the islands in batches, and executive officers came to the pools and dredged up the most usable men they could find. The custom sprang up, naturally, of dropping into these pools any lemons among the crew. Toward the end of the war this rummage-sale body of available personnel came to be almost solid citrus. In this floating group of unemployables, I thought, Ochiltree would have to sit out the war.

Meantime I was getting complaints from the ship's galley. I had tried him there early, of course, but he had scalded our best cook by upsetting a vat of soup on him. I now learned that Ochiltree was hanging around the galley again, getting in the way of the baker. The galley passages were narrow, and Ochiltree was big and slow, and the baker was a temperamental Swede. The first-class cook informed me that Ochiltree might find a bread knife in his midriff before too long.

I called in Ochiltree, and asked for an explanation. He had none, except that he liked to watch the baker; a fact I already knew. It occurred to me that he might be of some use to the baker. The Swede used unpleasant language when I suggested this to him. Aboard

Herman Wouk as an ensign circa 1942.
COURTESY OF HERMAN WOUK

destroyer-minesweepers an executive officer learned to accept such informality. I persisted, and the Swede grudgingly allowed that Ochiltree might not do too much damage if he were put to kneading dough.

Our Swede was not a bad baker, but he was not an outstanding one. His bread tasted all right. It was coarse and full of holes, and it dried up in a day, even out on the humid Pacific. Not long after Ochiltree went to work, compliments on the bread, hitherto unheard, were spoken in the wardroom. Soon the crew was praising the bread; and crews seldom praise anything in a destroyer. One day the captain commented on the bread. I passed the captain's remark on to the Swede. When I visited him, Ochiltree was bent over the trough, bare arms thrust into fragrant gray dough up to his elbow, kneading and kneading, with the happy far-off look in his eye of a cow chewing a cud of rich grass.

Shortly thereafter the Swede was transferred. I requested a replacement, but destroyer-minesweepers stood low on priority lists. We obtained bread from tenders, or from ships we were escorting, for a while. Desperation drove me to ask Ochiltree whether he thought he could bake bread. I did this without much hope, figuring that all we could lose was a batch of flour. Ochiltree shyly said he would give it a try.

One tends to romanticize the past, and it is possible that I have since eaten superior bread, but I do not think so. Ochlitree's bread was white, but not pasty; crusted, but never hard; it sliced well, it dried slowly, butter spread without tearing it, and butter tasted marvelous on this bread. You could eat a few slices of this bread with butter and coffee, and feel that you had feasted. It was *satisfying* bread, smooth, springy, with a superb smell. I despair of telling you how good Ochiltree's bread was. If you have ever eaten sublime bread, just once, at some out-of-the-way restaurant, or diner, or hotel; if you still remember it; if you have never tasted bread quite like it again; then what you ate on that occasion was something like the bread of Ochiltree.

We almost lost Ochiltree once.

The squadron commander of our minesweeper group was a notorious personnel-stealer. He would come aboard a ship, and if an offi cer's steward struck his fancy, or he liked the way a boatswain's mate was standing a deck watch, or he needed a good quartermaster, then he would coolly arrange for a transfer of the man he wanted to his flagship. Which commanding officer would have the bowels to object, when the squadron commander was the one who wrote his fitness reports? As it happened, our squadron was scattered wide, all over the Pacific, and we had not seen the flagship for months. It was late in the war, the great invasions were almost over, and our antiquated vessels were no longer operating in a body to do high-speed sweeps ahead of attacking forces. Some of the vessels had been declassified into AG's, towing targets or doing other mean harbor chores. The rest of us wandered at the pleasure of task group commanders, performing odd combat-zone jobs, mainly escorting.

One day toward sunset our ship steamed into Ulithi Atoll, and there was the flagship in South Anchorage, swinging to its chain. An exchange of blinker messages, and our skipper informed us that

Mr. Wouk delivers the seventh Spruance Lecture at the Naval War College in Newport, Rhode Island, in April 1980. He also delivered the initial Spruance Lecture in 1973. These lectures were subsequently published in the *Naval War College Review*.

NAVAL WAR COLLEGE MUSEUM

Captain X—— was coming aboard for dinner. All of us in the wardroom at once had the same thought: Ochiltree! If the squadron commander tasted that bread, all was over. He would kidnap our baker without a qualm. The captain and I held an urgent conference as we drew alongside a tender and threw over our lines.

The squadron commander was in excellent humor when he came aboard an hour later. But he seemed disappointed in the dinner, though it was Swiss steak, one of the best dishes in our cook's repertoire. Finally he remarked to our captain that he had heard rumors of a wonderful baker aboard our ship, but what was so good about this bread? Did the captain really think it was so much better than the bread on any other ship?

Our skipper took offense—as much as he could, in a seemly way, with a superior officer—and said that he *did* think it was marvelous bread, he had been boasting about it all over the Pacific, and he defied the squadron commander to produce a better loaf of Navy-baked bread. Captain X—— shook his head, glanced around at the other officers, and laughed. "Well, I don't want to seem rude, it's perfectly all right as bread goes," he said, "but we have better bread on our own ship. Come aboard tomorrow and see for yourself. You fellows have been in the forward area a little too long, maybe." Shortly afterward he left. He did not eat aboard again.

Just to be safe, I had borrowed quite a lot of bread from the tender alongside. It lay piled in our wardroom bread locker for days, insurance against the possibility that Captain X—— might return for a meal. Meantime, we regaled ourselves on the now twice-precious Ochiltree bread. At the end of the week, the flagship upped anchor and left the atoll. As it dwindled out beyond the first channel buoy, our mess boys fed the stale bread from the tender to the jellyfish and sharks that swarmed around our fantail. The shark that mattered was gone, successfully foiled.

DOUGLAS LEACH

DOUGLAS LEACH, Emeritus Professor of History at Vanderbilt, is a renowned historian who studied under Samuel Eliot Morison at Harvard, where he received his Ph.D. in 1952. His specialty is Early American History, and he has written books such as *Flintlock and Tomahawk: New England in King Philip's War* (1958) and *Arms for Empire: A Military History of the British Colonies in North America, 1607–1763* (1973).

Leach grew up in Providence, Rhode Island, and was greatly attached to his church youth group, even as he studied at Brown University. He was in the company of a friend from this group when he heard the news of Pearl Harbor. After graduating from college and entering the Navy's V-7 program, and during later naval duty, he kept in close touch with his friends through frequent visits to Providence, through visits with youth group members serving on other naval vessels, and through a church newsletter (named *The Odyssey*) that printed news of the young men and women throughout the war.

Because of this focus on friendship, Leach's memoir *Now Hear This*—which deals mainly with Leach's duty on board the USS *Elden* (DE-264) from the ship's commissioning in 1943 to near the end of the war—is gentler in tone than many naval memoirs of the

period. That personal charm offsets the memoir's sparseness of incident, which Leach attributes to the very great luck of his ship. As
he puts it, "By the time I left [the *Elden*] at Oakland she had steamed
more than one hundred thousand miles in two oceans, earning five
battle stars on the Asiatic-Pacific Area service ribbon.... Yet—almost
incredible fact—not once through all that did we ever sight an
enemy ship or plane." But there was much to recount nevertheless.

Often we remember shipmates who had some talent or grace—
and we remember them warmly. At other times, we recall individuals with character flaws—especially when they were part of our
chain of command. In his incompetence and paranoia, the commanding officer who Leach describes in this episode resembles
Captain Queeg in Herman Wouk's *The Caine Mutiny.* The executive officer on Leach's ship, however—unlike Lieutenant Maryk in
Wouk's book—took early action.

from

NOW HEAR THIS: THE MEMOIR OF A JUNIOR NAVAL OFFICER IN THE GREAT PACIFIC WAR

The *Elden*'s safe return to the great naval base at Pearl Harbor
brought many welcome changes. For one thing, we could again feel
secure, free from the possibility of imminent attack by enemy aircraft or surface vessels or, especially, submarines. Nighttime watches
now were less frequent for everyone, which meant that a full night's
sleep became the norm, sleep in a ship that was motionless and,
except for the rush of forced air below decks, relatively quiet. We
slept easy for a change. Our meals improved dramatically, with
fresh vegetables and fruit and real milk appearing daily on the table.
Again there was mail from home, our first in four weeks. The dates
on the letters were fairly recent, indicating that some postal sacks
of earlier date still were chasing the *Elden* around the ocean. When
the missing mail finally did arrive, it included some letters from as
far back as early September.

Lt. (jg) Douglas E. Leach at Oahu in November 1944.
Leach was feeling good during his first real liberty in five months,
but the ship would soon face problems with morale.
COURTESY OF DOUGLAS E. LEACH

Despite minor wartime deprivations, my family at home seemed to be thriving. Tom Buffum, now fully recovered from his dunking in the English Channel the previous June, had been assigned to new construction as executive officer of the fleet tug *ATR 79,* destined for the Pacific. The October issue of *The Odyssey* (expertly mimeographed at the church office by Trudy Kraus) carried on its cover a rollicking Halloween photograph of a radiant Clara Miller and George Turner biting at an apple suspended by a string. Clara, I learned, would soon be leaving for training as a Wave—another one of the old gang gone from home. The same issue published a cheery letter from Yeoman second class Mary Noyes, who took pride in being a member of the first all-Wave band in the entire Navy. Trudy reported on a recent Y.P.F outing on the shore of East Greenwich Bay. Also published was a letter from a Y.P.F.'er on *LST 917* in the Pacific, commenting on my previously reported reunion with Roger Hard. From "Uncle George" a little later came a typically sensitive message to all of Calvary's men and women in the service at a time when American casualties were mounting: "Dear friends, even if we do not talk in 'Thee' and 'Thou' we do have your eternal souls, even more than your beautiful bodies, on our heart and mind every day. We pray that you may through the very dark days ahead feel God's presence and care over you. As you talk with Him each day, may He bring you cheer enough to share with the men around you." It was "Uncle George" and Trudy, together with a corps of faithfuls such as Dottie Burdon, Patsy Farrow, Dick Johnson, Isabelle Kean, Carol and Hazel Lindquist, Bud Tucker, Elberta Waterman, and Grace Whitney, who kept the greetings coming, binding us all together in a warm web of mutual concern and remembrance. What a help that was in staving off the loneliness of operating far away in an all-male world of routine, discipline, and danger!

Soon after arriving back at Pearl we began seeing some of our shipmates depart for other assignments, their places being taken by newcomers. Among those who left the *Elden* at this time were our engineering officer Ned Lee and our chief steward Manzala, the latter being transferred to a heavy cruiser. Ned Lee's departure meant the loss of one of our tried and true originals, whose level-headed common sense and general good nature had been valuable assets. A welcome newcomer was Ens. Frank H. Krayer. The most significant change, however, occurred on the morning of 28 November when all hands mustered on the fantail for the *Elden*'s second transfer-of-command ceremony since commissioning. Our own able and congenial captain, Fred Hartman, relinquished his command to Ed Sneed, and proceeded to the command of the *Silverstein* (DE 534), a newer, slightly faster, more heavily armed ship. There went one more of the *Elden*'s original "plankowners." With this change, Jack Rickard became Captain Sneed's executive officer, moving across the wardroom passageway to the privacy of the single stateroom, while Leo Miller moved in with me. Frankly, few if any of the ship's company, officers especially, were pleased with the change of command, for Sneed was known to be problematical. He certainly had good intentions but seemed to lack both self-confidence and operational competence. In addition to these major deficiencies, he was known to be heavy on the bottle.

[Let me recount one example from an earlier port visit.] Alcohol was strictly prohibited aboard ship, but inevitably some of the more thirsty men would find or devise some form of relief, usually involving raw alcohol. Officers got ashore more often than enlisted men, which helped solve the problem for them, not always with salubrious results. Late one evening when I was OOD in Seeadler harbor, [Captain Hartman and his "exec" Sneed had] returned aboard together, the former perfectly in control of himself, the latter drunk and belligerent. When Sneed refused to subside, the disgusted captain finally ordered me to summon the master-at-arms and have him bring his night stick! So out blared the unusual command on the PA system: "Now hear this! The chief master-at-arms, lay up to the quarterdeck on the double, with a night stick!" Before you could blink twice, the hatches began spewing up sailors curious to know what was happening, even as the stalwart master-at-arms, billy club in hand, made his official appearance. Thus there was a sizable audience to see the spectacle of the ship's executive officer hoisted over the master-at-arms' shoulder and lugged away to his bunk to sleep it off.

[Such was the disposition of Ed Sneed, our new captain. . . .] Otherwise, what was happening to the tired old *Elden* during these days was a general sprucing up. Needed repairs were effected by yard personnel; old equipment was modified and new equipment added for increased efficiency. On the third anniversary of the Japanese attack on Pearl Harbor the ship entered Marine Railway Number 2, high and dry, to have her hull scraped and painted. When this was completed she looked almost as good as new.

By 13 December, after nearly four weeks in port, the *Elden* was again ready for sea. On that date we commenced the first of a series of short training cruises testing our combat effectiveness. Among our consorts during this period were the submarine *Pollack* (SS 180), the destroyer *Colhoun* (later to be sunk off Okinawa by kamikazes), the destroyer escort *Silverstein* (DE 534), and the amphibious command ships *Eldorado* (AGC 11) and *Estes* (AGC 12). With student officers and their instructors aboard, the *Elden* practiced shore bombardment and antiaircraft gunnery, expending nearly four hundred rounds of 3-inch ammunition as well as large quantities of 1.1-inch and 20-millimeter. Early in the morning of 21 December, when I had the watch, our formation underwent a simulated pre-dawn attack by friendly aircraft, always an impressive and exciting experience which made us doubly aware of the importance of good air cover, sharp evasive action, and rapid-fire gunnery. The next day, with the training completed, the *Elden* returned to Pearl and moored alongside the destroyer tender *Yosemite* (AD 19). . . .

During these weeks of renovation and training, Captain Sneed was trying to improve his own confidence and competence, without much real success. One time after the *Elden* had come in from sea, the captain brought her to the wrong mooring. Many of the officers, including our susceptible skipper, then went ashore, leaving Russ Morrow in charge of the ship. Scarcely had the captain disappeared from view when a Marine officer, sent by the base commander, arrived at our gangplank with a written order requiring the captain to move the ship to her assigned mooring immediately—or else! With no possibility of recalling the captain, Russ took the initiative and moved the *Elden* as required, thereby saving the skipper's hide. Later that night Russ spotted Captain Sneed weaving along the dock, obviously drunk and greatly agitated, looking for a ship that was not where he had left her. At last, finding her in the new and correct berth, he staggered aboard and yelled at Russ: "You stole my ship! I'm going to have you court-martialed!" Without stirring a hair, the object of this angry threat summoned a couple of petty officers and had them deposit the captain in his bunk.

On the evening of 10 January Captain Sneed again was ashore. About midnight, when most of us aboard were already asleep, he returned—sodden drunk—with the curious (and ironic) notion in his head that some of the crew were concealing liquor somewhere on the ship. Confronting the executive officer, Jack Rickard, he demanded that all hands be routed out of bed immediately to stand a captain's inspection for the purpose of discovering the imagined contraband. I was among the group of hastily clothed, sleepy-eyed officers who now assembled in the wardroom to be told of the captain's order. Of course we were outraged at this nonsense, and there was some discussion as to whether or not we should obey; fortunately, the cool heads of Jack Rickard and Russ Morrow prevailed and a decision was made to go through with the charade. Accordingly, the crew were required to crawl out of their bunks and stand to in their quarters while a drunken captain, trailed by his angry and embarrassed officers, stumbled through their midst on a futile hunt for imagined booze. It was a bad experience all round. A further touch of irony was added when, at about the same time, a barge came alongside and pumped into the *Elden*'s tanks twelve thousand gallons of fresh water!

Obviously, all of us on the *Elden* were confronted with a serious problem involving morale as well as the very safety of the ship and her crew. Not only was our commanding officer a heavy drinker, but he also remained insecure in the knowledge and skill necessary for safe and effective handling of the ship under way. Quite understandably, then, with the *Elden* likely to be involved soon in the next major operation against the Japanese, Jack Rickard faced an agonizing dilemma. What to do, without running onto the rocks of insubordination? A captain's authority and power he well knew; a really vindictive captain could make life hell for any individual under his command. Jack Rickard was by profession an attorney. So was Russ Morrow. That much, at least, was to our advantage, for neither would act precipitately or foolishly. As it happened, Jack's brother-in-law, a captain in the regular Navy, was stationed at Pearl Harbor. As soon as possible on the day after the midnight inspection Jack shared the problem with him, and was advised to consider the safety of the ship first and foremost, regardless of any possible consequences. So Jack whistled up his courage, went to the commodore of CortDiv 16, and told him about the midnight inspection. After that, things began to happen. It wasn't long before Jack and Russ together found themselves nervously reporting to DesPac (Headquarters, Pacific Fleet Destroyers) for an interview during which they freely and frankly stated the case. All this was accomplished, of course, without being revealed to the rest of the ship's company. Certainly I knew nothing of it. And there the matter appeared to rest.

Our next assignment was to help screen a formation of transports carrying Marines for amphibious training exercises at Maalaea Bay, Maui, as training for the next major assault. The *Elden* got under way at 0450 on 12 January, preceding the loaded transports. En route to Maui, with the officer in tactical command aboard the USS *Auburn* (AGC 10), we conducted tactical and gunnery exercises. Then, at Maalaea Bay, the *Elden* easily settled into the old familiar routine of figure-eight barrier patrol to protect the transports lying just off the beach. Except for the beauty of land and sea, the successive watches were tedious and largely uneventful, with our sonar pinging incessantly across the assigned arcs of search as we patrolled back and forth, back and forth.

Finally, on 17 January, having completed the amphibious exercises, the ships reformed for the return voyage to Oahu, with the screen commander in the USS *Fullam* (DD 474). We entered Pearl Harbor the next afternoon and began approaching our assigned mooring. As we did so, our signal watch began receiving a blinker message from ComDesPac ashore, a message whose import quickly became obvious, spreading like wildfire the whole length of the ship. Captain Sneed was being relieved of his command and transferred! Those of us stationed on the flying bridge, in the captain's presence, struggled to conceal our elation, but elsewhere the rejoicing was considerably less restrained. By supper time the officer designated to serve as the *Elden*'s next captain was on board, although the actual transfer-of-command ceremony did not take place until the next day. Quietly, in bitter disappointment, the displaced skipper left the ship forever. I felt sorry for him, a sad example of a man out of his depth, but I also was deeply grateful that the *Elden* would not have to sail under his command against the Japanese. The problem of command at sea is a critical one. It's a truism to say that authority and responsibility are inseparable—but how readily that can be forgotten. The relative isolation of a Navy ship at sea, even when in the company of other ships, places upon the skipper's shoulders an awesome responsibility to match his awesome authority. Upon his quick judgment may depend the lives of the entire ship's company. A mutual bond of confidence and trust is essential. In this regard, the contrast between the *Elden*'s first two captains on the one hand, and the third one on the other, is especially striking. The latter, for all his earnest trying, had simply failed to create that bond, and so he had to go. I give the Navy high marks for a decision showing that the brass did have regard for the safety and dignity of lesser ranks.

Lt. Comdr. J. F. Doubleday, our new skipper, came in like a breath of fresh sea air. He was a large man, jovial and hearty, with almost unbounded self-confidence, a fertile mind, and a taste for friendly kidding. Having already commanded another destroyer escort, he knew what he was about, which meant that on the scale of competence, too, we had come out of the exchange well ahead. Conversation at the wardroom table became more stimulating, while throughout the ship one could sense a revitalized spirit. In short, Captain Doubleday seemed to be exactly what the *Elden* needed. . . .

Early in the afternoon of 22 January the *Elden* got under way as sole escort for the *Anne Arundel* (AP 76) and the *Gen. M. L. Hersey* (AP 148), a pair of troop transports ordered to Eniwetok. As we slowly proceeded toward the Pearl Harbor exit, the *Elden*'s motor whaleboat was being hoisted to the davits on the port side amidships and secured for sea. A coxswain, Henry Duncan Jr., was standing on the bow of the motor whaleboat when suddenly, without warning, a rat-tail stopper parted, causing the forward falls to drop about six inches. This sudden drop was enough to throw Duncan off balance. Falling, he struck his head and plunged into the water. "Man overboard!" Quickly all engines were stopped and the ship went to General Quarters as the "man overboard" signal was run up to advise nearby ships of the emergency. Now the drill we had practiced so often became a grim reality, with a shipmate's life at stake. Topside all eyes were on the harbor water astern, but no head bobbed to the surface. Duncan had simply disappeared. Within less than three minutes of the accident our boat was in the water and beginning a search, with other boats in the vicinity assisting. After about twenty minutes of searching without success, we had to give up, recall the motor whaleboat, and continue sadly on our way out to the open sea. Later we were to learn that Duncan's body had been recovered in the harbor. The *Elden* had suffered her first fatality, and a young wife had to be notified.

HENRY G. BUGBEE JR.

H ENRY G. BUGBEE JR. graduated from Princeton with high honors in philosophy in 1936, and he was doing graduate work at the University of California at Berkeley when the war intervened. From August 1942 to January 1946 he served as a Naval Reserve officer, and except for eight weeks of initial training and eleven weeks of mine warfare training, he served entirely on "small ships with oak hulls" in the Pacific. In the war he got so caught up by his three years at sea that philosophy seemed utterly remote from him, and he could not imagine ever returning to a life of study. But eventually Bugbee did go back to school, and while teaching at Harvard after the war (he eventually settled at the University of Montana), he came to understand that, unknown to him at the time, his life at sea had been "an almost uninterrupted active meditation."

We understand some of that sense of meditation in reading the following passages, which are for a layperson some of the more accessible portions of his philosophical journal, *The Inward Morning: A Philosophical Exploration in Journal Form.* Upon reading this book, some of his friends told him, "You have written here as a man might write only near the end of his life." Bugbee responded, "[S]ince certain episodes in World War II that has been my sense of life." Bugbee intersperses his interpretations of experience with descriptions of combat and ends this segment with a character sketch of the ship's chief boatswain's mate who—simply through carrying out his naval duties with total earnestness—set the uniquely innocent and hopeful mood of the ship.

from

THE INWARD MORNING:
A PHILOSOPHICAL EXPLORATION IN JOURNAL FORM

Wednesday and Thursday, September 2 and 3

I've been thinking of the ship's companies whom I have known. A motley of backgrounds and personalities went into each crew, a job-lot of men into each ship. These hitherto divergent life streams converging at random, to pour into the ship's life. None of us exercised much choice in landing aboard a particular ship. And the life aboard ship itself had little to do with choice either in the company one kept or in the things one did. Furthermore we always sailed under orders merely handed down and subject to alteration without warning; the ship and all hands were snatched this way and that, and we could seldom see that our moves brought to culmination a purpose justifying the errands on which the ship was sent. Supervening upon these vagaries and the nebulous horizons into which our perspective ever trailed off was the senselessness of war itself. Bearing all this in mind it becomes interesting to reflect on how such a situation could make sense.

I would say that I have this situation to thank for being undeceived with respect to the fundamentality of choice. Relative to an attitude of choice our situation was as contingent as you please. Why were any of us where we were rather than somewhere else? Perhaps if the yeoman in some personnel office had not been a bit hung over on a certain morning, he would have stretched a bit farther to pick up another folder on men available for assignment, and one would not be just where he finds himself now. And if our communications officer had not spoken some bitter words to the offi-

Wise beyond his years, philosopher Henry Bugbee Jr.
poses in a bridge coat with pipe.
COURTESY OF HENRY BUGBEE JR.

cer in charge of communications back at the base, perhaps we
wouldn't be off on this thousand-mile jaunt, escorting a couple of
old scows to some godforsaken dot of land in mid-ocean.

We sail out of a staging-harbor with other ships of our class, heading for an invasion. Suddenly a sister ship breaks down; she needs
an engine part no one can supply, which it will take days to obtain.
She is out of the invasion, but we sail on. A year later we meet up
with her again, and this time we stand out to sea with her in a
typhoon. The last we see of her, she is fading into a flying shroud
of spray. Not hide nor hair nor plank of her is seen again. . . .

Sunday, September 6
As I think back to my shipmates, reaching back to them in memory, I find that they elude me, that I cannot really call them to mind,

except as I identify them in moments of their earnestness when they were conclusively defined in action. I can remember them when they were in earnest, and until I can remember them so, they do not come back alive to me. And every man I can so remember I realize that I have cared for and respected, and care for and respect all over again. And I see through the unevenness that would inevitably obtain between one's liking for one man and another. Each man had his defining moments—some rarely and some frequently, a few almost constantly. Now they would come singly for this man or that, and occasionally there were moments in which every last man of the ship stood forth revealed, three-dimensionally clear in the flash of a ship-embracing event.

Though I had sailed in other ships for nearly two years before I came to her, my clearest and most complete memory is of *YMS 319* and her men, with whom I lived for over a year. It had been her good fortune, in a sense not too perverse, to be assigned to the forward area in the Pacific not very long after her commissioning and shakedown. I cannot but see in that an element of good fortune on the evidence which struck me even as I swung over her side for the first time, as she lay at anchor in the harbor of Manus Island. She had just completed participation in her second invasion and had come through a typhoon. Here she lay, not so far short of halfway round the world from home, and facing no respite from sheer work and risk for an indefinitely protracted period to come. The ships I had sailed in before were seldom away from a liberty port for more than a week at a time, and had been based on no more austere place than the Hawaiian Islands. But here were thirty-five men who had participated in proving that a 137-foot minesweeper and patrol craft might operate like the larger units of the fleet, provisioning and fueling at sea for weeks of operation on end, with only occasional recourse to casual harbors for staging and repairs. Those men had come to live with a sense of mortal danger sure to come, already well confirmed. They had little to look forward to. Even the mail might be a month or more delayed, and sometimes had surely been lost. They had played a game or two of baseball in the past six months, had drunk a few beers, taken a few swims, and seen a movie or two, but "recreation" was mostly of the improvised hour off watch while under way, or the luxury of eight hours' sleep while riding the hook in an occasional safe harbor. And you could pick up the disc jockeys of the Jungle Network and the Voice of Freedom, or Tokyo Rose—out of the very air that brought suicide planes.

I came aboard the *319* with trepidation, to join the lives of utter strangers, a man untried by the circumstances they had known. Within my first hour aboard I savored something for which I was unprepared, something I could not really understand until I had drawn of the life of that ship. There was a prevailing cheerfulness and buoyancy about the ship, so marked and strange to me, I must admit, that I almost questioned its authenticity. In one or two of the officers, it is true, I sensed a shade of self-consciousness about it; were they trumping it up? No; I think they were trying to find refuge in the genuine quality that dwelt as a bond in that ship, a refuge from the nervousness to which we are liable when we must call the moves, prepared or not to do so. There had been a shattering explosion in another ship close aboard the *319* a couple of days before. A sister ship alongside had suffered casualties, had been reduced to a shambles as well. A reminder of past scenes, an adumbration of what scenes to come?

During my first hours aboard I discovered a man or two who conveyed exception from the pervasive liveliness; at that time Eddie Jones, the steward's mate, was sullen enough, and Soldahl, seaman first class, exuded reticence, a heaviness that hung like an atmospheric nimbus around him; it took quite a while before I came to know Soldahl, discovered the quick in him. But these and possibly two or three others were the exceptions, and I could even sense the prevailing atmosphere the more clearly as it resisted contamination here and there. I have said it was one of buoyancy and cheerfulness, but these terms are not sufficient in themselves. It would be still nearer the truth to say that the *319* was a ship of innocence and hope. I noticed refinement in the tone of speech and comportment here, beneath the stereotypes of the vernacular. I saw that this crew was not going through an act or marking time in the far-Pacific. And

I noticed that on the whole the men were good friends. I came to perceive them, sometimes one by one, sometimes all together.

All together for the first time as we got the ship under way and spent a day in antiaircraft practice. It was evident that they knew what they were doing. All together in that hour at the close of Christmas Day, of which I will say no more. Then there were times when one man would gather us all, as it were, into an epitome of expression. Such was the time when Chief Boatswain's Mate Johnson met a certain plane on our way to Lingayen Gulf.

Chief Johnson's battle station was in charge of damage control, placing him amidships by the damage control locker on the starboard side. He had long pled for a gun of his own with which he could occupy himself before any damage might occur. During twenty years in the Navy he had never served as a gunner, and some of the crew averred that he would not be able to hit a seagull perched on the tip of his gun. But at last an extra .50-caliber machine gun had been surreptitiously acquired, and here it was installed for him by the rail at his station. We were at General Quarters steaming in a large formation off Mindoro, awaiting the arrival of a group of suicide planes from the direction of Manila. How quiet it was.

Eight planes appeared in our bright and cloudless sky. As they headed for various ships of our group, the rending cannonade began. The danger of ships firing into one another increased as the planes came down. Out of a canopy of chaos a plane swept into range in a long, steep glide, heading for a ship forward of our beam on the starboard side. We opened up. The disciplined gunners on the Twenties and Twin-Fifties pounded away in bursts, and the Three Inch was blasting fast. Then I saw the chief: his small figure tense between the handles of his gun; his blond beard flowing down over the life jacket around his chest; his fingers frozen upon the trigger, the continuous stream of tracers flying from his gun; his whole frame shaking to the shattering recoil; the searing concentration with which he followed the plane.

Though it was his firing the whole drum without pause that burned out the rifling, it was as if the little man himself were making the prayer of his life and burning out the gun with the white fire of his soul, pouring out, pouring out, flowing toward the plane from where he stood. And I saw the plane brought to focus in the sky by the converging cone of fire from ours and other ships. It kept on and on, and as it came on without deviation toward its target it seemed to be standing still in the sky, hanging, hanging, hanging upon the air. In that hanging moment of the undeviating plane, in that moment when the chief became continuous fire, gun and plane came to seem one, so that we might as well have had the pilot aboard and the chief might have been at the controls of the plane. In that moment I saw beyond the war. Into this transcendence the chief carried us all.

Though provided with a new barrel, he never became a gunner. He was a seafaring man.

Monday, September 7
I remember Chief Johnson best from times that were not spectacular, which partook of the everyday concerns: setting the watch, considering the scope of the anchor chair upon a rising wind, positioning the fenders while we surged alongside other ships, checking and handling the sweep gear, catching up on a bit of scraping and painting here or there, discussing someone's complaint about someone else, and the rationing of the beer—which he kept from going awry. I remember the gravity in those sharp eyes and his habitually mild-mannered speech. I knew him as a man you could work with, whose basic dignity carried through even his moments of peevishness. Whatever stubbornness might lie on both sides of a disagreement with him, it tended to dissolve in the concern for the ship underlying the judgments he formed. . . .

During peacetime Raymond Johnson had never risen above the rate of coxswain, serving mostly aboard large ships. So it might have continued to be but for those exigencies which uniformly lifted in rate men whom the service had schooled by dint of years. Yet now he came to be a chief so fit for our small ship in war, setting that innocence and readiness with which the life of the ship was charmed, that I'm sure none of us could have put our finger on it at the time, and known our debt to him more than to any other man. The only outstanding feature of Boats was that long beard of his, and he shaved that off in time.

There was a night down in Tulagi when we were in floating dry dock. We'd spent the day in scraping the ship's bottom. Then, while the others slept, Boats and I fished the whole night through. We fished with hand-lines right off the dry dock. The fish kept us baiting up. There was little sound upon the passing night; no engines turning over, no sound of waves, only the listening stillness of the jungle along the shores of our narrow estuary and stars above. I knew, too, that Boats knew of the month-old news of my father's death.

EDWARD L. BEACH

A S RECOUNTED ABOVE (pages 115–16), Edward L. Beach's career as a novelist began in the 1950s, while he was naval aide to President Eisenhower. He had actually begun writing for the public in the latter days of World War II, however, while serving as executive officer of the USS *Tirante* (SS-420). Beach had served for two and one-half years (the last year as executive officer) aboard the submarine USS *Trigger* (SS-237), and when that vessel was lost, he began to write a memorial to the boat, intended for its crew's next of kin. He wrote an autobiographical account, had it cleared by the Navy, and when someone suggested publication, he sent the piece to the magazine *Blue Book,* which published it in 1946. The editor of that magazine asked for more, so Beach wrote another such story, and eventually several of his narratives (about various ships) were stitched together. *Submarine!* became a best-seller when published by Henry Holt in 1952.

The autobiographical account below recounts an episode that occurred during a war patrol of the *Tirante.* Incidentally, Beach's skipper, George Cross, received the Medal of Honor for his first war patrol aboard this vessel; for the same patrol, Beach was awarded the Navy Cross.

from

SUBMARINE!

The next night we received a message ordering us to proceed to a point off Tsingtao where ships running between China and Japan were reported to pass occasionally. It would take us a full-speed dash to reach the desired spot, but if we went more leisurely we might be out of action for a full extra day. And besides, orders were orders, to be carried out with dispatch. All night long we sped across the Yellow Sea.

The system we had evolved in *Tirante* was that I stayed up all night, more or less with the ready duty in case of a sudden emergency, and also to navigate. Just before diving, we called the skipper, and shortly afterward I would turn in until time for lunch. This day, however, I felt like a good breakfast, and left a call for 0800.

I ate leisurely and drank two cups of coffee before I began to sense that something was stirring. Then came a subdued clink of the annunciators, a faint whisper of hydraulic oil flow as the rudder went over. The gyro repeater in the wardroom overhead began to spin slowly. After a bit I heard someone in the control room tell someone else that there was pinging on the sound gear. One by one members of the ship's company began to drift by the wardroom—some one way, some another—but all, I noticed, in the direction of their battle stations. *Tirante* was girding her loins for battle, and it was time to go.

I gulp down the remains of the coffee, start for the conning tower. Pausing, I tell Roscoe Brown, one of our colored stewards, to call all the officers and tell them we'll be at battle stations soon.

Ed Campbell, I see, is already on the dive. As I swing onto the ladder leading to the conning tower, I hear the TDC start up. That means that Chub, or Gene Richley, is already there. George is looking through the periscope, and back by the TDC, Chub flashes me a huge, gap-toothed grin. The false tooth is out, which is Chub's way of getting ready for a fight.

Street is looking intently ahead. "That's them," he says, a bit ungrammatically. "Take a look."

There is a bad mirage effect on the horizon, but I can make out something which must be the mast of a ship, a shimmering something else which could be the tops of another.

"Better put it down again," says the skipper after a moment. "This mirage effect is tricky. It might look like a telephone pole to them."

That was something I hadn't thought of. He continued, "These are the most perfect sound conditions I've ever run into. We've heard them for nearly an hour before sighting them, and they shouldn't have any trouble bouncing an echo off us long before we're ready to shoot. We're going to have a tough approach and a rough time afterward."

"Shall I sound battle stations?" I ask him. It is obviously going to be quite a while before we fire torpedoes, but from what I've seen below it won't make much difference whether we sound the general alarm or not. George agrees with me, and the musical notes peal out. As we had expected, there is not a move below decks, but the "manned and ready" reports come through within seconds.

It isn't long before we can make out enough of the convoy to identify it. Two big ships and three escorts. The biggest looks like a passenger liner, with a long, square superstructure. The other is a freighter type. The three escorts are *Mikura*-class frigates—something like our destroyer escorts. All are zigzagging radically.

The approach is routine, except that we have to give unusual attention to the periscope to avoid being sighted. As the ships draw nearer we can see that both targets are crowded with soldiers, and that the three escorts have lookouts all over their decks. We identify the two big ships as *Nikko Maru,* an old passenger liner, and *Ramb II,* a brand-new, foreign-built freighter.

It is getting time to shoot. I check for the third time that all is ready, that the torpedoes need only pressure on the firing key to send them on their way. I watch George narrowly, to anticipate his every need, relay his orders, and receive reports for him. I also ceaselessly look over Chub's shoulder, and keep current on the tactical situation to have the latest dope for the skipper.

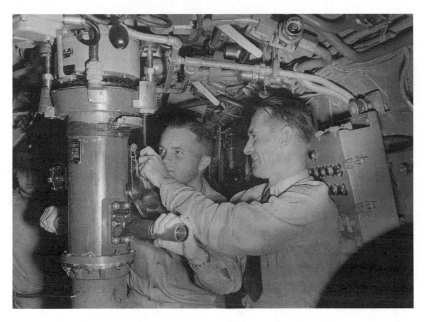

Edward Beach as a junior officer *(left)* stands at the periscope
while getting submarine training circa 1940.

"Stand by forward, two fish!" suddenly says Street. This is unexpected, and can only mean one thing. We've been detected, and one of the escorts is after us.

"Down 'scope. Escort, passing close aboard," George explains briefly. "I don't think he's spotted us. He's passing now. No signs of having got us on sound?" The last is a question directed at me.

Sonar is on him, and the pings are coming in awfully loud. "How close?" I whisper to the skipper.

"Two hundred yards," he whispers back. Too close to shoot now. The steady rhythm of his propellers comes strongly through the hull, grows steadily louder for several agonizing moments, then begins to recede. I heave a sigh of relief.

The escort is gone now, and from the setup on the TDC we can see it is time to shoot. George gets back on the periscope. I send to the forward torpedo room—we have no torpedoes left aft—to stand by with all six fish.

We wait two minutes. "Up, 'scope! Final bearing and shoot!"

"Stand by forward," I order.

"*Nikko*—bearing—mark!" The 'scope slides down. George nods at me.

"Zero three two!" from Karlesses. Chub turns the target-bearing dial a fraction of a degree. The correct solution light seems to flicker momentarily, then burns bright and steady.

"FIRE!" I shout. *Tirante* lurches three times.

The periscope is up again. "*Ramb,*" calls George. "Bearing—mark!"

"Three five seven-a-half." Chub's hand is a blur as he spins his bearing crank.

"Range—mark!"

"One six double oh." Chub doesn't have the bearing matched yet, so I grab the range crank and set the new range in myself.

"Angle on the bow, starboard fifteen," George calls out suddenly. This can't be right—it should be about forty. "Zig toward," the skipper adds—which explains that.

Feverishly we set in the new angle on the bow. It seems ages before the TDC catches up.

"Final bearing and shoot! Bearing—mark!"

"Zero zero two!"

"FIRE!" Number four torpedo goes out with a jolt.

"Angle on the bow zero!" He hasn't finished zigzagging. I hold up my hand to stop the next fish. Chub frantically grinds his crank.

"FIRE!" as soon as it is matched.

"Angle on the bow port fifteen!" George is giving us all the dope he can. Furiously Chub spins the little crank.

"FIRE!" Our last torpedo tube is emptied. Street spins the periscope.

"They've seen us," he growls. "Flag hoist on both ships. Probably means 'sub sighted.' *Ramb* has reversed course. Not a chance of hitting him."

WHRANNG! A tremendous explosion shakes the conning tower. George spins the periscope again.

"*Nikko!*" he shouts. "Hit aft! Blew his stern off!"

WHRANGG! "Another one! Amidships!"

WHRRANGG! "Three hits! He's done for! Going down on an even keel! The first hit was in the after well and blew his stern off. The second hit under the stack. The third hit under the forward well and blew his bow off!"

"How about *Ramb?*" I ask.

"No luck there at all. She's got clean away."

"Escorts?"

"Here—they—come! Take her down. Take her down *fast!*"

Ed Campbell has been waiting for that one. The diving planes go immediately to full dive. Then the sudden increase in pressure telling us that he has flooded negative and vented the tank. We ring up more speed to help him out, and *Tirante* claws for depth, hoping to get there before the ash cans arrive.

George crosses to the hatch, squats on the deck to speak more easily. "Keep her off the bottom, Ed. We've only got two hundred feet. Watch your angle carefully after we're down—it wouldn't take much of one to send one end of the ship into the mud."

At that moment the first depth charge goes off, and it's a good one. WHAM! Our sturdy hull shudders and the piping twangs. WHAM! WHAM! A couple of men lose their footing. WHAM! Still closer. A cloud of cork dust rises into the air. WHAM! WHAM! WHAM! WHAM! I have been holding more tightly than I realized to a piece of periscope drainage line in the conning tower overhead. Now I wish I hadn't—as I massage a tingling hand. George, standing with arms folded and feet spread apart, manages a grin. "That'll teach you," he says.

I'm not the only one who has relearned one of the tricks of the trade. The sonar operator is doubled up in agony: he had forgotten to take off his headphones, or at least to tone down his amplifier when the explosions came.

We have a slight respite, then another barrage bangs around us. After this one the skipper sends me through the ship to take stock of the situation and cheer up the lads. The latter part is a hard assignment. This is by no means the first time I've heard close depth charges, and *Tirante,* besides being brand-new, is a whole lot more rugged in design than *Trigger* was. But after all, it takes only one bull's-eye—and *Trigger*'s disappearance is fresh in my mind.

Throughout the ship, however, all hands are taking the beating stoically and with confidence. Despite the nerve-racking pounding, the tremendous noises of the separate explosions, the trip-hammer blows of the concussions themselves, they go quietly about their business. The experienced submarine sailors, by their example, leaven the reactions of those youngsters on their first patrol. In chief petty officers' quarters I come upon the ultimate in calmness. Remley, chief of the boat, on watch for many hours, had been sent by Ed Campbell to get some rest. He is carrying out orders, sound asleep on his bunk. The effect on the rest of the sailors is terrific.

As I look at him, another saintly series of close explosions shakes the ship, adding more dust and debris to that already strewn about the decks. Remley's eyelids flicker, then relax once more, and I walk gently away.

But it is in the forward torpedo room that I find the most remarkable reaction to a depth charging. Everyone is going about with a broad smile which somehow belies the strained look around the eyes. It seems that our Korean prisoners had been helping mule-haul the big torpedoes in and out of the tubes. Our men had told them, by sign language, that the torpedoes were meant for the Nips and this seemed to please them mightily, especially a few hours ago, when six fish had been hauled part way out, checked, and pushed back into their tubes. There had been many ribald gestures depicting what they hoped these fish would do to the Japs, and the Koreans had cheered for each one when it was fired.

When the hits came in, there had been more cheers which, so far as the Koreans were concerned, continued indiscriminately well into the first barrage of depth charges. The amusement was over the antics of the prisoners when they realized that there had been only six torpedoes but that there were many more than six explosions.

This much of the story I get between attacks, but the Koreans are nowhere to be seen, until a quivering canvas cot, rigged under an empty torpedo rack, is pointed out. Moans come softly from a blanket draped over it. I lift up one end, and there is one of our

Korean friends, hands clasped over his head, eyeballs rolling, moaning away.

Back in the conning tower I report everything normal, and receive the welcome news that we now have three ships working on us.

Street and I hold a small council of war. The time seems propitious to spring our surprise on the enemy. In the after torpedo room, covered with a tarpaulin, we have a little half-pint torpedo which, for want of a better name, goes by that of "Cutie." Cutie is an affectionate little fellow, always wanting to nuzzle up to fellows bigger than he is. His attentions are not very popular, however, as they are apt to terminate violently. Cutie is a homing torpedo.

"I've already told the after room to load it," says George. "Go on back with Chub and be sure they don't make any noise." I hurry away, for it's important to carry out this job quietly. Running silent as we are, the sound of chain hoists must not be permitted to get out into the water. Enemy tactics for a single ship attacking a submarine are usually to ping. With two ships they will alternately listen and echo-range, but with three there is always one listening.

Back in the conning tower once more, "We've got to wait till one of them makes another run on us," says the skipper. "Cutie hasn't much range and we've got to give the little fellow a chance to reach his target."

We do more than that. We take two runs in succession before there comes one to George's liking. Then, speaking softly over the phones, we give the order to let Cutie go.

Minutes pass. We had fired the little fish in the middle of a depth-charge run. Could it work its way through the roaring explosions? Would not its mechanism be damaged by the concussions which managed so to shake *Tirante*'s tough hide? We listen with growing impatience.

BANG! One tin can's screws stop abruptly. A subdued cheer rings out in *Tirante*'s conning tower—subdued, because there are still two others up there. And then, over the sound gear, comes the most eerie sound either George Street or I have ever heard. Distinctly audible in the receiver is the sound of voices in distress. We cannot make out what they are crying: they do not sound American, but they are obviously screaming in terror. The only explanation is that the Jap was nearly overhead when hit, and that the cries of his personnel were carried through the water. In sound tests conducted in training I had heard the human voice transmitted in this way, but this is the first time, so far as we know, of such an instance in combat.

In a few moments the other two escorts are back at us. Trembling and shuddering under the successive concussions, *Tirante* works her way toward deeper water, wishing that she had two more Cuties, that there were some way of striking back at her tormentors.

"Ned," says the skipper suddenly, "it looks as though this will be a busy night for you, keeping out of the way of these fellows. No doubt they'll expect us to surface after nightfall, and have some kind of search plan to find us. I can handle things right now. You go below and get some rest." So saying, he gives me a winning smile and a shove toward the hatch.

"I'm not tired, sir," I start to say, realizing all at once that I am.

"Goddamnit, Ned, that's an order! I want you fresh tonight!"

While undergoing depth-charge attack it is customary to secure unnecessary personnel, partly to make it easier on those who still must stay on duty, and partly to conserve oxygen by reducing the activity of the others. Besides, I had been up all night and most of the previous day, and as George said, would have a full night again. So rationalizing to myself, I climbed down from the conning tower and headed forward. When I reached the wardroom, an idea came to mind.

Seated there were all the officers who had already been secured— by coincidence the group included several who were on their first patrol. It was a tense bunch. There was not a thing any of them could do to help matters, which made things just that much worse. The game had degenerated into a contest between our skipper and the two tin can skippers, with an undetermined factor—how well the Portsmouth Navy Yard could build a submarine hull—in the balance.

Just as I arrived the screws of one of the enemy vessels became suddenly very audible, right through the thick steel hull. Someone said, "Here we come again."

Another voice: "We can't keep this up forever. Wonder how long our battery can hold out?"

I waited to hear no more. Stepping in, I announced that I had been up all night, and meant to get some sleep, and suggested that some of them do the same. The statement caught them by surprise—evidently they had not seen Remley.

The first of four close ones caught us as I climbed into my bunk, but resolutely I got in and lay there. With my head alongside the skin of the ship I could clearly hear the propeller beats, and knew when to expect the charges. I turned my face to the bulkhead so that no one would see my eyelids quiver, and forced myself to lie still.

I felt cold. The heat of my body was going right out into the Yellow Sea. It was warm within the ship, too warm, but the cold sea was sapping the heat right out of us. I realized that I was shivering, and then I realized it was mainly because I was afraid.

In the distance the swish-swish-swish-swish-swish of the propellers belonging to the chap who had dropped the last load took on a new note. At first it seemed that he was turning for a new run; but then another set increased in intensity, while those of the first remained steady.

Swish-swish-swish-swish-swish-swish-SWISH-SWISH-SWISH-SWISH-SWISHSWISHSWISHSWISH—*He must be right over us now—listen to that son of a bitch come*—SWISHSWISHSWISH-SWISH. *Drop, you bastard! Drop your . . . sonsabitching charges! Drop and be God damned to hell!* SWISHSWISHSWISHSWISH-SWISHSWISHSWISHSWISHSWISHclickclickclick—*Here they come here they come here they come here they come!* WHAM! WHAM! WHAM!

My pillow is wet beneath my face, and I can feel my mind reach deep into slumber with the relaxation of tension. But it is wide awake again for the next run, and the next, and the next.

And then, somehow, the explosions seemed to lose some of their authority, seemed to draw away from us, and I slept.

EDWARD P. STAFFORD

A FTER HIS COMMAND tour aboard subchaser *692* (see pages 61–66), Stafford was ordered home for more training and then assigned to the USS *Abercrombie*. The following passages reflect, first, a brief period of workup in March 1945, which the *Abercrombie* spent in the captured anchorage at Leyte Gulf, and during which the officers occasionally got to the small club ashore. Second, Stafford describes the intense conflict with kamikazes off Okinawa that took place from late March until May.

from

LITTLE SHIP, BIG WAR

One of the creature comforts in Leyte Gulf was a truly delightful little officers' club on the southern shore of the island of Samar. It was known as the DesPac (for Destroyers Pacific) Café. Its membership card displayed graceful green palms, and one could buy books of twenty-five-cent chits for three dollars, good for a dozen drinks. In that benign climate, the little club had open sides and a peaked, thatched roof covering a large, square mahogany bar surrounded by tables. There was a regulation, stateside jukebox which filled the place with the tunes and songs of peace and home—Frank Sinatra, Bing Crosby, the Andrews Sisters, Benny Goodman, the Mills Brothers, both Dorseys, Glenn Miller, Ella Fitzgerald, Les Brown, Patti Page, Harry James. On any evening when *Abercrombie* happened to be moored within a reasonable distance, the whaleboat (before disaster befell it) would take two or three of her officers over for a couple of pleasant hours of relaxation and conversation.

On one such evening it was my turn, and I went over with Keith Wheeling. The DesPac Café was crowded with khaki uniforms. Japanese lanterns hung in the surrounding palms and lighted the short path up from the dock. The moon was bright. The music was full and mellow but not so loud that it interfered with conversation. We bought beers and sat down at one of the tables. Then we noticed that one of the khaki uniforms surrounded by a dozen others at the bar was shaped in a disturbingly different and disturbingly familiar way, and that it came with softly wavy brown hair and a young, animated, unutterably feminine face.

The sight of that attractive little nurse was an emotional, psychological and even physical shock that would seem exaggerated and incredible to a man leading a normal life. But at Leyte in the spring of 1944, no one was living a normal life. I was twenty-six years old. It had been seven months since I had been in the same room with a warm, living, flesh-and-blood woman. During that time, except for dreams, which I could not control, and the surges of longing released by my wife's occasional letters, a vital part of my life, as of any man's life, had been necessarily excised. In wartime in the Western Pacific, the world contained only gray ships, green islands, blue sea, and men—there was effectively no such thing as a woman. The two-dimensional shadows a noisy projector caused to flicker across the movie screens of an evening were only tantalizing symbols from another world.

But over there at the bar, that was no symbol! I felt a little dazed, as though I had been solidly hit in a boxing match. My pulse quickened. In the cool of the tropic evening I felt flushed. My palms were damp. My mouth was dry. My attention span shrank toward zero. I drank my beer, got another and drank that too, and another. They

Edward Stafford, newly promoted to lieutenant,
was ordered to the USS *Abercrombie* in 1944.
COURTESY OF EDWARD P. STAFFORD

were no help. I got up and moved across the room almost like a
sleepwalker toward the semicircle of khaki backs. Somehow I pen-
etrated the circle until I was close enough to sense her female fragrance and feel her warmth. I said something and she replied. The
words are gone. Her eyes were clear and they looked directly into
mine with—what? Interest. Perhaps tinged with compassion. My
breathing actually became shallow and I had difficulty speaking.
But there were too many other voices, other faces, other bodies. It
was hopeless, without even a conscious realization of what it was
that was hopeless. I went away, had another beer, tried to regain

some measure of composure. Then, suddenly, the club was closing, people were moving out and down the lantern-lighted path to the dock—and the lovely little nurse was beside me, close, her small warm hand in mine, our bodies touching as we walked. She said something like "I just want to be with *you*," and I said something lyrical like "Jesus Christ!" or "Thank God!"

It was probably "Thank God" because that was literally how I felt. I had received a gift, unasked for, undeserved, but straight from heaven. The obvious question—what was I going to do with such a gift?—never entered my mind. I was beyond logical or even coherent thought. I was going to take this warm, affectionate, compassionate little creature home and love her forever. Home? The *Abercrombie,* of course; there was no other. I put my arm around her and pulled her close. The whaleboat was waiting. I helped her aboard and forward under the canvas canopy. Keith must have followed, sitting across from us. I ordered the coxswain to shove off and make the ship. He jerked his lanyard, the bell clanged once, then four times rapidly, and we were off. I turned and kissed my gift from heaven. Her mouth was unbearably sweet and she clung to me. Keith, the boat crew, all in the same twenty-six feet, did not exist. We kissed again. Surprisingly, after the months of deprivation, I did not feel urgently lustful, rather hungry and tender and blissfully happy.

Leyte Gulf was calm and quiet in the moonlight, and the whaleboat churned purposefully out toward the low, dark silhouette of DE 343, a couple of miles away. But about halfway out, the night was shattered by the roar of another engine close aboard, and a voice full of authority hailed us.

"Stop your engine and lie to! This is Captain Something of the hospital ship *Something.* You have one of my nurses aboard. She is to return to the ship!"

The whaleboat's bell clanged twice and the diesel died to idle. We drifted while the other boat came alongside. It was a thirty-knot "skimmer" of the type used by heavy ships to whisk their VIPs around an anchorage. In the stern stood a full captain, the moonlight glistening on his gold-braided visor and the silver eagles on his shirt. The little railroad tracks on my own collar had never looked so puny. Reality had returned. The gods were taking back their present.

The unwelcome transfer was duly accomplished with only the quick, strong squeeze of a small hand for good-bye, and the skimmer departed with an angry bellow of her big engine and a smother of spray.

That was it. A mini-romance. A love affair in twenty minutes. I never saw her again. I never even knew her name.

The next morning in the wardroom Keith said to me, "What the hell were you going to do with her when you got her aboard?"

"Mr. Wheeling," I told him, unashamedly pulling rank for the first and only time with Keith, "that's none of your goddamn business!"

*   *   *

[The] USS *Abercrombie* now began the most dangerous and deadly two months of her short existence. She was part of a sea battle like no other in history, one in which naval forces were denied the freedom of movement and surprise provided by the open ocean, and were required instead to remain in a closely restricted area well known to the enemy in order to protect and support ground forces ashore. From late March until late June the Japanese knew exactly where to find the concentration of U.S. warships upon which the battle for Okinawa depended. And they also knew, whatever their propaganda, that defeat on Okinawa would eventually and inevitably mean defeat on the sacred home islands themselves. So they threw everything they had at that ring of gray ships—the *Yamato* and her escorts, the Baka, and kamikazes by the hundreds in wave after bloody wave—and the American men-of-war, supported by carrier- and land-based air patrols, fought back with bitter, stubborn courage—for eighty-seven days. The result was the longest and costliest naval campaign of the greatest of all wars, a campaign in which casualties afloat rivaled those ashore, in which U.S. losses of destroyer-type warships were so heavy that at times the issue hung in the balance. . . .

[In particular,] on Friday the twenty-fifth [of May], kamikazes gave DE 343 the busiest night of her life. It was perfect kamikaze weather, clear and with the full moon that *Abercrombie*'s men had learned to dread. The DE was in station A38, a five-thousand-yard sector of the Inner Screen about halfway between Ie Shima and "Point Bolo" on Okinawa, steaming at ten knots on courses 078 and 258 degrees. With bogies all over the scope, the ship was fully buttoned up and every weapon manned. A defensive system was in effect which had been developed under the unprecedented and peculiar circumstances of warfare in the waters off Okinawa, a situation in which warships were tethered for long periods to fixed locations in close vicinity to prominent landmarks where they could be readily located and attacked. Although *Abercrombie* had a main director which could aim and fire both 5-inch guns from the bridge, and a director for each 40-millimeter, all guns were in local control with gunners ordered to open fire as soon as they could see the target. To help them find that target as quickly as possible, the sound-powered phone circuits were cross-connected so that the gunners could hear the ranges and bearings of the enemy reported by the radar operators in CIC. Most often the SA radar would pick up the bogey first and track it in until it appeared on the surface-search (SL) gear. The captain and the OOD could then watch it on the small remote radar scope on the bridge and maneuver the ship to keep the enemy on the beam where all but the offside Twenties could bear.

At about 0140 on the mid-watch, one of the bogies which had been circling off to starboard apparently sighted DE 343. On radar the little white blip suddenly straightened out and began closing rapidly on a steady bearing. The engine order telegraph jingled, a puff of dark smoke belched from the stack, the turbines began to whine and the ship surged forward, ready for battle. On the bridge scope it looked as though the plane were circling to come in astern—the same tactic used with fatally successful results on *Kimberly*, *Dickerson* and others. Katschinski, his eyes fixed on the scope, kept turning to starboard, swinging the stern away, keeping all guns clear. But the speed differential—20 knots to 180—was against him, and when the twin-engine Betty bomber popped into sight in the flash of a single 3-inch round from the DE astern, it was well back on the starboard quarter.

Gunner's mate third Bob Hawthorne, gun captain on Mount 41, saw it first through a set of binoculars he had borrowed from quartermaster Howard Amos for exactly this purpose. It was a sight to make a strong man quail—the big bomber close and boring straight in, the two props whirling with blue exhaust flames sputtering behind them, the roar of the engine building, the nose aimed directly at him, the whole mass seeming to be driving right down his throat. But Bob Hawthorne didn't quail at all. Since neither Harry Hensler, the trainer, nor Red Henderson, the pointer, had yet seen the plane, Hawthorne pushed Hensler out of the trainer's seat and took over, spinning the wheel to bring the twin muzzles around to the target bearing, and yelling across to Henderson, "Down a little, Red, down, down, a little more." Then Hawthorne hit the firing key, and the Forty began hammering out its two-pound high-explosive rounds, cherry-red balls lancing out into the dark, nearly three a second. "Up a little, Red, now down a little," Hawthorne coached; and steady in train, raising and lowering slightly in elevation, the twin Forties banged away straight into the teeth of the enemy.

After the first few tracers, Henderson picked up the target and needed no more coaching. Both men now held the nose of the incoming plane on the X at the dead center of their cobweb sights. Its barrels level with the water, so low was the kamikaze, Mount 42 stood its ground in the face of what looked like imminent obliteration. Close above and behind Hawthorne and Henderson, Tom Rutters and Sloan Duncan jammed four-round clips down into the slotted loaders, while Chicken Clinedinst, Al Deaton and Jim Hensley kept them supplied with clips from the ready-ammunition locker. With the 40-millimeter tracers pointing out the target, the two aft Twenties on the starboard side got into action. But it was Hawthorne's Forty on which life or death depended. He and Henderson watched a couple of red balls clip close above the plane, then two went under, tearing into the sea below it. Then another hit the water, bounced up and detonated on the enemy's right engine, which exploded with a blinding white flash. For an instant the plane kept coming. Then the right wing broke off at the engine, flipped up and back into the night sky; the plane rolled right, the stub of the wing dug into the sea, the bomber cartwheeled in a fountain of spray, came to rest and settled out of sight ten yards from *Abercrombie's* stern. Buckets of seawater splashed onto the main deck aft. Hawthorne and Henderson thought they could make out two heads in the white water where the plane had been. In the sudden silence of the guns, from topside fore and aft, from engine and firerooms and after steering, from repair party stations in passageways and living spaces, from CIC and radio and pilothouse, DE 343 rang with shouted cheers of relief and deliverance as the tension broke. If it had been up to *Abercrombie's* crew that night, Bob Hawthorne would have been elected President of the Universe for Life.

But that bloody night was not yet over. Bogies swarmed across the scope like flies scouting for carrion. Four times DE 343's radar men watched as fast-moving blips closed and merged with the slower ones of ships, and on the bridge at the moment of merge, they could see bursts of fire as another ship was crashed. Antiaircraft fire, explosions, patches of flame, and a couple of huge, flaring fires marked the vicinity of Yonton Field; and the next day we learned that the enemy had sent five Sally bombers with suicide teams to make belly landings and destroy parked planes and fuel supplies. Four had been shot down, but one team had destroyed some planes, damaged others and fired seventy thousand gallons of aviation gasoline before being exterminated.

An hour after shooting down the Betty, *Abercrombie's* guns opened up on a similar plane, which crossed astern, low and slow, apparently in search of a juicier target.

Then just at the end of the mid-watch it was *Abercrombie's* turn again. The second attack began in the same way as the first, with a circling bogey suddenly closing straight and fast from starboard. This time, Katschinski was able to keep it broad on the beam. In the midships closet and passageway of Repair II, we heard radar report the plane one mile out—then "one five double oh," then "one oh double oh." Under our bottoms, as we sat on the steel deck, we could feel the turbines pick up speed and hear the pitch of their humming rise. The deck slanted as the rudder was put hard over to starboard. "Range eight double oh." "Range five double oh." In another second or two came the heavy hammering of the Forties from fore and aft, next the faster chattering of Twenties, hideously noisy because Number Five was almost directly over our heads, and tough on the nerves because when the Twenties opened up, we *knew* the attacking plane was close. And when they kept firing in a sustained, steady way, we knew he was still on his way in.

Then came the unmistakable roar of an aircraft engine so close overhead that we all instinctively ducked. The Forties and Twenties went silent, but in a moment the ship shook with the booming of the forward 5-inch, firing repeatedly and at equal intervals of about ten seconds.

"He's circling the bow," Don Wood reported from under his big talker's helmet. "Fifty-one is firing at his exhaust flames. Looks like he's coming in again."

As tough as it was for the men topside, directly exposed to the impact of the kamikaze, and for the engineers below the waterline, surrounded by pipes full of scalding steam, I think this kind of action was hardest on the men of the repair parties. Topside and below, a man had things to do—search, aim, load, fire, pass magazines or clips, steer, watch the radar, turn a throttle wheel, open a valve. Even the men in the handling rooms for the 5-inch guns, under dogged-down doors and hatches far below the waterline, surrounded by explosives, passing their fifty-four-pound projectiles and twenty-eight-pound cases up through scuttles to the mount, had something to do, something to occupy hands, body and mind. A man in a repair party had nothing to do; his job began only when the ship was hit. Until then he had simply to sit deep inside the hull, watertight doors and hatches closed around him, ventilation off, blind except for the eerie glow of red battle lights, wait, and try to piece together from the sounds of the ship and the fragmentary report of a talker the events outside on which his life depended.

Thus, below decks, we waited in tense silence for the kamikaze to attempt again to sink us, ordering our minds not to think of what we knew had happened to other ships like ours and other men like us in situations much like this.

The second attack was a nearly exact repetition of the first. Again the kamikaze (now identified as a single-engine Hamp) came in low and fast from the starboard beam. Again the Forties opened up, then the Twenties, but earlier this time since the gunners knew what they were looking for. Again came the crescendo of engine sounds close overhead and even louder than before. However, now there was a difference. A clattering of Twenties broke out along the port side, lasted for perhaps fifteen seconds, and stopped. Dead, suspenseful silence after all the firing. Then from above our heads came another burst of unrestrained, profane cheering. Forty minutes later, with the scopes at least temporarily clear, General Quarters was secured and we found out what had happened. After the first attack and as the kamikaze was beginning his second run, Tom Parlon had ordered the port Twenties to elevate to their maximum angles, pointing nearly straight up at the zenith, and be ready to open fire as (and if) the plane passed over again. On his first pass, the Hamp had just missed the top of the stack, nearly clipping the mast with his right wing. The second time he was even lower, skimming across the torpedo tubes between the stack and Mount 42, and burning from half a dozen hits. But that time the port Twenties were waiting for him, laced his belly full of high-explosive rounds at point-blank range as he went over, and followed him unmercifully into the darkness until he tumbled into the sea a few hundred yards away. A short-lived pool of burning gasoline fell rapidly astern and flickered out. Score: *Abercrombie* three, kamikazes zero.

But that was not a final score. The deadly game continued.

After the clear, moonlit night, daylight brought a heavy, low overcast and occasional rain, the kind of weather that the sailors on the ping line prayed for. But despite the weather, bogies reappeared on the fringes of the radar scopes, and after a respite of three and a half hours, DE 343 went back to General Quarters. At 0800 she joined up with two other ships for mutual protection, and the three steamed back and forth on the patrol line in column with three hundred yards between ships—*Abercrombie, Roper* (APD 20) and *Gosselin* (APD 126). At 0925, with flash red in effect and with *Abercrombie* leading the little column on a course of due south, the starboard lookout reported a single-engine enemy plane, a Zeke, on the starboard quarter (bearing three hundred degrees true) about four miles away and closing. The guns on all three ships were on him instantly, but before a single round was fired, it appeared that shooting would not be required. Right on the Zeke's tail appeared two Marine Corsairs pouring bullets into the enemy. We could see the red blinking of the .50 calibers along the Corsairs' wings and the gray smoke streaming back. The Zeke began to smoke. It looked as though the plane would go down at any second. It seemed to falter, but caught itself and steadied. The pilot banked right, then left, weaving and skidding, the Corsairs still blazing away. It was up to the Marines. None of the ships could fire for fear of hitting them. A mile out the Zeke was headed straight for *Abercrombie*'s stern, but by then she was doing better than twenty knots and pulling away to the plane's right. It tried to turn right to follow, but one of the Corsairs was close on its right wing, firing. The Zeke leveled its wings again and flew straight into the starboard bow of the *Roper,* three hundred yards astern. A gout of thick black smoke sprang up at the APD's bow, red flame at its base. It blew away in a few seconds, leaving a thin column of gray-white smoke and a jagged round hole about four feet in diameter. Flames flickered redly inside the hole. There was no sign of the crew of the forward 3-inch gun.

Abercrombie circled back, looking for survivors, found none, and pulled alongside the wounded APD with all hoses led out and full fire main pressure at their nozzles, ready to help with the fire fighting. But *Roper,* thirty-odd years young and, in a previous incarnation as a destroyer, a veteran of the Battle of the Atlantic, needed no help. With *Abercrombie* escorting her just to be safe, she retired slowly to the Hagushi anchorage to tend to her wounds and her wounded.

By 1100 *Abercrombie* was back on patrol in the Inner Screen. . . .

KENNETH DODSON

FROM 1925 TO 1942, Kenneth Dodson served in the U.S. Merchant Marine, working his way up from deck boy to master of a freighter. In late November 1941 his vessel ran "scared, blacked out and answering the challenges of all the Allied forces" from Hong Kong to Seattle; it was apparently the last American ship to leave Hong Kong before the outbreak of war. After a couple of adventurous merchant voyages in 1942, Dodson accepted a commission in the Navy—at the cost of three-fourths of his salary, precious time at home, and the command of his own vessel. Having worked as a Navy instructor for a few months, Dodson was assigned to the transport USS *Pierce* (APA-50) in early 1943. He served successively as boat group commander, navigator, and executive officer of this ship, which participated in operations from Makin to Okinawa—that is, in all the great invasions of the Central Pacific drive toward Japan.

Dodson wrote long letters to his wife throughout the war, letters which she in turn sent on to relatives. Someone showed one of his letters to the poet Carl Sandburg (the letter from which selections are printed below), and Sandburg wrote the naval officer, asking to use excerpts from Dodson's letters in his novel *Remembrance Rock*. When, after the war, Dodson was involuntarily retired from the Navy because of wartime injuries (he spent a full year in a naval hospital), he remembered Sandburg's encouragement and decided to apply under the GI Bill to study creative writing. The eventual result was Dodson's novel *Away All Boats,* by far the best novel about amphibious warfare. Dodson later wrote other books based on his maritime career, and he always kept up a warm correspondence with Sandburg, whom he hosted at his home while the poet gave readings throughout the Pacific Northwest. Dodson admired the poet's vision. Sandburg, from the first, had recognized the seaman's unusual powers of observation.

Note: The letter reproduced here describes events during the Kwajalein invasion, a battle that took place in February 1944, earlier than other events described in this section. But it is placed here because, in Dodson's description of his visit to this newly conquered island, we begin to sense the end of the war.

from

A LETTER HOME

At sea, Feb. 9, 1944

Darling Letha,

It is high time you had another letter, isn't it? The old censorship is easing up somewhat. We are allowed to say that we were down in the Marshalls and took part in the capture of Kwajalein Atoll. We are allowed to say whether or not we have left the place. I sent off an airmail letter to you from Kwajalein, saw it take off in the four-engined Coronado which took Admiral Nimitz back to Pearl; hope that you get it without delay so as to know that your old man is still eating his meals regularly.

I suppose that you have read that our losses were lighter than they were in the Gilberts. It was a much harder place to take than Makin, but the job was much better organized and executed. The naval and aerial bombardment was terrific. The Japs had every few square yards of Kwajalein Island proper, where we made our main attack, fortified. They had twin-mount 5-inch all-purpose guns at all strong points, and they had their fire areas very accurately computed, so that they could lay their fire where they wished. The whole island bristled with guns, and we discovered that under every house and hut on the whole place was one or more pillboxes. These were used as cellar storage places, for magazines for the guns nearby, for bomb shelters and for the last desperate stand that they made against our final invasion. Most of the pillboxes were connected by underground tunnels. You will probably read a pretty good description of how the landing was made in the papers and magazines. Somehow, it seems hard to talk about it. Makin was something exciting and new. This was a vastly more complicated effort, a terrific blitz concentrated on a ring of small islands, the capture of the first Japanese territory made by anyone in this war.

The island is quiet now, excepting for the roar of patrol planes in the lagoon, and the occasional blast of a closed-over pillbox by the cleanup demolition squads. Kwajalein was a pretty island, with the usual thick tropical foliage and tall coco palms. Now it is seared and blasted beyond human comprehension. And the stink of death is everywhere. It is the awfullest, wretching stench imaginable. We made our initial landing on the west end of the island, only five hundred yards wide. It was the most strongly fortified part of the island, but the idea was to knock out the Jap artillery, and then storm the end where they couldn't flank our men with cross fire. . . .

[T]he complicated landing job went through without a hitch. Then it was up to the infantrymen who went on driving from pillbox to pillbox, using high explosives, hand grenades, and flamethrowers to smoke the Japs out. The Japs would run underground and keep popping up behind again, which is why so many of our men were shot in the seat of their pants. All the time dive-bombers, and naval gunfire, delivered on call. By afternoon the smoke poured out and up high into the sky all over the islands being attacked. Every now and then gas oil and ammunition dumps would be blown up. The explosions and the gunfire shook the ship. The roar was never ending. Then came the smoke and the stench, getting worse every day, until we were heartily glad to leave the place.

I went in and landed on the beach where the first assault was made. The destruction and death was beyond belief. Where coco palms and green foliage had stood was nothing but a desolate stretch of shell craters and hillocks of upthrown coral. Not a tree stood alive, just broken and jagged stumps on the tallest of which (about ten feet) were a maze of army telephone wires. Shattered guns pointed at crazy angles, blasted clear of their steel and concrete mounts. There were strong points, magazines and pillboxes, made of coconut logs, sand, coral, cement and reinforced with steel, all blasted open. And there were the dead. Some of the Japanese had been dead from the first bombardment, the day before we landed. Their bodies were seared and bloated, and the stench was sickening. I saw one half buried in a pillbox. You could not tell whether he had on any clothes or not. The skin was burned off his back and his head lay a few feet from his body. Another looked like a bronze statue in Golden Gate Park. He lay forward in a crouch, helmet still on, both hands holding on to a coconut log of his pillbox. There were many, many others. I lie in bed at night remembering how they looked, and that awful sweetish sickening stench of powder, and kerosene and decaying human flesh, and I wonder, after all, what war is all about. I feel sorry for those Japs in a way. They died courageously after a stubborn, last-ditch, hopeless fight. They fought for the things they had been taught to believe in, with their poor little bundles with pictures of their wives and kiddies tied to their belts. They fought treacherously, selling their lives as dearly as they could. Had they been on the winning side they would have shown us no mercy. They pushed native women and kids ahead of them. Sometimes one would surrender; go back into his pillbox after another, and then thirty or so would open fire from inside as our men closed in. Fortunately for us, most of their tricks had been tried before, elsewhere, and our men were trained to look out for them.

Time after time they were called upon to surrender by our Japanese-American interpreters. Almost invariably they refused, and then our men closed in with explosives and hand grenades, and those terrible flamethrowers. On one island there was a submarine

The "bureau of stars"—navigator Ken Dodson and his assistant,
Ensign Ranson, on board the USS *Pierce* in the South China Sea,
January 7, 1945.

COURTESY OF KENNETH DODSON

sailor in a shell crater who refused to surrender. They squirted oil
on him twice with a flamethrower which refused to ignite. It saved
his life, for as he stood there wiping the oil out of his eyes, a soldier reached over and pulled him out by his feet. They fought like
wild men, but seemed to make rather meek prisoners, once captured. Most of them seemed dazed from concussion, and amazed
at the size of our fleet anchored in their lagoon. One of them pointed
at the ships, jabbered to his captured officer, and then spit in the
Jap officer's face. Probably the man who told him the U.S. fleet was
all sunk. Another looked in a startled way and exclaimed to the
interpreter that he didn't know that there were so many ships in
the world. He couldn't have come from a big Japanese seaport town,
but it was a lot of ships.

Some of the smaller islands were not strongly defended, and escaped the spoliation of a heavy barrage. One of them had the prettiest beach of coral sand I have ever seen. I have a bag of this beautiful sand. There was no death on that beach. I'm hoping to send it on to you to use in a goldfish bowl. The sand would have to be washed in several changes of fresh water to get out the salt. It is the prettiest sand I have ever seen. I thought perhaps Mark could cut off the top of a glass jar for you, or you could buy a small aquarium, and have some goldfish with some green plant life and this pretty sand in the bottom. Dickie would be thrilled with a goldfish, if we could keep him from turning it over on the floor.

One of our planes was shot down the second day. I was looking at it with binoculars when it was hit and burst suddenly into an awful sheet of flame. The plane sideslipped down towards the water, parts of it falling off as it fell toward our boats in the lagoon beneath. One of the men in it fell out, his parachute opening too late just as he hit the water alongside one of our boats. I found myself praying for him even as he fell. Ensign Hoeffner was bringing wounded out to the *Pierce.* The body nearly hit his boat on one side, and the plane on the other. He got hold of the parachute and pulled the poor broken body in. Every bone was broken, some protruding through the flesh, all of his clothes and hair and skin were burnt off. There was no identification. One of the wounded men began to vomit. Carl cut off the parachute and let the poor broken body go. They brought the parachute aboard to the bridge. That night as I was on watch I had the queerest feeling, as if the pilot was very close to me. I went over to the wooden Jap bucket that held the chute and felt the soft silk with my hand and said, "I'm sorry, fellow." He may have been a nice clean boy like George, or Arvid.

We are going to fight and work our heads off to win this war. But we are fighting because we bungled the last peace, and we must never let it happen again. They can't tell me war is a fine and noble thing. I wish they could see the difference between the Saturday morning parades at Alameda, and the stench of Kwajalein. General Sherman had no idea how right he was. He said, "War is hell." I heard a blinded veteran of the last war say that, low and bitter. It didn't sound like it reads in print.

One night I worked with my boys until midnight transferring sixty-two wounded men to a hospital ship. Some groaned, some talked out of their head. One poor kid screamed thru grit teeth from the pain of moving his terrible bone fractures. We worked as gently as we could, swearing inwardly at the stupidity of moving badly wounded a second time when we had the best of medical care here. One fine-looking tall boy extended over both ends of his stretcher. He was shot thru the leg and the bone was shattered. For some reason I felt compelled to ask him where he was from. He said, "Southeast Oregon," and mentioned a small town near Ashland. I told him my brother-in-law had a fox farm at Eagle Point. We were just picking him up to put him in the boat, and he smiled in the moonlight and said, "Eagle Point Fox Farm. I know him. He sure has beautiful foxes. He sure has beautiful foxes." He gripped my hand hard, and then we picked up his litter and lowered it into the boat to start him on his way back home. Well, I'd got thru all the groaning and the boy who couldn't help screaming thru his grit teeth, and kept a stiff upper lip, but as that smiling kid left, I had to rub away the tears with my fist. I hate war.

Here we are in the third year of it, and it is just beginning to come home to me. I know we all love our country more than we ever did. But the average soldier and sailor wants to get the war over as soon as possible and go home.

It leaves a stamp on you. You take a bath and don't feel clean. You want a spiritual purge of the whole stinking business. You feel like you want to kneel at the altar and pray. You feel like you'd like to be baptized, and have communion. You want to lie on the grass on a windy hill in the summertime and smell the clean drying grasses and watch the cumulus swimming by in the blue of the sky. You want to have your arms around one very near and dear to you and snuggle your head deep beside your beloved one and feel the tenderness of her lips on yours, and the clean warm living scent that is her. And then sleep and sleep, and there shall be no more war, no parting, no killing, no smell of death; just peace.

Well, this has been about the most morbid letter I've ever written. Don't take it too bad. I'm very healthy and eat my three square meals (out of tin cans). . . .

Must close up now, have early supper and go on watch. The old trade wind is blowing dead ahead, and it feels good and fresh in our faces. The soldiers are laughing and telling stories outside the port. Life goes on.

Boy, are we looking forward to mail next week. Hope you did your stuff, honey, for I'm ready for a long session reading letters from you.

Bye for now.
I love you
your husband
Kennie

GOING HOME

ROBERT EDSON LEE

ROBERT EDSON LEE was finishing a degree at Iowa State University when the Japanese attacked Pearl Harbor, and in 1943 he was commissioned as a Naval Reserve officer, eventually to be designated a "hull repair specialist." His wartime duty first took him to East Coast ports such as New York City, and these many months of off-and-on duty allowed him to explore the cultural life of the east. After the war he was to follow up this experience and become a professor of English at the University of Colorado and an author of works of criticism on several American writers.

But in 1944, the repair ship to which he had been assigned—USS *Hamul* (AK-30)—deployed from New York to the Western Pacific, in particular to Ulithi Atoll, where it tended ships of the Okinawa invasion force. Lee was then transferred to a floating dry dock, where he was serving at the war's end. To the young officer's dismay, he was still in the Pacific serving aboard this unglamorous vessel more than half a year later. Besides occasional visits ashore, Lee's main entertainment up to this point was being required to play acey-deucy after dinner with the laid-back captain of the dry dock.

The subject of the following selection is the falling off of standards and the general laxness in this Navy byway, a negligence that brought about a conflict between the disillusioned young reserve officer and a strict "regular Navy" captain who suddenly reported aboard. Lee's account forms part of a chapter of his fine memoir, *To the War,* which appeared in 1968.

from

TO THE WAR

I wanted to go back home. We all did. Wasn't the war over?

Patriotism was a scarce commodity in the postwar period. It had never been, to my eyes, very visible, except perhaps in a few crackpots. I don't mean that we all didn't get a thrill out of the United States flag; we did, of course, but it was rather like Pavlov's dog. More motivating in the war was the sense of a certain work that had to be done; we knew no more why it had to be done than we knew why we had been born, but there was the feeling of: Get the job done and then we can get on to something else; and so we labored and won the war. The end of the war, however, made any further labor meaningless. So there was great scorn for the refrigerator-type patriotism so evident in the star-spangled advertisements in American magazines (the attitude that we were fighting for the American way of life, for our Homes, Mothers, and Refrigerators), yet there was also a secret urge to have, to get back to, to possess what we had "won." We saw no reason why we should not, each of us, return to the States not only immediately, but also before anyone else.

Even before Hiroshima, the point system of demobilization began to dominate our thinking. I believe the Navy's first directive on discharge came out August 5, 1945; fifty-three points were necessary for Naval Reserve officer discharge, based on one point for each year of age and three points for each year of Navy duty. By that reckoning, I had thirty-three points and was five years from discharge. By the end of August, the war ended, the point system was revised; but I still had two years to go until discharge. By October, under the next point system, I could reasonably expect to be out in one year. The new point system of November—half a point for each year of age, half a point for every month in the Navy, and a quarter point for every month overseas—would put me out on exactly May 2, 1946. A later refinement added twenty-five days' "proceed" time before discharge, April 7 in my case, provided a relief had been furnished. That was still eight months after the end of the war and nearly intolerable, but it was within the realm of the foreseeable and a base from which to plan my future. Needless to say, I lived only to accumulate points, as everyone else, and I grew to hate the whole bloody military system, as did everyone else.

Demobilization of millions of men from all over the world; administrative "snafu" (situation normal, all fucked up); congressmen drumming up votes by crying "Bring the boys home"—it is not surprising that twenty thousand servicemen in the Manila area held an illegal protest meeting in Rizal Stadium on March 7, 1946. Army or Navy mimeograph machines were used to churn out thousands of sheets of antimilitary protest. ("Those are as brothers whose bodies have shared fear, or shared harm, or shared hurt or indignity.") In short, none of us gave a good goddamn about "winning the peace." We just wanted to go home.

At Mariveles, [Philippines,] we did what we could to expedite the demobilization. Our dry dock still belonged to the Army, and boats assigned to the Army had to have their hulls scraped of barnacles whether the war ended or no. Nevertheless, some of our crew had been overseas more than two years, and in October we were able to ship out some thirty skilled men. These were replaced in November by twenty-five nonrated (unskilled) seamen, all age nineteen. After these had been more or less trained, we shipped out thirty-seven men just before Christmas. They were replaced by ten men. (Eight of these, incidentally, were named Smith, and one had no given names at all, just two initials. We could always get somebody for a job on the dock by yelling out "Smith!") However, someone ashore goofed up: we got in January copies of orders for sixty rated men who had been assigned to us. So we discharged old hands as fast as we could; but when the new men arrived in February, there were only twenty-seven of them and they were nonrated (and with names like Calaiacovo, Manaszkiewicz, and Didomenico). The net result was that our skilled crew of 120 had been reduced to an unskilled crew of 60.

The same shuffle took place among the officers; the force of three deck officers dropped to two, the captain and myself. I found to my dismay that I was now executive officer, docking officer, maintenance officer, commissary officer, first division officer, second division officer, education officer, welfare and recreation officer, gunnery officer, diving officer, photography officer, postal officer, public relations officer, and damage control officer. Not only that, the two warrant officers were replaced by only one new man. And then the skipper was replaced, too. Captain B—— arrived on a Monday, and Captain A—— left early on Tuesday.

* * *

"I never should have relieved him! I never should have let him go! Navy Regs makes it quite clear that a ship must be in good order before a command can be relieved. Why, this is unbelievable!"

"Yes, sir."

"Do you know that when I came on board last night, there was no deck watch?"

"Yes, sir. You see, when the movie is on, the deck watch can't see the screen from the gangway; so it's gotten that he was allowed to move away from there for the movie."

"Not any more, he doesn't! Is that clear?"

"Yes, sir."

"And the man down there now. Do you mean to say he is allowed to stand watch in dungarees?"

"Yes, sir, I guess so, sir."

"You get him into whites, immediately! Whites for the gangway watch, whites for the boat crew, and whites for the liberty party as well."

"Captain, if you don't mind my suggesting it, it's either muddy or dusty in Mariveles; so for the liberty party to wear whites would be, well, ridiculous."

"Whites for the gangway watch, the boat crew, *and* the liberty party. *Is that clear?*"

Robert Edson Lee, then a lieutenant (junior grade), at Ulithi Atoll
in 1945; a photo of his repair ship sits on the desk. Shortly after this
photo was taken, Lee was transferred to a floating dry dock.

COURTESY OF JEANNE DUPLAN LEE

"Yes, sir."

"Next, I want to know about docking. That tug in there now.
When are you going to bring her out?"

"*Me,* sir? Well, sir, it's due to come out tomorrow morning, only
I think I should mention that I personally have never docked or
undocked anything without making a mess out of it."

"Aren't you the docking officer?"

"Yes, sir, but only for two days now. The executive officer that
left, *he* was the docking officer, and we—well, I just was never really
trained—my God, can't *you*—"

"I never should have taken command! What *have* you people
been doing? When was this deck painted last?"

"Not since I've been here, and that would be eight months and
ten days now, sir."

"Isn't that the responsibility of the first lieutenant? Weren't you the first lieutenant all that time?"

"Yes, sir, and we tried, sir. The men did start chipping off the rust, but they lost all the chipping hammers overboard, and we've tried every time we went to Manila to get more hammers, but—"

"You mean the men *threw* the hammers overboard so they wouldn't have to work. Didn't Captain A—— do anything about it? Just what did Captain A—— do?"

"If you mean, sir, did he keep a tight ship, well, no, I guess he didn't. After the war ended, you know, and we lost most of our rated men and—"

"Well, Mr. Lee, I want to make it perfectly clear that that was Captain A—— and yesterday, but today I'm in command, and you are the executive officer, and that means that you execute *my* orders, and *I* am going to keep a taut ship. *Is* that clear?"

"Yes, sir."

"And one more thing. I'm used to bad coffee in the Navy, but I've never had anything like this."

"Well, sir, the coffee beans we have. They were loaded down into the hold when this dock left the States, and, well, sir, that's been over two years now."

"And *you* are the commissary officer?"

"Yes, sir."

"Do you think—oh. *You're* a *Reserve* officer."

"Yes, sir."

"How long have you been overseas?"

"Thirteen months and twenty-two days, sir."

"And when do you expect to be discharged?"

"April 7, sir. Forty-four more days, counting today."

"I never! Never! Ah, well, so be it. We'll have to make do with what we have, Mr. Lee. We'll have to learn to get along with each other."

*   *   *

Captain B—— worked the skin off my ass, and I hated his guts. I used to go over to the Blue Goose and get tight and tell all my troubles to Ida, but even that wasn't very satisfying, for things had changed. Mariveles had become pretty dull. The law of supply and demand worked inexorably, and the price of Black Label Scotch Whiskey of Great Age dropped from ten pesos to seven. The cathouses had multiplied, from two to eight, and the price there dropped from ten pesos to five. Then a Catholic chaplain showed up in the area, insisted that the whole industry be shut down, and after a certain date that any remaining prostitutes be put under arrest. One of our old hands made a valiant, futile attempt to smuggle to Manila on our tug six girls and two pimps. And after that excitement was over, somebody marked out a baseball diamond, which seemed to satisfy the taste of the replacements, so different from that of our veterans.

(Two or three of the girls I had met were now pregnant and without husbands, their men demobilized. I heard of one colored man who paid off his obligation with $250, both parties satisfied.)

Whenever I could get away from Captain B——, I used to go hunting in the hills, either with the new warrant officer or with a carpenter, or alone, but never alone after José Sorreál warned me about pythons. We went after iguana or the wild caribou or wild boars, and this was really exciting. We carried rifles and pistols and hiked in the brown-grass savannas past the abandoned rusted trucks, souvenirs of the Battle of Bataan of 1942. It was quite something when an iguana a yard long or more, startled by our approach, would hurry (as fast as a running dog) out of an old foxhole and slither noisily through the dry grass. It was equally great to come across at dusk, finally, a family of wild boars, completely surprised by our approach, as we were by them, and so there was time enough and we were close enough to see the long curved tusks, yellow, turning brown at the base, before they stampeded off, luckily away from us, not toward us.

And we grew mustaches, those of us on the dock that were old enough, and I have a picture of myself, the sere hills in the background, the rifle over my shoulder, the pistol slung from a web belt, and just the shadow of something under my nose.

We met the Catholic chaplain one day and virtually without introduction launched into an argument about evolution. He was unbelievably fundamentalist, nearly denying that Darwin had ever existed, let alone any validity to his theories. Then abruptly we went with him on his search for a small American cemetery, which he found, finally, overgrown with weeds, some of the graves opened and robbed for the sake of the gold fillings in the teeth.

Once, after a long hike, the warrant officer and I found a hot spring bubbling out of the ground with noxious sulfur fumes. A small pond had formed there, so we pulled off our shoes and pants and dangled our legs in the soothing hot water—until a Filipino came by and told us this had been a favorite place for lepers.

Back on board the bastard dock, we chipped that goddamn deck to bare metal, burnished it, and put on three fucking coats of paint.

I wanted so desperately to go home. The brown hills of Bataan were not the hills of my home. There, in the spring, tiny white trillium would have fallen like snow.

*   *   *

Suddenly, in March, the Army pulled out of Mariveles. The tents came down one by one, the trucks hauled everything out over the road to San Fernando. Almost overnight there was nothing left in town but the decorated Christmas tree in front of the federal building (the radar "window" for tinsel blowing, glittering in the wind). Suddenly, there were no more boats to dock. We were idle. Ominously, Captain B—— [like Captain A——] began to play acey-deucy with me after every meal.

Suddenly, the orders came through: the Army was turning us back to the Navy as of April 1. And suddenly my own discharge orders came through: "When relieved and when directed, on or after April 7 . . . proceed home." But immediately after that came the dock's orders: to depart by tow on or after April 1 for decommissioning in the United States. I did not panic immediately because I knew that the dock could never get ready to leave on time, and in fact secondary orders came through the next day to hold up the dock until a dredge had been taken on board, the dredge to be unloaded at Guam. Then came copies of the orders for my relief, an Ensign F——, presently somewhere in the Philippines, and the skipper assured me he would let me go the moment my relief came on board—and so we went through a flurry of preparation, the dock to go one way and I the other.

Except, April 7 rolled around and nothing happened. (General Homma was executed at 0130 on April 3.) Everything was delayed while typhoon winds and rain swept the area. Then promptly on April 10, the dredge arrived to be floated into the dock, brought to Mariveles by the same seagoing tug that would take the dock to Guam and then to the States. I *begged* the captain to release me without a relief.

"You know I couldn't do that. We're down to half a crew. It's the typhoon season. You can't expect me to do all the work by myself."

He was right, of course. But I *couldn't* wait the week after week after week it would take for the dry dock to be towed back to the States, and so I didn't give up hope.

By noon April 11, the dredge was loaded and everything secured for sea. Suddenly, a radio message from PhilSeaFron—someone to go in to Manila (my relief, of course!)—and after hours we located an Army boat that would take me in—four hours one way and no promise that they could get me back (I didn't care!). But when I got to PhilSeaFron at 1800, the man I had to see had, of course, quit for the day. They'd get a message to the dock to hold it, and there was a BOQ where I could spend the night.

On April 12, at 0800, I presented myself to X——.

"Ah, yes. You people all loaded? Ready to go? I called you in because there are some papers here, some inventories that have to be done before decommissioning. Thought you'd have lots of time to work on them under way. A relief? For you? Why, don't be silly, man. I'm overdue for relief myself, and if a live body showed up here, I certainly wouldn't let him get out to you. But you'd better get a move on and get back to the dock."

I think I shouted. I was content enough to miss the fucking departure of the fucking dock, but I knew damn well the skipper wouldn't shit without me, and what the good goddamn was I supposed to use for transportation?

Presently, I was the sole passenger in a Navy crash boat, a PT boat, skimming across Manila Bay at twenty-two knots. The four-hour trip took just one hour and twenty-five minutes—and I said my good-bye to Manila, Corregidor, and Bataan in style and in bitterness. I could have written the sign I'd seen in Manila: "Give it back to the Japs!"

* * *

It took us fourteen bloody days to go the sixteen hundred miles to Guam. I saw nothing. We passed Mindoro and Panay and Negros and Bohola and Leyte and came out through the Surigao Straits. We passed over the Mindanao Deep, and the water was purple-black. We passed through storms that held us nearly motionless for hours. The dredge inside the dock weighed four thousand tons, and the wind broadside set up a periodic roll to the dock; a ten-degree roll strained the hundred cleat blocks holding the dredge in place; but we rolled to starboard several times as far as seventeen degrees. We arrived in Guam on April 28—and we calculated that, after we left Guam, it would still take fifty or sixty days to get back to the States. And I was *past* eligible for immediate discharge, my points were up, and I *had* to get home.

And there, in Guam, was my relief, waiting to come on board. I could have kissed him.

* * *

"Now, Lee, *think* a moment. Ensign F—— got his commission a month ago. He was *flown* out here. *He has never been on a boat.* Why, he doesn't even know port from starboard. You don't for a moment think that he can handle the red tape of the day-to-day life around here, let alone life at sea, do you, now? Can you conceive of my trying to sleep while that *boy* had the watch? Do I have to remind you that this dock nearly tipped over that night on the way here? Think what that *boy* would do in an emergency. If we had *anybody* on board who had *any* experience *at all*—but you can't honestly ask me to accept that *boy* as your relief."

"Sir, my orders say 'on or after April 7.' It is now April 28. My orders say 'when relieved,' and F—— is my relief."

"Your orders also say 'when directed.' Now, you just get yourself ashore to the personnel office and sit there until they can come up with a *qualified* relief."

So I did just that, for days and days. The dredge was unloaded without my help. Ensign F —— busied himself getting supplies for the long voyage ahead—I wouldn't even talk to him. I sat in the personnel office ashore. I begged, I shouted, I cried, I threatened, I tried bribery, and I got discharges for eighteen more men and eight replacements, but nothing for myself.

On our last afternoon in Guam, I went over to the officers' club and got drunk.

When I got back to the dock, too late for dinner, to my dazed horror I saw that the skipper had waited for me in the mess, waited for me to play acey-deucy—and that did it.

"Is that why you're keeping me on board, so you'll have somebody to play acey-deucy with for the next two goddamn months? Sir? Honestly, now, isn't it just for your personal convenience that you're keeping me, so I can entertain you?"

Ensign F—— and the warrant officer left the mess room in embarrassment, but I continued.

"You just don't seem to understand the difference between regular Navy and Naval Reserve, do you? Some people might like this kind of life, but I just want you to know, I loathe it, I really loathe it. I signed up for the duration, sure, but the war has been over so many months I can't count them—and anyway I am legally entitled to my discharge *right now*. I've got to get back before this goddamn garbage scow gets back. Look, I'm going back to college. You know the rate we're going I'd never be out in time for the fall semester. Don't you understand? I never did get acclimatized out here and I damn well don't like it. That doesn't matter to you, though, does it? You're just taking it out on me because I'm not regular Navy and don't want to be, and trying to see just how much shit I'll put up with, and I'm here to tell you, sir! that I've just about had enough!"

Oh, God, I don't want to hear myself any more. For twenty years, I have stood before good, honest Captain B—— and insulted him!

Finally, he could take no more. He ordered me to be silent.

I sat there at the mess table, furious, not quite silent, muttering to myself. After a time, Captain B—— reached behind him and brought out the acey-deucy set. He opened up the board, he sorted out the red and black pieces, he put the dice in the dice cup, rattled them, but did not shake them out; instead, he passed the dice cup to me. I hesitated—and then played.

I beat him five games in a row.

Then we sat there in the dusk (the mess boy too frightened to come in to turn on the lights) and we did not speak, though we lighted cigarette after cigarette.

Outside, over the speaker system, came the movie call: "Screen detail, lay up to the screen. Cobb, Powers, Kovalski, Cox."

And finally I apologized—which was all he had waited for—and Captain B—— said, "Do you think you can get everything in order to turn over to Ensign F—— before you leave tomorrow?"

LOUIS AUCHINCLOSS

LOUIS AUCHINCLOSS was in command of *LST-130* when the war ended. Although his small ship was in California, he was ordered to take it back to Japan, to the port city of Sasebo, and later to Guam. As mentioned above (pages 180–81), Auchincloss had started writing again during this tour of duty, his confidence buoyed up partly by his felt success as a naval officer.

Auchincloss was detached from his ship while still overseas. In the passage below, he narrates his last days as a naval officer, as well as his mental attempt to come to terms with his wartime experience.

from

A WRITER'S CAPITAL

At Guam I at last received orders detaching me from the *LST 130* and sending me to the United States on an APA. It was a strange and delectable feeling to be a passenger again. But it turned out that I had one final duty. I was singled out of a group of officers in Portland and placed in charge of a troop train carrying three thousand sailors to New York City. Christmas was approaching, the war was over; the men, although still in the Navy, considered themselves civilians. The disciplinary problems can be imagined. In the long cold trip the breakdown of heating and lighting in some of the cars did not help. Liquor, though forbidden, abounded. At first, like a good lieutenant, I insisted on making my morning and evening inspection of the entire train. I would have done this to the end had I not been saved by a politic group of chief petty officers.

In the Navy these represent a necessary compromise between the hard-nosed idealism of the regular officers and the more natural simplicity of the enlisted men. Sly, cynical, unimpressed, shoulder-shrugging, they address themselves, like eunuchs in an Eastern court, to the basic machinery of government. The delegation which came to my stateroom pointed out to me politely that if I continued to inspect the train, it was only a matter of time before I was knocked over the head with a bottle. This would be a mutiny; the train would be stopped; nobody, including the chiefs, would get home for Christmas. Would I agree to let them run the train? We worked it out that I would stay in my stateroom and receive their reports, like an oriental potentate in a forbidden city, from behind a closed door. Most appropriately, I had in my bag, as reading material for the trip, some volumes of Gibbon.

In my isolation on that rowdy train on those dull frigid days, I did a lot of thinking. All of my small, puffy pride at being the skipper of a tiny unit in a great nation victorious over the forces of evil seemed to blow away before the drunken racket of those three thousand men. What is the sense of inferiority, born so deep in the would-be intellectual of the twentieth century, which makes him respect animal behavior as if it were possessed of some greater reality? Why did I have to assume that everything from which I naturally recoiled had to have a greater validity in the scheme of things than anything which attracted me? Why did I feel that anyone on that train was a wit more "fundamental" than I was?

I brooded over the four war years. I had served in two oceans. I had seen petty bureaucrats obsessed with their trivial bickering in the damp heat of Central America. I had seen violent storms and submarine attacks in the Atlantic. I had watched London under the buzz bombs. I had sat on the tank deck of a ship loaded with ammunition watching while a bomb demolition squad, a few feet away, with fingers moving so slowly that they seemed to be still, had inched an unexploded shell out of a truck and lowered it into the sea on a sick bay stretcher. I had seen German nurses, prisoners, come on board our ship screeching "Heil Hitler" and had sat with one of them who had swallowed poison while a pharmacist's mate tried to save her. I had driven in a jeep through the atomized ruins of Nagasaki. And what did it all amount to? Had I ever really been away from home? Had I once been scratched? Had I gone a single day without three meals? Had I gone a single day without shaving?

Some time later I came across a passage in a book by Henry de Montherlant which seemed exactly to fit me:

> Some men seem to repudiate the tragic. In small things as well as great. There is a street accident; they are never there to see it. Bombs and shells can swirl about them; they are never touched. It is not that they are more timid than others or even that they keep themselves in the shelter. On the contrary, they may have a yearning for the tragic test. It makes no matter: drama never strikes where they are. They go through wars and revolutions without ever seeing a corpse. Without ever really taking in what it is that turns a man into a corpse. They are always safely preserved— bourgeois in spite of themselves.

And so what? That was what I was beginning to ask myself in that long train ride home. Wasn't the bourgeois as real as the Hemingway or Montherlant hero? If you prick him, will he not bleed? If you tickle him, will he not laugh? Was there any point, in the one life that he was given, for him to fuss over what he was not? Oh, how obvious these conclusions seem! And yet a man can spend his whole existence never learning the simple lesson that he has only one life and that if he fails to do what he wants with it, nobody else really cares. As my train approached New York, I had a sense of jubilation at all that was over and at all that lay before me. I thought I might have achieved some kind of independence from my ghosts. I didn't know it then, but I had a long way still to go.

The officers who met the train were horrified at the state in which they found it. They suggested that there had been drinking on board and threatened me with a formal investigation. But when they received the report of the muster of the men, their expressions suddenly changed. The muster was complete. Not one man was missing! Every other train had lost at least a dozen crossing the continent, because men got off at the stops. How had I managed to accomplish my remarkable feat?

"They were too drunk to get off," was all I could mutter.

ACKNOWLEDGMENTS

While listening to a radio discussion about biology writer Lewis Thomas, the comment that Thomas "had once served in the Navy" caught my ear. I wondered—had Thomas ever written anything about his naval experience? I drove by the university library and found there in one of Thomas's books a chapter entitled "Guam and Okinawa" in which he described his wartime naval service as a medical researcher. That was the beginning of a long search for excellent writers who had seen naval duty and who at some time had written an account of that experience (by no means everybody does so).

I knew, of course, to look for material from Wouk, Michener, Morison, and Beach, and I had hunches and research successes of my own. But many of the names of writers came one by one from the recollections of people I talked to.

For example, my colleagues at the University of New Orleans helped. Carol Gelderman mentioned Louis Auchincloss's experience on LSTs (Carol had just written *Louis Auchincloss: A Writer's Life*), and Liz Penfield put me on to her friend, aviator Gordon Forbes. Also most helpful were those I visited in Annapolis. The staff at the Naval Institute (Paul Wilderson and Paul Stillwell, especially) pointed me to long-term Navy people like William Lederer and Edward Stafford. Alice Creighton, in the special collections department of the Naval Academy's Nimitz Library, mentioned academy graduate Dan Gallery, while Jack Sweetman had me read the fine memoir by Robert Edson Lee.

And if you can catch Ken Hagen at the doors of Nimitz Library for fifteen minutes, that time is likely to prove more valuable than hours of other research. He gave me many good ideas—although, again, not every writer he mentioned had written about his naval duty. But that was my challenge, to check all these suggestions out. My appreciation to all these who so freely gave me their help and their advice.

I also would like to thank all the librarians who assisted me in various ways, particularly Johnny Powers, Bob Heriard, and the rest of the reference staff at the University of New Orleans library, who bore with my ignorance and answered so many questions, and Nancy Radonovich and the interlibrary loan staff, who helped me procure a book or two a week for well over a year in pursuit of this quirky project.

I owe a large debt to Ed Socola (himself a World War II-era naval officer), along with Cooper Mackin, Dennis Quinn, and Herb Johnson for reading the manuscript and offering their suggestions. Many thanks. Thanks also to my editor, Linda O'Doughda, to Susan Brook, who assisted in securing the photos, and to Anita Roberts-Long, my research assistant. And as always, loving thanks to my wife and family, who unfailingly humored my enthusiasm and who occasionally even could be cajoled into listening to a paragraph or two.

ABOUT THE EDITOR

Robert Shenk saw his initial Navy duty during the Vietnam War, serving as communications officer of the destroyer *Harry E. Hubbard* (DD 748) during two deployments to Southeast Asia, and as senior patrol officer for River Patrol Division 535 in the Republic of Vietnam. Having earned his Ph.D. from the University of Kansas in 1976, he continued to serve in various naval reserve units and returned to active duty with the Navy in 1979 to teach English first at the U.S. Air Force Academy and then at the U.S. Naval Academy. He is currently professor of English at the University of New Orleans, where he has taught since 1985. He retired from the Naval Reserve as a captain in 1993.

Shenk is the editor of *The Left-Handed Monkey Wrench: Stories and Essays by Richard McKenna* (Naval Institute Press, 1984) and author of *The Sinners Progress: A Study of Madness in English Renaissance Drama* (Universität Salzburg). He has also written introductions for two books—Richard McKenna's *The Sand Pebbles* and Kenneth Dodson's *Away All Boats*—for the Naval Institute's Classics of Naval Literature series. His *Guide to Naval Writing* (Naval Institute Press, 1990) will see a second edition in spring 1997. Shenk has published some twenty articles on literary works by authors from Homer to Robert Frost and on classical rhetoric and technical writing.

The **Naval Institute Press** is the book-publishing arm of the U.S. Naval Institute, a private, nonprofit, membership society for sea service professionals and others who share an interest in naval and maritime affairs. Established in 1873 at the U.S. Naval Academy in Annapolis, Maryland, where its offices remain today, the Naval Institute has members worldwide.

Members of the Naval Institute support the education programs of the society and receive the influential monthly magazine *Proceedings* and discounts on fine nautical prints and on ship and aircraft photos. They also have access to the transcripts of the Institute's Oral History Program and get discounted admission to any of the Institute-sponsored seminars offered around the country.

The Naval Institute also publishes *Naval History* magazine. This colorful bimonthly is filled with entertaining and thought-provoking articles, first-person reminiscences, and dramatic art and photography. Members receive a discount on *Naval History* subscriptions.

The Naval Institute's book-publishing program, begun in 1898 with basic guides to naval practices, has broadened its scope in recent years to include books of more general interest. Now the Naval Institute Press publishes about 100 titles each year, ranging from how-to books on boating and navigation to battle histories, biographies, ship and aircraft guides, and novels. Institute members receive discounts of 20 to 50 percent on the Press's nearly 600 books in print.

Full-time students are eligible for special half-price membership rates. Life memberships are also available.

For a free catalog describing Naval Institute Press books currently available, and for further information about subscribing to *Naval History* magazine or about joining the U.S. Naval Institute, please write to:

Membership Department
U.S. Naval Institute
118 Maryland Avenue
Annapolis, MD 21402-5035
Telephone: (800) 233-8764
Fax: (410) 269-7940
Web address: www.usni.org